A Companion to
Andrei Platonov's
*The Foundation Pit* ——————————————

Studies in Russian and Slavic Literatures,
Cultures and History

Series Editor: Lazar Fleishman

# A Companion to Andrei Platonov's *The Foundation Pit*

Thomas Seifrid
University of Southern California

Boston
2009

Copyright © 2009 Academic Studies Press
All rights reserved

ISBN 978-1-934843-57-4

Book design by Ivan Grave

Published by Academic Studies Press in 2009
28 Montfern Avenue
Brighton, MA 02135, USA
press@academicstudiespress.com
www.academicstudiespress.com

# CONTENTS

**CHAPTER ONE**
Platonov's Life . . . . . . . . . . . . . . . . . . . . . . . . . . . . . . 1

**CHAPTER TWO**
Intellectual Influences on Platonov . . . . . . . . . . . . . . . . . . 33

**CHAPTER THREE**
The Literary Context of *The Foundation Pit* . . . . . . . . . . . . . . 59

**CHAPTER FOUR**
The Political Context of *The Foundation Pit* . . . . . . . . . . . . . 81

**CHAPTER FIVE**
*The Foundation Pit* Itself . . . . . . . . . . . . . . . . . . . . . . . 103
    The generic context of Platonov's tale: the production novel . . 105
    Platonov's refraction of the production novel in
        *The Foundation Pit* . . . . . . . . . . . . . . . . . . . . . . . 110
    Principal characters . . . . . . . . . . . . . . . . . . . . . . . 130
    Important symbols
        The proletarian home/tower . . . . . . . . . . . . . . . . . . 142
        Excavation . . . . . . . . . . . . . . . . . . . . . . . . . . . 149
    The language of Platonov's text . . . . . . . . . . . . . . . . . 154
    Selected annotations of events and situations in
        *The Foundation Pit* . . . . . . . . . . . . . . . . . . . . . . . 173

Index . . . . . . . . . . . . . . . . . . . . . . . . . . . . . . . . . . 187

*Andrei Platonov, 1950*

# Chapter 1

# Platonov's Life

For someone justly considered one of the major figures of twentieth-century literature, Platonov left behind a surprisingly meager collection of written or other materials from which his biography can be reconstructed. The paucity of biographical materials in his case is mostly a legacy of the Stalin period of Soviet history in which he lived most of his life, when private documents could be turned into incriminating evidence in the event of a search by the agents of the NKVD (the Stalinist secret police). But even against this background the material is sparse. Platonov kept a series of notebooks in which he wrote down ideas for literary works and technical inventions, and these have been published in recent years; but they reveal almost nothing of his private life and even relatively little about the composition of his literary works. He is not known to have kept a diary, though many of his contemporaries did, sometimes prolifically (see, for example, those collected in Garros, et al., *Intimacy and Terror. Soviet Diaries of the 1930s* and those discussed in Hellbeck, *Revolution on My Mind. Writing a Diary under Stalin*). Some letters by and to him have survived and been published, but not very many. Reminiscences by some of his acquaintances have also been published, but few of their authors seems to have known Platonov particularly closely—or, since some of these reminiscences were published in the Soviet era, to have been willing to say much about Platonov's views. At various times from the 1920s–1940s Platonov filled out questionnaires for one or another journal or literary organization, but the information in them is sometimes contradictory and we lack even a full account of his non-literary employment for various land-reclamation agencies in the 1920s and 1930s. In general Platonov seems to have been more

## Chapter One

inclined to discard than to preserve things he had written; his wife Mariia Aleksandrovna occasionally even had to rescue his literary manuscripts from the garbage.* The account of Andrei Platonov's life is thus mostly an account of his literary career, behind which one gains only glimpses of his private self and experiences.

The writer we know as Andrei Platonov was born Andrei Platonovich Klimentov, on 16 August (28 August, new style) 1899 in Iamskaia Sloboda, a suburb of the provincial Russian city of Voronezh (the suburb's name means "coachman's settlement," and would originally have designated an area in which coachmen were allowed to live without paying certain taxes).** On a questionnaire he filled out in the 1920s he once gave his class origin as *meshchanin* (roughly, petit bourgeois). His paternal grandfather was a watchmaker, and in a letter to Platonov's brother written late in his life his father also referred to himself as *meshchanin*; but Platonov's father, Platon Firsovich Klimentov, worked on the railway throughout his adult life, and in his late teens Platonov worked on the railway, too, so that his claim to come from a proletarian background was entirely legitimate (Inozemtseva 98; *Sochineniia* I-2, 351). Indeed, in this sense he was one of the few genuinely proletarian writers to emerge in the years immediately following the October Revolution of 1917, and the press continued to refer to him as a proletarian writer even after critics had attacked him for his "counterrevolutionary" views (Langerak 208).

---

\*     Andrei Platonov, *Zapisnye knizhki. Materialy k biografii,* 2nd ed., foreword N.V. Kornienko (Moscow: IMLI RAN, 2006), 13. Hereafter this and other works by Platonov will be referred to by title alone (e.g., *Zapisnye knizhki, Sochineniia,* etc.).

\*\*    There is some confusion over the exact date of Platonov's birth. Soviet-era sources give it as 20 August (1 September, new style) 1899 (see for example Vasil'ev 4). More recent Russian scholarship, however, pushes the date back by four days to 16/28 August. See, for example, V. P. Zaraiskaia and N.V. Kornienko, *Andrei Platonov. Zhizn' i tvorchestvo* (Moscow: Pashkov dom, 2001) accessed online at: http://orel.rsl.ru/nettext/bibliograf/platonov/platonov.htm on 13 January 2009. I have assumed that the recent scholarship is accurate.

Platonov's father was hardly a simple worker, however. He had several inventions to his credit (a device for attaching bands to the wheels of locomotives, another for rolling pipes) and for one of them, a device which simplified the mounting of drive cylinders on locomotives, he received a patent (Inozemtseva 103, n. 16; *Sochineniia* I–2, 351). Although images of suffering mothers arguably play a more important role in Platonov's works than do those of fathers, Platon Klimentov's influence on his son is explicit. Platonov's decision sometime in 1920 to adopt "Platonov" rather than Klimentov as his surname, was almost certainly meant to honor his father, perhaps under the influence of the Russian philosopher Nikolai Fedorov, whose vision of a utopian resurrection of ancestors emphasized the importance of paternal filiation in particular (another, albeit less likely, possibility is that he wanted to suggest an affinity for the Greek philosopher Plato, whose name in Russian is "Platon"; in any event, Platonov left no explanation for his change of surname). Platonov's attempts when still a teen-ager to construct a *perpetuum mobile* were likely influenced by his inventor-father (see M.Iu., Preface to *Golubaia glubina*, ix), as was his own invention later in life of an electrical scale (a report filed by the OGPU agent assigned to him stated that he was able to live off the award he received for it; Shentalinskii 19). In 1920 in the *Voronezhskaia kommuna* newspaper Platonov published an homage to his father and two other Voronezh workers that was clearly meant to serve as a nomination for the recently instituted "Hero of Labor" award ("Geroi truda. Kuznets, slesar' i liteishchik," in *Sochineniia* I–2, 101–5). Alexander Maltsev, the protagonist of the story "In the Fierce and Beautiful World" ("V prekrasnom i iarostnom mire," 1941) who is tragically blinded by lightning yet continues to drive his locomotive, is also partly modelled on Platonov's father.

Platonov attended parochial school until he was thirteen, then completed four years of public school. In October 1918 he enrolled at Voronezh University with the intention of studying physics and mathematics, but soon switched to the department of history, where he studied until the following May. He soon transferred from

Chapter One _____

there as well, however, to the electrotechnical department of the Voronezh Railway's polytechnical institute, from which he graduated in 1921.* The vacillation between technologically-oriented science and the empathetic interpretation of human life (through history, for example) was to characterize virtually the whole of Platonov's career, and seems to represent some fundamental divide in his intellectual temperament. Because his father could not support a family of eleven children on his own, Platonov, the oldest child, had to begin working when he was only fourteen (*Tvorchestvo Andreia Platonova* 229). His first job was as an errand-boy in the offices of the "Rossiia" insurance company, then he worked as an engineer's assistant for the South-Eastern railway. He also he worked in a foundry, then again, in 1917–1918 (i.e., during the Revolution) in the repair facility of the Voronezh railway (Inozemtseva 99; Kommentarii 449). His work on the railway—in that era a symbol of industrial modernity—made an especially strong impression on him, and scenes involving trains and train wrecks appear in some of his most significant literary works. "Without having finished technical school," Platonov wrote to his wife in 1922, "I was hurriedly assigned to a locomotive as an engineer's assistant. The phrase about the revolution being the locomotive of history for me turned into a strange and pleasant feeling: recalling it I worked especially hard on the locomotive" (Platonova 161).

It was common in Soviet culture from the 1930s onward to claim early allegiance to the Bolshevik cause where none had in fact existed, but Platonov seems to have welcomed the Bolshevik Revolution of October 1917 with genuine enthusiasm—perhaps, as his later articles suggest, in the utopian hope that it would remake not just social but physical existence as well. The front line of the civil war which followed the Revolution passed directly through Voronezh: the forces of the White general Denikin briefly occupied the city in the fall of 1919 until it was retaken by the Red Army on October 24. In later years Platonov gave conflicting information about his involvement

\* I. Iu. Aleinikova, *et al.*, commentary to Andrei Platonov, *Sochineniia* (Moscow: IMLI RAN, 2004), I-1: 449–50. Hereafter referred to as "Kommentarii."

in military affairs in this period, stating on a questionnaire he filled out in 1923 that he did not serve in the Red Army, but claiming in an autobiographical sketch he wrote in 1942 (during another war) that he had been mobilized in 1919. Most likely as an employee of the railroad he was automatically absorbed within the war effort. In the 1942 autobiography he indicates that he volunteered as an infantryman for a "special division" (*chast' osobogo naznacheniia*; Inozemtseva 97), a fact which, if true, may have meant that he had some experience of requisitioning grain from peasants, a common assignment for such units; but the length and nature of this service remain unverified (Kommentarii 450–1; Shubina 141).

Somewhere around the age of twelve or thirteen, even earlier than he began working, Platonov began writing poetry. Although he is now known as one of the most significant Russian prose writers of the twentieth century, his first serious literary publication was a collection of poems called *The Blue Depth. A Book of Verse* (*Golubaia glubina. Kniga stikhov*), which was brought out in Krasnodar in 1922 by the Burevestnik publishing house (the name means "Stormy Petrel," and was taken from a 1901 poem by Maxim Gorky). *Golubaia glubina* had little impact on the development of post-revolutionary Russian poetry (though it did attract a brief review by the Symbolist poet Valery Briusov, who praised Platonov's peculiar talent while noting the derivative and awkward manner of many of the poems) but it already exhibits what were to become key traits of Platonov as a writer. The most striking feature of the collection as a whole is its dualism, the way its poems sort themselves out into two groups of distinctly different tone and subject matter. To one belong poems which develop rural or folk-oriented motifs in a lugubrious mood reminiscent of such "peasant" poets in the Russian tradition as Alexei Kol'tsov and Nikolai Nekrasov, together with poems expressing vaguely Symbolist "longings" for an unattainable otherworld or sentimental empathy for nature (in the preface to the volume Platonov thanks his schoolteacher Appolinaria Nikolaevna, who taught him "that there is a fairy-tale sung by the heart about Mankind, whose native ties are with 'all that breathes,' with the grass and the beasts, and not about some all-powerful God who is alien to the tempestuous green earth and separated from the sky by infinity"; *Golubaia glubina* vi; also *Kommentarii* 467). The poem "The Wanderer" ("Strannik")—a recurring figure in many of Platonov's works—for example, imagines the poet opening the door late at night to a wanderer, then leaving together "with the last star/to search for our grandfather's truth" even though "we can't even understand the grass" (*Sochineniia* I-1, 288). In a review of Platonov's 1930 collection of stories *Proiskhozhdenie mastera* published in the Leningrad journal *Zvezda* the critic M. Maizel' was later to note, sardonically, how attracted Platonov seemed to be to "humble peasant pilgrims (*podvizhniki*) lit by the halo of christian humility" (195). The poems in this group were almost certainly written when Platonov was in his teens.

The other group of poems in *Golubaia glubina* express a discordantly different militant enthusiasm for the October Revolution, which clearly provided significant stimulus for Platonov's development as a writer. Indeed, with the exception of the early poems and a few early, autobiographically-oriented stories his entire *oeuvre* can be viewed as a complex *response* to the Revolution, and it is in this sense that he is a profoundly Soviet writer. His works, including *The Foundation Pit*, are simply unthinkable apart from the Bolshevik Revolution and the political and social changes to which it led. The poems in this second group are dominated by industrial motifs which betray the influence of the so-called Proletarian Culture movement (in its Russian abbreviation, "Proletkul't") and the kind of impassioned odes on factory themes cultivated by such worker-poets as Alexei Gastev, Mikhail Gerasimov, Vladimir Kirillov, and Nikolai Liashko. Gerasimov's "Song About Iron" ("Pesn' o zheleze," 1917), for example, enthuses that "In iron there is strength/It has raised up giants/On the rusty juice of its ore;/Forward we march, my brothers/In an iron platoon/Under the flaming banner of labor!" Kirillov's "Iron Messiah" ("Zheleznaia messiia," 1918) depicts a mighty proletarian who is "the savior and ruler of the world" and who "strides across the deeps of the seas" in order to "bring it a new sun, destroying thrones and prisons, erasing boundaries and borders." In similar spirit Platonov's "To the Universe" ("Vselennoi") vows that "We will extinguish the tired sun/And ignite a different light in the universe/ We will give people iron souls/and sweep the planets from their paths with fire" (*Golubaia glubina* 6). "The Dynamo-Machine" ("Dinamo-mashina") similarly insists that "Until night, until death we are at the machine, and with it alone/We do not pray, we do not love, we will die as we were born: at this iron face/Our hands are regulators of electric current...An electric flame has poured a different life into us" (*Golubaia glubina* 28).

The contrast between these poems with their stentorious proclamation of the new world of factories, collective labor, and machines—which are placed first in the volume—and the sentimental, meditative intonations of the other poems in the collection was not lost on the audience at Voronezh's "Iron Pen" café where Platonov gave readings in the months after the Revolution, and in the preface to *Golubaia glubina* the editor and publisher G.Z. Litvin-Molotov, Platonov's sponsor in those years, even felt compelled to offer a sociological explanation of his protegé's duality as a reflection of the Russian proletariat's relatively recent emergence from the peasant class (Kommentarii 476–8). For his part, however, Platonov seems to have been concerned not with the opposition but with finding some kind of link, some "native bond between weeds, the beggar woman, the field song and electricity, locomotives, and the whistle which shakes the earth" (*Golubaia glubina* vi). In a sense the two scenic parts of *The Foundation Pit*, the digging of the pit in order to erect the Proletarian Home and the collectivization of agriculture in a nearby village, preserve both this duality and the attempt to find unifying themes within it.

With Litvin-Molotov's sponsorship Platonov quickly gained notice on the Voronezh literary scene (Litvin-Molotov was to play an important role a few years later when, as the director of the publishing house *Molodaia gvardiia*, he helped Platonov find entry to the Moscow literary world). Platonov registered as a journalist for the local press in 1920, and several "literary evenings" were organized

Chapter One

to discuss his works—especially, at this stage, the "poetry of the worker Platonov," who, his listeners agreed, was a "rare self-taught writer of considerable promise" (Inozemtseva 92). He also began publishing newspaper articles and delivering intellectually ambitious talks on a wide range of philosophical, literary, and political topics, from reports on the effects of the drought in the Volga region and earnestly intended proposals for inventions (such as a system which would allow planes to fly along telegraph lines like inverted trolleybuses) to bold pronouncements on the future organization of human labor, the nature of consciousness, sex, and the death of God. Fueled by a young man's utopian response to the Revolution, these outpourings were typically written in haste and rather than forming a coherent system present us, as the editors of his collected works put it, with "a bundle, a clump (*klubok, sgustok*) filled with all the contradictions of his intellectual searching" (Kommentarii 490). They nonetheless provide a catalog of early influences on Platonov, and for all their inconsistencies the articles are united by Platonov's fervent hope in those years that the Bolshevik Revolution would transform not just Russian society but human physical existence in general. As Platonov wrote to his wife in 1922, in essence imposing a cosmic dimension on Marx's famous dictum that philosophy should not just analyze the world but change it, "We should love the universe that could be, not the one that is" (Platonova 162).

In the years immediately following the Revolution, however, writing was not Platonov's only profession, and not even his principal one. After graduating from the Voronezh Polytechnical Institute in 1924 he began work as a land reclamation engineer for the Voronezh region, with additional responsibilitites for introducing electricity into local agriculture and planning a hydroelectric installation on the Don River ("...Ia derzhalsia i rabotal'," 115, n.7). This "second" career was far more important to his sense of himself as a writer than even, say, Chekhov's training as a physician was to his, or Nabokov's entomological pursuits were to his (Kornienko even suggests that Platonov's various early writings are realized in different "languages," 15). As late as 1931, in a questionnaire he filled out for the journal *Na literaturnom postu*, Platonov stated that he considered "electrotechnology" to be his main profession ("... Ia derzhalsia i rabotal'," 117). A particularly important stimulus for his work in land reclamation and electrification was the severe drought which struck the Volga region in 1921. As Platonov explained in a 1924 autobiographical statement, having seen the effects of the resulting famine he felt could no longer occupy himself "with a contemplative activity, literature" (Kommentarii 466; though several of his stories of the 1920s feature desperately starving peasant characters). In the early 1920s Platonov left journalism altogether in order to devote himself to his work as an engineer, a decision possibly influenced by such theoreticians associated with the avant-garde journal *LEF* as Nikolai Chuzhak and Boris Arvatov, who believed that labor represented a more authentic form of human creativity which would eventually replace art (Langerak 40). In his Voronezh journalism Platonov himself often expressed the belief that the real "construction" of socialism must take place within the physical, not the cultural, realm. "In the era of socialist construction it is impossible to be a 'pure' writer' ("Otvet na anketu 'Kakoi nam nuzhen pistatel'," 287).

Unlike the majority of Soviet writers in the 1920s and 1930s, who traveled in "brigades" to observe such labor projects as the digging of the White Sea canal or the construction of the industrial city of Magnitogorsk so that their descriptions would inspire other Soviet laborers, Platonov thus had direct, physical experience of the construction of socialism in the Russian countryside. From May 1923 to May 1926 he worked for the Voronezh branch of *Gubzemupravlenie* (the Russian acronym for Regional Agency for Land Management, most often shortened to Gubzemuprav), overseeing the agency's efforts to prevent future droughts. As the certificate issued to him when he left Voronezh indicates, during his work in the region he excavated 763 ponds, dug 331 wells, drained 7600 *desiatin*s of land and irrigated 30, built bridges and dams and installed three electrical stations (Kommentarii 456–7; Platonova 163). At one point he was even paid a visit by the Formalist literary theoretician Viktor

Shklovsky, who descended by plane to one of Platonov's work sites. "Comrade Platonov is a land reclamation engineer," Shklovsky wrote in *The Third Factory* (*Tret'ia fabrika*). "He's a worker, about twenty-six years old...Platonov is very busy...The desert is encroaching. Water seeps away beneath the earth and flows there in huge subterranean rivers...Platonov spoke also about literature, about Rozanov, and about the fact that it's impossible to describe sunsets and how one ought not to write stories" (Shklovskii 126, 129).

Platonov did write at least one "technological" work in this period, the popularizing brochure *Electrification* (*Elektrifikatsiia*) which was published in Voronezh by the state publisher Gosizdat in 1921—but, his words to Shklovsky notwithstanding, he also began to write stories, many of which directly reflect his experiences as a land reclamation engineer. "Il'ich's Extinguished Lamp" ("O potukhshei lampe Il'icha," 1926), for example, recounts the efforts of a young man who has taken a course on electrical technology while in the Red Army to build an electrical generator and a mill in his native village of Rogachevka. After considerable effort, with only meager resources at his disposal, he manages to install both and plans to start them up ceremoniously on the anniversary of the Revolution. The owners of the local windmill, however, sabotage his efforts. The tale was closely based on Platonov's own experiences—even down to the name of the village—but the editor of the journal in which it first appeared changed the title to the more optimistic "How Il'ich's Lamp Was Lit" ("Kak zazhglas' lampa Il'icha") and omitted the ending in which the generator is wrecked (Langerak 99, 225, n. 154; "Il'ich" was Lenin's patronym, and the lamp is his because of the campaign he led to extend electricity to the Russian countryside). A closely related story is "Electricity's Native Land" ("Rodina elektrichestva"), in which an engineer is sent at the height of the 1921 drought to install an electrical generator in a remote village.* Once there the

---

\* In the two-volume collection of Platonov's works published by Khudozhestvennaia literatura in 1978 the date for this story is given as 1926. Kornienko, however, suggests that it may have been written in the late 1930s ("Ot 'Rodiny elektrichestva' k 'Tekhnicheskomu romanu', i obratno" 1). In

engineer discovers that the villagers have converted a motorcycle into a generator, which they fuel with *samogon*—Russian moonshine. With no proper tools available, the engineer manages to construct a pump so that the generator can be used to irrigate the village's parched fields. But the episode ends ambivalently when the old man tending the still falls asleep and it explodes—leaving the fate of the new technology in rural Russia unresolved. "Masters of the Meadows" ("Lugovye mastera," 1927) situates its similar portrait of rural life in a tale of how peasants from a village called Red Guard (formerly Gozhevo) obtain technical help in order to dredge the local river and prevent it from flooding the surrounding fields.

Less immediately reflective of Platonov's work as an engineer, but clearly inspired by the utopian ideas he associated with technology, is a series of science fiction tales he wrote in the 1920s. Unlike the articles he wrote for the Voronezh press, which predict the eventual triumph of proletarian "consciousness" over the inert "matter" of the world, however, Platonov's science fiction stories manifest a conspicuous ambivalence by anticipating either the failure of the given scheme to change anything, or outright catastrophe. "A Satan of Thought" ("Satana mysli," 1922), for example, embodies the kind of dualism evident in the poems of *Golubaia glubina*. Its engineer-hero had once been a "tender, sad child who loved his mother, the wattle fences of his home, the field, and the sky above them all" (*Sobranie sochinenii v trekh tomakh* I 32) but now he despises human weakness (a distinctly Nietzschean note). At the behest of the "World Congress of Workers' Masses" he undertakes to develop an explosive so powerful it would allow him to reshape the earth's geology. His study of matter, however, reveals to him that it is imprisoned in immutable physical laws, and before he is able to detonate anything he goes mad and wanders the earth mourning a former love (and not unlike Nebuchadnezzar in the Book of Daniel, punished for his pride). "The Lunar Bomb" ("Lunnaia bomba," 1926) fantasizes

> either case it clearly draws on Platonov's experiences as a land reclamation engineer in the mid–1920s.

about escaping earthly existence altogether by potraying a hero who successfully builds a space vehicle (the influence of Konstantin Tsiolkovsky, father of Soviet rocketry, on this and several other of Platonov's early stories is unmistakeable). As the hero approaches the moon, however, he discovers its to be nothing but "desert, dead mineral, and platinum twilight" (*Sobranie sochinenii v trekh tomakh* I 58) and he suicidally decides to exit his spacecraft. "The Ethereal Path" ("Efirnyi trakt," 1926) offers a still more elaborate version of the same motifs. Its engineer-hero—and all these engineer-heroes are forebears of Prushevsky in *The Foundation Pit*—experiences an epiphanic revelation that the cosmos is in fact biological in essence and consists mostly of the "corpses" of electrons. He hypothesizes that if these can be "fed" to living electrons, the result will be a materialist utopia in which metals and other substances can be produced at will. He never succeeds in applying his idea, however, and most of the tale's elaborate plot (which at one point has the hero visit Riverside, California) involves his and his assistants' scientific doubts and lonely wanderings.

Platonov's work as a land reclamation engineer also provided him with his first entrée to events on a national scale. In May 1924 he attended the First All-Russian Hydrological Congress in Moscow and later that year visited the construction site of the Volkhov hydroelectric plant in northwestern Russia, at that point the largest of its kind in the country (Verin, "Istoriia odnoi komandirovki" 103–4). In February 1926 he attended the First All-Russian Conference on Land-Reclamation in Moscow and was elected to the Central Committee of the Union of Agricultural and Forestry Work (Kornienko 18). In June 1926 he moved to Moscow with his wife and son in order to work for the Central Committee of the Union of Agricultural and Forestry Work, which provided him with housing in the Central Home for Specialists (*Tsentral'nyi dom spetsialistov*), a residence for technicians needed in Soviet industry—where, however, he ran into a series of conflicts (Langerak 75). Nor was the position with the Agricultural Union particularly successful for Platonov. It lasted all of four weeks, after which, as Platonov later described his plight, he found himself "in unfamiliar Moscow, with a family but with no income...My child became ill and every day I would take valuable specialized books, without which I couldn't work, to the Chinese wall. In order to feed my child I sold them" (quoted in Kornienko 19; Platonov had married Mariia Aleksandrovna Kashintseva [1903–1983] in 1921; their son Platon, whom they nicknamed Totik or Tosha, was born in 1920, their daughter Mariia in 1944; *Zapisnye knizhki* 315).\*  Platonov complained that for two of the four weeks all he was able to do at the Union of Agriculture was try to defend his institutional interests, with no chance of getting any practical work done; but in a letter to the editor and literary theoretician Alexander Voronsky he also blamed his being fired from his engineering position on his "passion for reflection, for wanting to write about things" ("strast' k razmyshleniiu, pisatel'stvu")—an attestation which in retrospect suggests there is an autobiographical basis to the situation in which Voshchev, the hero of *The Foundation Pit*, finds himself at the opening of the tale (quoted in Kommentarii 499; Langerak 77). Something of this loner's restlessness with organizations may also explain Platonov's relations with the Communist Party. Platonov had been a member of the Party in 1920–1921, but left it for what he later called "inexcusable" and "immature" reasons, which apparently had to do with a lack of patience for endless meetings where he had to sit through clumsy discussions of articles in *Pravda* which he had no trouble understanding on his own (Inozemtseva 100; Kommentarii 453). His attempts to rejoin the Party in 1924–1926 were unsuccessful (Langerak 75).

At some point—Platonov's employment history is surprisingly hard to ascertain with any precision—he went back to work for Gubzemuprav, which this time sent him to oversee land reclamation projects in the provincial city of Tambov. There, from December 1926 to March 1927, he experienced bitter frustration with the local

\*  The "Chinese wall" actually had nothing to do with China but was based on the similarity between the adjective *kitaiskii*, "Chinese," and an old Russian word "kita" referring to bundles of sticks out of which a former wall on that site had been made.

bureacrats, who regarded him as a Moscow "big-shot" and from the moment he arrived engaged in stalling tactics and schemed to undermine his work. In letters he wrote to his wife from Tambov he laments that it has become for him a "Gogolian province," his room there a "prison cell." "In the future this 'Tambov' will become a symbol for me, like a bad dream in the remote Tambov night dissipated in the morning only by the hope of seeing you." He devoted his evenings in Tambov to working on one of his most significant works of the 1920s, "The Locks of Epiphany" ("Epifanskie shliuzy"), imploring his wife when he sent the manuscript off to her that she not let any editors alter its unusual literary style, which he called "part Slavonic ornamentation, a kind of viscous speech" ("otchasti slavianskoi viaz'iu—tiaguchim slogom"; Platonova 164–7).

In 1927 following the Tambov debacle Platonov resigned from Gubzemuprav and returned to Moscow, where he continued some technical work but increasingly began to devote himself once again to a career as a writer—a less institutionalized, but by that token also less certain, occupation in the 1920s than it was to become in the 1930s, when all writers were required to belong to the Union of Soviet Writers. Despite his early enthusiasm for Proletkul't and brief affiliation with a related proletarian group called The Smithy, Platonov did not attach himself to any of the literary factions struggling for cultural dominance in the late 1920s, even though doing so would undoubtedly have made publication easier for him (Kommentarii 493).

All the same Platonov now began to establish himself as a presence on the national literary scene. His stories began to appear in important venues such as *Krasnaia nov'* and *Novyi mir*, two of the leading literary journals published in the capital (Langerak 93), and in the summer of 1927 he published *The Locks of Epiphany. Stories* (*Epifanskie shliuzy. Rasskazy*), a collection which gathered some of his most important works of the mid–1920s. Although it went largely unremarked in the central Soviet press, the volume drew a positive response from Maxim Gorky, doyen of Soviet letters, who recommended it several times in letters to other writers (Langerak 90).

What unites many of the stories in the collection, even as it anticipates *The Foundation Pit*, is the attitude of what might be called ironic loyalty to the Soviet cause which runs through them. Loyalty, in that the stories reveal Platonov's obvious sympathy with the aims of the Soviet project for building a socialist society—at least, as he interprets them, which is to say, in technological and physical rather than social terms; but ironic as well, because the efforts to change human existence which he portrays are routinely either frustrated by a recalcitrant Soviet bureaucracy or fail because the technology brought to bear on some task is woefully inadequate.

The title story of the collection, "Epifanskie shliuzy," for example, portrays the efforts of an eighteenth-century English engineer named Bertrand Perry to build a canal between the Don and Oka rivers at the behest of Peter the Great. Perry has to contend with hostile local officals and the peasants conscripted to work on his project die in droves, but he survives these trials and manages to excavate the bed for the canal—only to realize that he has overestimated the region's rainfall and that the canal will not even contain enough water to float a small boat. In a more sardonic vein "The City of Gradov" ("Gorod Gradov") satirizes provincial bureaucracy by portraying the efforts of an official named Shmakov who is sent to a remote town called Gradov to straighten out its murky administrative affairs (the town's name, based on the Slavic root meaning "city," already suggests an epitomizing tautology). Once there, however, Shmakov turns out to be not a reformer but a utopian theoretician of bureaucracy in his own right, author of a work called *Notes of a Government Man* which praises the clerk as "the most valuable agent of Soviet history" and bureaucracy as the only force capable of uniting the Soviet state. The story assimilates Platonov's own experiences in Tambov to a tradition of satires on provincial bureaucracy going back to such pre-revolutionary writers as Saltykov-Shchedrin (author of "The History of a Town" ["Istoriia odnogo goroda"], an evident model for Platonov's tale) and Nikolai Gogol (whose play *The Inspector General* Platonov effectively inverts by making the inspector the theoretician of bureaucracy). Platonov was also very likely responding to the recent Fifteenth Congress of the Communist Party in 1926, which criticized bureaucracy as an impediment to socialist development (Kornienko 67); but as hostile critics soon began to point out, "Gorod Gradov" flirts with the suggestion that bureaucracy is not a temporary or local aberration but a defining element of Soviet political life.

A closely related work of 1927 was "The Innermost Man" ("Sokrovennyi chelovek"), whose hero, a simple peasant named Pukhov, makes his way to Moscow to see firsthand whether socialism is doing anything to alleviate the physical plight of the proletariat. Pukhov is something of a holy fool but his naivety masks a pragmatic skepticism toward everything he sees and Platonov turns his tale into a picaresque survey of the bureaucratic and technological shortcomings of the Soviet project (Solzhenitsyn incidentally adapted this device of reviewing the system from the social "below" in the figure of the peasant-hero of his *One Day in the Life of Ivan Denisovich*—whose surname, Shukhov, echoes that of Platonov's hero). Voronsky, who liked the story, called Pukhov a "Russian Eulenspiegel"; but the picaresque genre, with its playful and satirical proclivities, was already at odds with the dominant tendencies of Soviet literature in 1927, and the ambivalence toward Soviet endeavors suggested by the figure of Pukhov began to risk implicating Platonov himself.

Platonov's most significant literary endeavor in 1927 was the writing of his first novel, *Chevengur*, which he completed in early 1928. A meandering tale of how a semi-educated band of workers and peasants tries to create a communist utopia in the remote steppes, *Chevengur* is in fact the only completed novel by him which we possess (*The Foundation Pit* belongs to a shorter genre known in Russian as *povest'*, or tale). *A Technical Novel* (*Tekhnicheskii roman*), an expansion of the story "Rodina elektrichestva," which was to have been published by Khudozhestvennaia literatura in 1933 (Langerak 94–5) and *Happy Moscow* (*Schastlivaia Moskva*), Platonov's attempt at a socialist realist novel on which he worked from 1932–1936, were never finished. *A Journey from Leningrad to Moscow* (*Puteshestvie iz Leningrada v Moskvu*), on which he worked in 1937 and whose title suggests an ironic updating of the late eighteenth-century writer Alexander Radishchev's moralizing *Journey from St. Petersburg to Moscow* (*Puteshestvie iz Sankt-Peterburga v Moskvu*), we know of only from a handful of references to it in biographical documents; the manuscript itself was lost. *Chevengur* itself was never published in its entirety in Russia until 1988. In 1927–1928 Platonov managed only to publish parts of it as separate stories—the opening of the novel, as "The Origins of a Master" ("Proiskhozhdenie mastera"), another early fragment, as "An Adventure" ("Prikliuchenie"), other segments as "The Fisherman's Descendant" ("Potomok rybaka") and "Builders of the Country" ("Stroiteli strany")—but these often appeared with alterations which angered Platonov, who wrote to Nikolai Zamoshkin, editor of *Novyi mir*, that he absolved himself of all responsibility for editorial changes made to "Prikliuchenie" by the journal ("Pis'ma A.P. Platonova 1927–1936 godov" 163). The novel as a whole had been scheduled for publication by Federatsiia in 1929, and had even been typeset, but was withdrawn at the last minute for ideological reasons. Platonov wrote to Gorky pleading that he had written his novel with "completely different intentions" than the "counterrevolutionary" ones the editors at Federatsia perceived in it; but Gorky wrote back in September 1929 to tell him that no publisher would take on a manuscript like that of *Chevengur*, with its "anarchistic" mood and its portrayal of revolutionaries as "half-wits" (*Gor'kii i sovetskie pisateli* 313–4). Litvin-Molotov, to whose Molodaia gvardia Platonov submitted the manuscript before he offered it to Federatsiia, told him that the novel seemed to cast doubt on the very idea of building socialism "in one country" (Stalin's slogan) and that no publisher could accept it in its present form (Langerak 186–7).

1928–1929, the years immediately prior to the writing of *The Foundation Pit*, were turbulent ones for Platonov in which his continuing achievements as a writer took place in an atmosphere of increasing political tension. Collections of his stories continued to be brought out by important, "central" presses (two by Molodaia gvardia in 1928, *Masters of the Meadows. A Story* [*Lugovye mastera. Rasskaz*] and *The Innermost Man. Tales* [*Sokrovennyi chelovek.*

Povesti], as well as *The Origins of a Master. A Tale* [*Proizkhozhdenie mastera. Povest'*] by Federatsiia in 1929) but these incremental successes did not alleviate his personal difficulties. He continued to find it difficult to arrange permanent housing for himself and his family, and the relatively minor trouble over the publication of *Chevengur* turned out to have been a foretaste of the much harsher attacks he was about to face.

In the summer of 1928 Platonov together with the writer Boris Pil'niak toured a newly created administrative district, the Central Black-Earth Region, to which his native Voronezh belonged. The two of them then co-authored a satirical account of their travels entitled "Che-Che-O" (the title is the local pronunciation of the initials for the new administrative entity, which in standard Russian would be Tse-Che-O; Langerak 205). "Co-authored" may be an overstatement. Platonov later insisted that it was he who had written the sketch, with Pil'niak only making a few changes which in fact worsened the final text ("'...Ia derzhalsia i rabotal'," 106). Their collaboration nonetheless continued in fall 1928, when Platonov, still without a permanent home, stayed at Pil'niak's dacha outside of Moscow. Together they worked on another project in a satirical vein, the play *Fools on the Periphery* (*Duraki na periferii*), the main theme of which—the naïve and primitive form of communism, bordering on anarchy, desired by the locals instead of the "scientific" and bureaucratic form imposed by the Party—was close to that of Pil'niak's own controversial recent novel, *Mahogany* (*Krasnoe derevo*), which he then subsequently and penitently rewrote as a paean to Stalinist construction titled *The Volga Empties into the Caspian Sea* (*Volga vpadaet v kaspiiskoe more*).

Unfortunately Platonov was caught up at this juncture in the vicious campaign mounted against Pil'niak and another fellow-traveler, Evgeny Zamyatin (author of the dystopian fable *We*), by the critics of the Russian Association of Proletarian Writers (known by its Russian initials as RAPP). "Che-Che-O" caught the critics' attention as well, though the negative reviews it received were probably aimed at Pil'niak—by far the more famous author—rather than at

Platonov. Some of the reviews even failed to mention Platonov at all (Langerak 84). One that unfortunately did not fail to do so was that by V. Strel'nikova, who in the September 28, 1929 issue of the newspaper *Vecherniaia Moskva* charged Platonov with the sin of "being under the influence of Pil'niak" (a state of affairs for which Russian has a single noun, *podpil'niakovshchina*). Strel'nikova singled out for particular criticism Platonov's "Epifanskie shliuzy," homing in on its implied parallel between the "inflated projects" of the Petrine era and those of the present-day Soviet Union. She further accused Platonov of portraying the Russian people as a primitive nation unfit for modernity, and, in the story "Gorod Gradov," of blaming the Soviet regime itself for the bureaucratic habits of its government. Platonov published a spirited reply in *Literaturnaia gazeta*—still something one could do in 1929—in which he cited Lenin and Engels in support of his views and pointed out tendentious omissions in Strel'nikova's quotations from his story. In this instance the editors of *Literaturnaia gazeta* stood up for Platonov, appending a note in which they agreed that he had made mistakes but dismissing Strel'nikova's characterization of him as anti-Soviet (for Platonov's response see "Protiv khalturnykh sudei").

Strel'nikova most likely mounted her attack on "Che-Che-O" in the spirit of the RAPP campaign against Pil'niak and other fellow travelers, but her vitriolic response to Platonov may also have been sharpened by the fact that between the publication of "Che-Che-O" in the December 1928 issue of *Novyi mir* and the publication of her review nine months later the social and political climate had changed dramatically, in ways which retrospectively made the Platonov-Pil'niak satirical romp through the state's economic mismanagement acquire seditious overtones. In April 1929, at the Plenum of the Sixteenth Party Congress, Stalin announced the new economic initiative of the Five-Year Plan—an event which radically altered life on all levels of Soviet society in ways which were impossible for any one to ignore. The nuances of Platonov's response to Stalin's initiative, which was not reflexively dismissive, are to be seen in *The Foundation Pit*. Nonetheless what stands out about the shorter works he devoted

Chapter One

to the topic in 1929—which is to say, virtually everything he wrote that year—is their irony and skepticism.*

The story "Doubting Makar" ("Usomnivshiisia Makar"), for example, which Platonov surprisingly managed to publish in 1929 in the journal *Oktiabr'*, a RAPP outlet, continues the approach of "Sokrovennyi chelovek" by presenting its survey of the first Five-Year Plan and all its energetic undertakings from the perspective of a simple-minded poor peasant, the Makar of the title whose name evokes the canonical "poor man" of Russian literature (such as Makar Devushkin in Dostoevsky's *Poor Folk*, as well as perhaps Gorky's more recent "Makar Chudra"). Like Pukhov in "Sokrovennyi chelovek," Makar sets off for Moscow to see what technological wonders have been accomplished there. He finds workers engaged in constructing an "eternal building," much like that projected in *The Foundation Pit*; but he also finds a government run by bureaucrats. In the story's strangest episode he has a dream in which he sees a statue of a "scientific man" whose gaze is directed toward the future and who therefore cannot see the "private Makar" standing before him. When Makar asks the monument how he should fit into Soviet society, his question is met with silence. When he approaches the monument and touches it, it collapses. The episode recasts a famous scene in Pushkin's "The Bronze Horseman," traditionally read as an indictment of post-Petrine tsarist power, in which a poor clerk named Evgeny dares to shake his fist at the monument to Peter the Great. Moreover when Makar ends up in an insane asylum, the cure he undergoes involves reading the very speeches Lenin wrote just before his death in which he was critical of Stalin—thus daringly underscoring the suggestion that the "scientific man" is Stalin (Langerak 213–4).

---

\*   In addition to works of short fiction Platonov planned and partly wrote a cycle of "true tales" (*byli*) with titles like "The Wise Farm," "Listen to the story about a peasant who outwitted the entire government," "Listen now to the short tale of Filat the poor peasant"; they typically portray a poor peasant who arrives in Moscow in search of the meaning of life and skeptically confronts work on the Five-year Plan (Kornienko 132–3).

"Usomnivshiisia Makar" also attracted the attention of Leopold Averbakh himself, leader of RAPP, who in November 1929 vented his anger in an article titled "On the Large Scale and the Private Makars" ("O tselostnykh masshtabakh i chastnykh Makarakh"). The article was first published in *Oktiabr'* then reprinted in *Na literaturnom postu*—the principal RAPP organ—then once again in the still more visible *Pravda*. Satire is good, Averbakh began disingenuously, but Platonov's story is not aimed at correcting minor flaws in Soviet life. It is, rather, a "nihilist, anti-government" mockery suffused with anarchist sentiments in which "private Makars" and their petty concerns are elevated above the grand schemes of socialist construction. After the blizzard of invective released in Averbakh's serially republished attack *Oktiabr'* retracted and declared that it had, in fact, been a "mistake" to publish Platonov's stories (the journal had also published a shorter work by Platonov called "A Resident of the State" ["Gosudarstvennyi zhitel'"] in the same year).

It was in the midst of all this, then, that Platonov began taking notes for what was to become *The Foundation Pit*, which he finished sometime in the summer or fall of 1930 (the time-span indicated in one of the manuscripts of the work, December 1929—April 1930, once thought to indicate the period of its composition, is now thought to indicate the temporal setting of the events it portrays; *Kotlovan* 117–8). At that point he had recently turned thirty and was still having conflicts with the land reclamation section of Narkomzem (Kornienko 136, 150). Nor, unfortunately for Platonov, was the fiasco of the *Oktiabr'* publications the end of his political troubles. In 1931 in the journal *Krasnaia nov'*—erstwhile flagship of moderate, fellow-traveling Marxists—published a work of his entitled "For Future Use. A Poor-peasant Chronicle" ("Vprok. Bedniatskaia khronika") which again offered a skeptical survey of a Five-Year Plan initiative from the vantage point of a simple peasant, this time the campaign to collectivize Soviet agriculture. Two issues later, in the same journal, the arch-loyalist writer and secretary of RAPP Alexander Fadeev published a diatribe in which he accused Platonov of being nothing less than a "kulak agent" masquerading as a simple peasant, determined to undermine collectivization in order to prepare the way for a "kulak utopia" (273, 277). Echoing the journal *Oktiabr'*'s earlier craven retraction, *Krasnaia nov'* now appended its own apologetic note to Fadeev's "review" in which it endorsed his perspective and declared it to have been a "crude error" to publish Platonov's work on its pages. That both Fadeev and *Krasnaia nov'* leapt with such unambiguous swiftness to condemn Platonov may have had to do with the personal reaction of Stalin himself. According to one legend, he was infuriated by "Vprok" and wrote the word "bastard!" in its margins; according to another, he told Fadeev to "give it to [Platonov] real good (*vmazat'*, lit. "smear it in his face"), so that he remembers it in the future (*vprok*)" (Shentalinskii 19).

Given the harsh realities of life in the Stalinist Soviet Union, Platonov's only hope at this point, if he wished to continue as a writer, was to recant and make a display of reforming himself. On 9 June 1931 he wrote a letter to *Pravda* and *Literaturnaia gazeta* in which he painfully renounced all his previous literary works (thus repeating a gesture performed by such nineteenth-century writers as Nikolai Gogol and Leo Tolstoy, both of whom underwent a spiritual crisis, but in markedly different moral and political conditions) and lamented the "contradiction between this author's intentions and his activities" which had led to the expression of counterrevolutionary ideas rather than the proletarian worldview he thought he had possessed. In February 1932 the All-Russian Union of Soviet Writers (a relatively mild organization, in those years of RAPP-feulled animosity, of which Pil'niak had recently been head) held a closed-door meeting for the express purpose of discussing Platonov's situation. "Over the past year Platonov has become very popular," remarked P.A. Pavlenko in his opening statement, with an irony no RAPP critic would have allowed himself, "everywhere you turn he is being 'dekulakized' as a writer of hostile views who conveys ideas inappropriate for a Soviet writer" ("'... Ia derzhalsia i rabotal'," 98). During the meeting Platonov suggests that in his early work experiences he may have picked up, as if it were some kind of virus, the world view of "backwards workers, anarchist workers" even though he had no organizational contacts with any anarchists ("'...Ia derzhalsia i rabotal'," 100–4).

In a July 1932 letter to Gorky Platonov lamented that it was "impossible to bear the stamp of class enemy" (Perkhin 229–30) and that "to be rejected by one's class while remaining close to it inwardly is far greater torment than to recognize that you are alien to it" (quoted in Kornienko 166). The letter appears to have gone unanswered, and the ultimate result of the "Vprok" affair was that from 1931–1934 no journal or press would publish Platonov's work. The legend which once circulated that he was reduced to working as a janitor in the main residence of the Writers' Union was no more than that, but Platonov nonetheless continued to endure difficult material circumstances (in February of 1931 he even wrote to Leopold Averbakh, who had recently savaged him in the press, pleading for assistance in finding a place to live because "three plus years without an apartment is beyond anyone's limit of endurance"; "Pis'ma A.P. Platonova 1927–1936 godov" 164). He did not stop writing, however. In late 1931-early 1932, for example, he worked on the tale "The Juvenile Sea" ("Iuvenil'noe more"), an attempt at a more compliant work in which the heroine struggles to overfulfill the meat-production quota on a collective farm (the work, though, was first published only in 1986). He also turned to drama, writing *The Barrel-Organ* (*Sharmanka*) in 1930, *The Dirigible* (*Dirizhabl'*) in 1931, *High Tension* (*Vysokoe napriazhenie*) in 1931–1932, and *14 Little Red Huts* (*14 krasnykh izbushek*) in 1932. Like his prose works, they combine fervent support for socialism as a remedy for the physical sufferings of the proletariat with scenes bordering the surreal and scarcely veiled irony toward the bureaucracy and propaganda filling the everyday life of Soviet citizens. None was staged in his lifetime.

Platonov's situation began to improve somewhat in 1934. He was denied permission to travel to the construction site of the White Sea canal, to the glory of which a massive collective literary work was being produced under the sponsorship of the Writers' Union; but he was allowed to make a trip for similar purposes to Central Asia.

## Chapter One

The stark desert landscapes he encountered there, which he saw as an iconic representation of the difficulty of human survival and the decay of civilizations, fascinated him, and he wrote one of the masterpieces of this later period of his career under their influence. "Dzhan" (a Turkmen word meaning "soul," which is the title of its English translation) recounts the efforts of a young Turkmen who has received a scientific education in Moscow to locate his native tribe in the desert and bring them out of nomadic existence and into modern Soviet civilization. In one version of the tale he succeeds, but in another, almost certainly the original version, the effort at collectivizing the *dzhan* fails and they wander off into the desert once more.

Further evidence that Platonov was making a concerted effort to transform himself into an acceptable Soviet writer is his work from 1932–1936 on *Happy Moscow* (*Schastlivaia Moskva*), an attempt at a socialist realist novel which, however, approaches its task so idiosyncratically that one wonders whether Platonov seriously expected it to be published (it was not). In 1936, the journal *Literaturnyi kritik*, which normally published criticism rather than original fiction, took the unprecedented step of printing two of Platonov's stories, "Fro" and "Immortality" ("Bessmertie"). Both are minor masterpieces of psychological prose ("Fro" focuses on the sorrows of a wife, Afrosinya, left behind by a husband whose perennial absences are the result of his dedication to building socialism; "Bessmertie" portrays the loneliness of a loyal railway worker posted to a remote station); but one casualty of the "Vprok" debacle was the strange and complex idiom in which he had written the most innovative of his works in the late 1920s, *Chevengur* and *The Foundation Pit* in particular. In order to be published Platonov now had to write in a simpler and more normalized narrative style (a concession made by many other writers of the 1920s as well: as Soviet culture moved into the Stalin era all forms of artistic expression were expected to drop formal experimentation and become more "accessible" to the masses). Even in the later works occasional turns of phrase suggest the brilliant oddities of his earlier career, however, and nothing Platonov ever wrote could be called fully conformist.

Platonov himself escaped the horrendous purges which the Stalinist regime inflicted on Soviet society in 1937 and 1938, but his son did not. In 1938 Platon ("Tosha"), then still a teen-ager, was arrested and accused of plotting to blow up the Kremlin. The charge was flagrantly untrue, but the point of the arrest may have been instead to threaten Platonov himself. A friend of Platonov's, Emil' Mindlin, recalls Platonov telling him how he and his wife travelled to the provincial town to which their son had been taken and stood for hours in the snow staring at the high walls of the prison in the futile hope of gaining some glimpse of him (49). Tosha, who was already in frail health, was sent to a labor camp. He was released in 1941 but had by that time contracted tuberculosis, from which he died in January 1943.

In the later years of his life Platonov published a handful of stories while continuing to work in safer, nonliterary genres. In the late 1930s he wrote a series of book reviews, which were collected in the volume *Reflections of a Reader* (*Razmyshleniia chitatelia*) published by Sovietskii pisatel' in 1939. From October 1942 until the end of the war he served as a front-line correspondent for the army newspaper *Krasnaia zvezda*, producing a series of sketches and stories from the war which, while portraying the heroism of Soviet soldiers, nonetheless subtly exude a sense of world-weariness and even pacifism (as one critic complained). In the late 1940s, with the backing of Mikhail Sholokhov (author of *The Quiet Don*), Platonov published adaptations of Russian and Bashkir folktales for children (collected in *The Magical Ring* [*Volshebnoe kol'tso*] and *Bashkir Folk Tales* [*Bashkirskie narodnye skazki*]). In reality, though, from the early 1930s to the end of his life Platonov pursued but never gained full acceptance by the Soviet literary authorities. He was never assured of steady income from his writing, and was always vulnerable to reawakened critical and institutional ire. In retrospect *The Foundation Pit* and the works written in close temporal proximity to it represent something of a watershed in his life and *oeuvre*, though it is a matter of some dispute among scholars how fundamentally the accomplished later works like "Dzhan" and "Fro" differ in outlook from those of the 1920s and early 1930s.

Platonov fell seriously ill in the late 1940s with tuberculosis, which he probably caught from his son when he returned from the labor camp. Photos taken of him in these last years show a gaunt, ailing, and sadly resigned man. He died on 5 Janury 1951. Since Platonov's death his works have enjoyed two posthumous returns (Malygina 9). The publication in 1958, during the cultural period known as the "thaw" which followed Stalin's death, of his *Selected Stories* (*Izbrannye rasskazy*), made at least some of his tamer, later stories available to Soviet readers who in many cases had never even heard of him. Further collections containing works that were acceptable to the tastes of Soviet literary officialdom continued to appear in the 1960s, 1970s, and early 1980s. The second and more significant wave of republication, however, began in the late 1980s, when first the policy of *perestroika* and then the collapse of the Soviet Union made full publication of all Platonov's works, together with all the extant biographical materials, finally possible. The culmination of this process is the publication, currently in progress, of a scholarly edition of his complete collected works by the Russian Academy of Sciences.

## A SELECTED LIST OF PLATONOV'S WORKS IN ENGLISH

*Chevengur.* Trans Anthony Olcott. Ann Arbor, MI: Ardis, 1978.
*Collected Works.* Ann Arbor, MI: Ardis, 1978.
*The Fierce and Beautiful World.* Introduction by Tatyana Tolstaya. New York: NYRB Classics, 2000.
*The Foundation Pit*:
   (note: *The Foundation Pit*—*Kotlovan* in Russian—was first published in 1973 by Ardis Press of Ann Arbor, Michigan, based on a text which had been smuggled out of the Soviet Union. Unfortunately this text contained minor omissions and transpositions, which therefore appear in the first translation by Mirra Ginsburg published in 1975 and the 1978 translation by Thomas P. Whitney. *Kotlovan* first appeared in Russia in 1987, in the journal *Novyi mir*. A full text of the work in Russian which corresponds to the extant typescripts in Platonov's archive can be found in the 2000 Nauka edition, which also provides extensive information on the various drafts and their variations. The Chandler and Meerson translation follows this corrected text.)
      Trans. Robert and Elizabeth Chandler and Olga Meerson. New York: NYRB, 2009.
      Trans. Robert Chandler. London: Harvill, 1996.
      Trans. Mirra Ginsburg. Evanston, IL: Northwestern UP, 1994.
      Trans. Thomas P. Whitney. Ann Arbor: MI: Ardis, 1973
*Happy Moscow.* Trans. Robert and Elizabeth Chandler, with an introduction by Eric Naiman. London: Harvill Press, 2001.
*The Portable Platonov.* Glas: New Russian Writing. Moscow: Glas, 1999.
*The Return and Other Stories.* Trans. Angela Livingstone and Robert Chandler. London: Harvill Press, 1999.
*Soul and Other Stories.* Trans. Robert Chandler and Olga Meerson, with an introduction by Robert Chandler and afterword by John Berger. New York: NYRB Classics, 2007.

## REFERENCES

Averbakh, L. "O tselostnykh masshtabakh i chastnykh Makarakh." *Na literaturnom postu*, nos. 21–22 (1929): 10–17. Reprint: N.V. Kornienko and E.D. Shubina, eds. *Andrei Platonov. Vospominaniia sovremennikov. Materialy k biografii*. Moscow: Sovremennyi pisatel', 1994. 256–67.

Briusov, V. "Sredi stikhov." *Pechat' i revoliutsiia*, no. 6 (1923): 69–70.

Fadeev, A. "Ob odnoi kulatskoi khronike." *Krasnaia nov'*, no. 506 (1931): 206–9. Reprint: N.V. Kornienko and E.D. Shubina, eds. *Andrei Platonov. Vospominaniia sovremennikov. Materialy k biografii*. Moscow: Sovremennyi pisatel', 1994. 268–78.

Garros, Véronique, Natalia Korenevskaya, Thomas Lahusen, and Carol A. Flath. *Intimacy and Terror. Soviet Diaries of the 1930s*. New York: New Press, 1997.

Gor'kii, Maxim. "Gor'kii—A.P. Platonov." *Literaturnoe nasledstvo*. Vol. 70. *Gor'kii i sovetskie pisateli. Neizdannaia perepiska*. Moscow: AN SSSR, 1963. 313–15.

Hellbeck, Jochen. *Revolution on My Mind. Writing a Diary under Stalin*. Cambridge: Harvard University Press, 2006.

Inozemtseva, E. "Platonov v Voronezhe." *Pod'em*, no. 2 (1971): 91–103.

Kornienko, N.V. *Istoriia teksta i biografiia A. P. Platonova (1926–1946). Zdes' i teper'*, no. 1 (1993).

———. "Ot 'Rodiny elektrichestva' k 'Tekhnicheskomu romanu', i obratno: Metamorfozy teksta Platonova 30-kh godov." http://streetuniver.narod.ru/o_platonove_kornienko_tex_roman.pdf (accessed February 5, 2009).

Langerak, Tomas. *Andrei Platonov. Materialy dlia biografii 1899–1929 gg.* Amsterdam: Pegasus, 1995.

Maizel', M. "Oshibki mastera." *Zvezda*, no. 4 (1930): 195–202.

Malygina, N.M. *Andrei Platonov. Poetika "Vozvrashcheniia"*. Moscow: TEIS, 2005.

Mindlin, Emil'. "Andrei Platonov." In N.V. Kornienko and E.D. Shubina, eds. *Andrei Platonov. Vospominaniia sovremennikov. Materialy k biografii*. Moscow: Sovremennyi pisatel', 1994. 31–51.

Oleinikov, O. Iu., et al. "Kommentarii." In Andrei Platonov, *Sochineniia. Tom pervyi. 1918-1927. Kniga pervaia. Rasskazy. Stikhotvoreniia*. Moscow: IMLI RAN, 2004. 447–639.

Perkhin, V.V. "Dva pis'ma Andreia Platonova." *Russkaia literatura*, no. 1 (1990): 228–32.

Platonov, A.P. *Golubaia glubina. Kniga stikhov*. Krasnodar: Burevestnik, 1922.

———. "'...Ia derzhalsia i rabotal'. Stanitsa biografii Andreia Platonova (K 90-letiiu pisatelia)." *Pamir*, no. 6, 1989, 97–118.

———. *Kotlovan. Tekst. Materialy tvorcheskoi istorii*. Introduction by V. Iu. Viugin. Commentary by V.Iu. Viugin, T.M. Vakhitova, and V.A. Prokof'ev. St. Petersburg: Nauka, 2000.

———. "Otvet na anketu 'Kakoi nam nuzhen pistatel'." In N.V. Kornienko and E.D. Shubina, eds. Andrei Platonov. Vospominaniia sovremennikov. Materialy k biografii. Moscow: Sovremennyi pisatel', 1994. 286–8.

———. "Pis'ma A.P. Platonova 1927–1936 godov." *Volga*, no. 8, 1989. 163–5.

———. "Protiv khalturnykh sudei (Otvet V. Strel'nikovoi)." *Literaturnaia gazeta*, no. 26 (14 October 1929): 2.

———. *Sobranie sochinenii v trekh tomakh*. Moscow: Sovetskaia Rossiia, 1984.

———. *Tekhnicheskii roman. Ogonek* 19, no. 3277 (May 1990): 19–22; 20, no. 3278 (May 1990): 20–3.

———. *Zapisnye knizhki. Materialy k biografii*. 2nd edition. Foreword N.V. Kornienko. Moscow: IMLI RAN, 2006.

Platonova, M. "...Zhivia glavnoi zhiz'niu (A. Platonov v pis'makh k zhene, dokumentakh i ocherkah)." *Volga*, no. 9 (1975): 160–78.

Shentalinskii, V. Preface to A. Platonov, *Tekhnicheskii roman. Ogonek* 19, no. 3277 (May 1990): 19–22.

Shklovskii, Viktor. *Tret'ia fabrika*. Moscow: Artel' pisatelei 'Krug,' 1926.

Shubina, E. "Sozertsatel' i delatel' (1899–1926)." In N.V. Kornienko and E.D. Shubina, eds. *Andrei Platonov. Vospominaniia sovremennikov. Materialy k biografii*. Moscow: Sovremennyi pisatel', 1994. 138–54.

Skobelev, V.P., et al., eds. *Tvorchestvo A. Platonova. Stat'i i soobshcheniia*. Voronoezh: Izdatel'stvo Voronezhskogo universiteta, 1970.

## Chapter One

Strel'nikova, V. "'Razoblachiteli' sotsializma. O podpil'niachnikakh." *Vecherniaia Moskva* (28 September 1929).

Vasil'ev, Vladimir. *Andrei Platonov. Ocherk zhizni i tvorchestva*. Moscow: Sovremennik, 1982.

Verin, Vladimir. "'Ia zhe rabotal sovsem s drugimi chuvstvami...'." *Literaturnaia gazeta*, no. 17 (27 April 1988): 4.

———. "Istoriia odnoi komandirovki." *Sever*, no. 10 (1986): 103–5.

Chapter 2

# Intellectual Influences on Platonov

The phenomenon of Soviet "proletarian" or "revolutionary" literature was more varied than is sometimes assumed in the west, but even so Platonov occupied an idiosyncratic position within his intellectual context. His worldview is complex and sometimes contradictory, eluding reduction to any single doctrine or set of intellectual influences. Even the ideas one finds in his works that were popular in the late 1910s and 1920s in Russia tend to sound there in ways peculiar to Platonov. Ideas often appear in his works in a subtly ironic mode which signals neither full endorsement nor mocking rejection but something closer to resignation and emotional distance. Even in his most ardently ideological phase, the period immediately following the Revolution when he worked as a journalist in Voronezh, his aggressive espousal of such things as the ascendancy of proletarian "consciousness" or the triumph of technology over matter could alternate with somber intimations of human weakness or, as in the poetry collection *Golubaia glubina*, melancholic longing for rural simplicity.

Essentially self-taught in the field of letters, Platonov was nonetheless both an intellectual and an ideological writer, in the sense that his fictional works are to a significant extent *responses to* a series of ideologies and philosophies that animated Soviet culture in his day, not least the dominant ideology of Stalinism as it began to emerge in the late 1920s. To be fully understood his works have to be read against the background of these motivating ideas: the events and imagery in his stories, novels, and plays frequently allude to specific doctrines and the characters' speech is nothing if not littered with fragments of recognizable ideological or philosophical discourse. This is especially true of a work like *The Foundation Pit*, which was written in a period of ideological intensity in Soviet life.

Even early in his career it was evident that Platonov was an avid reader who was aware of some of the central preoccupations of Russian intellectual life in the era of revolution. The very first notebook he began keeping, in 1921, for example, opens with a quotation in Russian from Nietzsche's *Thus Spake Zarathustra*, deployed, it would seem, in a gesture of audacious radicalism of the sort he espoused in the years immediately following the revolution: "God is dead, now we want the superman to live" (in the original this is in fact "all the *gods* are dead": "Tot sind alle Götter: nun wollen wir, daß der Übermensch lebe"). Although awareness of Nietzsche's legacy was later suppressed in the Soviet Union, he exerted a significant influence on an array of Soviet intellectuals from the revolutionary period and on into Stalinism—even forming, for some scholars, one of the unacknowledged pillars of Stalinist thought (see Rosenthal).

In the description of Platonov as a land reclamation engineer working in the field that the Formalist literary theoretician Victor Shklovsky left after touring the Voronezh region in the early 1920s he records him speaking, as they sat on the terrace of a village house one evening, "about literature, about Rozanov" (129). The notes to the Russian edition of Platonov's collected works also state that the discovery of Rozanov's writings was "one of the intellectual events" of Platonov's life in the summer of 1920 (Kommentarii 328). Vasily Rozanov (1856–1919) was a journalist and writer who more than any one else in the Russian fin-de-siècle was responsible for introducing the hitherto taboo theme of sexuality and gender identity (his *Moonlight People* [*Liudi lunnogo sveta*] is a mediation on the meaning of homosexuality) into Russian culture. Shklovsky does not record what works by Rozanov Platonov spoke of, but the preoccupation with human physicality in Platonov's own works exemplifies a kind of discourse that became possible within Russian culture only after Rozanov and to a significant degree in response to his writings (see Tolstaia's remark to this effect, 314). Rozanov's *An Apocalypse of Our Time* (*Apokalipsis nashego vremeni*) may also have appealed to the young Platonov's attraction to chiliastic visions. A similar "decadent" influence was the German historian Oswald Spengler's 1917 *The Decline of the West*, which was widely read in early Soviet Russia. Platonov occasionally invokes Spengler's name on the subject of bourgeois decline in some of his Voronezh journalism—and an unpublished essay of ca. 1922 entitled "The Symphony of Consciousness" ("Simfonia soznaniia") is essentialy a review of Spengler's thought—though it is possible that Platonov knew Spengler's ideas from a collection of essays on them by leading Russian philosophers (*Oswald Spengler and the Decline of Europe*, 1922, which featured essays by Fedor Stepun, Sergei Frank, and Nikolai Berdiaev, among others) rather than from the original (*Sobranie sochinenii* I-2, 399). A related general presence in Platonov's thought is the late nineteenth-century religious philosopher Vladimir Solov'ev (1853–1900). Although he is not particularly important as a direct influence on any of Platonov's works, with the possible exception of some of the early poems, Solov'ev's notions of Godmanhood (i.e., human aspiration toward ultimate divinity) and the unity of the cosmos through the person of the divine Sophia, or holy Wisdom, shaped the turn-of-the-century Russian atmosphere of chiliastic longings and were important for both Vasily Rozanov and Nikolai Fedorov, who did influence Platonov directly.

When it comes to explicit influences, however, far more significant to the development of Platonov's writing were various forms of "bolshevik utopianism."* "Bolshevik" is the more appropriate modifier

---

\*   See also Bethea. *The Foundation Pit* is distinctly less *utopian* than the earlier *Chevengur*, in that it devotes hardly any space to the depiction of an ideal society. Unlike the eccentrics of Chevengur, who try out all sorts of exotically literal schemes for transforming their social existence, the characters in the later tale have essentially been reduced to longing for rescue from their existential plight; or perhaps the utopian initiative in that tale has been implicitly displaced by the claims of the Stalinist Five-Year Plan. Nonetheless *The Foundation Pit* exemplifies the same tension Bethea identifies in *Chevengur* between utopianism, in the sense of longing for a "no-place" where a perfect society exists or might be formed, and apocalypticism, in the sense of a longing for or anticipation of the end of time (a tension which Bethea argues is characteristic of the whole tradition of utopian thought in Russia).

here than "Soviet" because the doctrines in question belong more properly to the pre- and immediately post-Revolutionary period of heady intellectual ferment than to the era of more established official ideology (and with that, intellectual conformity) which settled in as the decade of the 1920s wore on. Nor does Marxism *per se*, as a philosophical and political doctrine, play much of a role in Platonov's thought. Although he clearly had read Marx and Engels, there is little evidence that their writings meant much to him intellectually. In this he was not unlike many other young, ardent supporters of the Bolshevik cause who would have seconded the poet Vladimir Mayakovsky when he intoned—with ominous cultural implications—in his "At Full Voice" ("Vo ves' golos"): "We opened every volume of Marx/The way you open shutters in your home/But *even without reading* we knew/Which camp to march with and in which to fight" (emphasis added, TS).

Chief among these heady influences is Alexander Bogdanov (real name A.A. Malinovskii, 1873–1928), whose theories of proletarian culture, in particular his project for a utopian form of science which he called "tectology" Platonov invokes often in his Voronezh journalism and stories of the 1920s. Bogdanov was an important figure in the early years of the Bolshevik faction of Russia's Social Democratic party, at least until he and Lenin had a falling out in 1909. Where Lenin obsessively devoted his attention to politics, however, Bogdanov devoted his to science—more specifially, to the question of the nature of scientific knowledge and its possible utopian implications.

Bogdanov's views represented a curious twist on the Marxist notion of the cultural "superstructure" and its economic "base." As one scholar comments, "For Bogdanov, science, art, and ideology did not merely *reflect* the socioeconomic structure, but played a crucial role in *organizing* and therefore *creating* that structure" (McClelland 408). Inspired in part by the "empiriocriticism" of the Austrian physicist Ernst Mach and the philosopher Richard Avenarius, which sought to relate all knowledge and thought to pure experience, Bogdanov elaborated his own philosophy of "empiriomonism," which argued that the material and the spiritual realms are not fundamentally distinct but merely different aspects of human experience of the world (on empiriocriticism see Blackburn 31). He revised Marx's claim that "social being determines social consciousness" by asserting that "social existence and social consciousness in the exact meaning of these words are identical" (see also the discussion in Seifrid 26–7). He then argued that the physical world had no existence apart from human consciousness of it—which consciousness, however, he believed resided not in individual minds but in the collective form of "socially organized experience." It was this emphasis on collective, especially proletarian, experience that signalled his Marxist heritage and set him apart from the "bourgeois" Mach and Avenarius. History for Bogdanov was primarily the record of sentient being's efforts to gain mastery over the world, and he believed that it was the destiny of the working class to realize the epistemological truth behind reality and on its basis unite *all* forms of knowledge in a "universal organizational science" he labelled "tectology" (which some have suggested anticipated Norbert Weiner's cybernetics by two decades or so). This grand synthesis of human knowledge would in turn make it possible to organize that knowledge in such a way as to restructure reality according to human needs (since the real restructuring takes place in collective consciousness).

Bogdanov seems earnestly to have believed that this doctrine was just a variation on Marxist materialism, but its heretical swerve toward philosophical idealism was obvious, and Lenin furiously rebutted Bogdanov's ideas in what was to become his principal philosophical work (though the arguments in it hardly rise to the level of that discipline), *Materialism and Empiriocriticism* (1909). Despite his philosophical differences with Lenin, Bogdanov remained prominent in efforts to promote proletarian culture (founding schools for Russian workers together with Maxim Gorky, for example) and became the leader of the Proletkul't movement that flourished in Soviet Russia from 1917–1920, which is almost certainly how Platonov encountered his ideas. Bogdanov's original education had been in medicine, and, never timid in the application of his theories, he died in 1928 as the result of a botched experiment he performed on himself in the Institute for Blood Transfusion he had founded in 1926.

Chapter Two

The utopian prospect of these ideas held enormous appeal for an intellectually ambitious young man from the provinces, as Platonov was in the years following the Revolution, and Platonov's Voronezh journalism at times reads as though it were meant to be a platform for disseminating the doctrine of tectology. In an article addressed "To Beginning Proletarian Writers and Poets" ("K nachinaiushchim proletarskim poetam i pisateliam," published in the newspaper *Zheleznyi put'*), for example, he explains that in the long dark period of bourgeois history which the Revolution brought to an end, people were nothing but "weak corporeal individuals." The proletariat's industrial experience, however, has taught it to "pour its isolated powers into a powerful stream of organized endeavors." One of these is art, which he defines as the process through which the forces of nature pass through human nature. The period in which art concentrated on mere inner experience is now giving way to one in which artistic creativity will be expressed in actions directed against the physical world. The article "Proletarian Poetry" ("Proletarskaia poeziia") which Platonov published in the journal *Kuznitsa* in 1921 develops these ideas more extensively. It begins by announcing, with the teleological conviction characteristic of Marxism and Bolshevism, that history leads inexorably toward the victory of humanity over the "disorganized" forces of the cosmos. History's endpoint, Platonov states, lies in a comprehension (*postizhenie*) of the world's essence which will yield the "complete organization" of knowledge about the world. His emphasis in this address to proletarian writers falls again on the nature of art, which he claims involves the "organization of the symbols of things, words." There is a characteristic hint of compromise or even resignation in this definition ("people have begun not with the reorganization of reality itself but with the easier, more manageable task of restructuring symbols") but Platonov nonetheless assures his readers that the organization of symbols runs parallel to "work on the organization and the transformation of reality, of matter itself." (*Sochineniia* I–2, 162–5). Another note of Bogdanovian "organization" sounds in the article "The Creative Newspaper" ("Tvorcheskaia gazeta," published in *Voronezhskaia kommuna*), where

Platonov defines newspapers as the "everyday working thought of society which organizes its activity." Without explaining exactly how, he declares that newspapers embody the "enduring, uninterrupted consciousness of the proletariat which directs its blows against nature." If in the hands of the bourgeousie newspapers fed class conflict, then under communism, he confidently predicts, they will be "transformed into a weapon in humanity's struggle against the cosmic elements." In order to do this the proletarian newspaper must become a means for "creating consciousness," which at this stage he seems to believe involves simply allowing the proletariat to express its views (*Sochineniia* I–2, 128–30).

Platonov could be contradictory, arguing on the one hand, in a manner sympathetic with Bogdanov's ideas, that historical progress entailed humanity's ascent from the realm of matter to that of *consciousness* (as in "At the Founding of the Kingdom of Consciousness" ["U nachala tsarstva soznaniia," *Voronezhskaia kommuna*], when he dismisses the bourgeois era as having been dominated by sex and emotion; or in "On the Culture of Harnessed Light and Comprehended Electricity" ["O kul'ture zapriazhennogo sveta i poznannogo elektrichestva," *Iskusstvo i teatr*] which claims that in the past human culture had devoted itself mostly to producing gametes and therefore could not raise itself above the level of vegetative existence); but on the other hand insisting that history marches forward from metaphysics to physics, from idea to *matter* (or, as he declares in "The Revolution of the 'Spirit'" ["Revoliutsiia 'dukha'," *Ogni*], spirit is nothing but an excresence on matter, and "there are no values for us outside of matter"). Part of the reason for this inconsistency has to do with the justifiably (at least from a philosophical point of view) precarious status that Bogdanov's ideas enjoyed in relation to official Bolshevik ideology (Lenin had, after all, condemned Bogdanov as a closet idealist). The assertions of the primacy of matter may thus represent an effort in effect to correct the idealist swerve in Bogdanov's thought. But there is an underlying rhetorical or emotional, if not logical, consistency in his Voronezh-era proclamations: he condemns anything which threatens to leave humanity in bondage to the physical world. If the triumph of "organizing" consciousness promises a liberation from the trials of existence, then some sort of reign of "consciounsess" is the proletariat's welcome destiny. If, on the other hand, idealism, the valuation of nonmaterial entities, seems to mean passive subservience to the physical world, it is rejected in favor of a materialism which will alter that world.

Most scholars of Platonov see the early infatuation with Bogdanov in the Voronezh journalism giving way, with the passage of time and his cumulative experiences as a land reclamation engineer, to skepticism and irony—over whether the "organization" of the material world in "consciousness" is truly possible, over whether it is even desireable. But Bogdanov's ideas flit in and out of Platonov's literary works of the 1920s, especially in his science fiction stories, such as "A Satan of Thought" ("Satana mysli"), "The Lunar Bomb" ("Lunnaia bomba"), and "The Ethereal Path" ("Efirnyi trakt"), all of which portray efforts by scientist-heroes to use a synthetic knowledge of the physical world to transform it—and Platonov may have been inspired to write science fiction in general by the precedent of Bogdanov himself, who had written two science fiction novels, *Red Star* (1908) and *Engineer Menni* (1911; both have been translated into English). At the very least Bogdanov's influence is evident as late as the period in which Platonov was writing *The Foundation Pit*, in which the engineer Prushevsky clearly understands his otherwise conventional Five-Year Plan construction project in philosophical terms derived from Bogdanov's "empiriomonism."

A related set of ideas that influenced Platonov in the 1920s involved the radically revisionist understanding of art promoted by the "left-" wing Soviet aestheticians Nikolai Chuzhak, Sergei Tret'iakov, and Boris Arvatov—"left" in the context of early Soviet culture meaning members of the pre-revolutionary avant-garde, adherents of such movements as Futurism and Constructivism, especially those who in the Soviet era had associated themselves with the journal *LEF* (for "Left Front of Art"). Particulary evident in Platonov's works is their idea of "life-creation," which held that real artistic activity should be directed toward life itself rather than any narrowly aesthetic sphere, with "activity" understood as meaning exclusively the creation of a socialist society; and "productionism," which called on artists to abandon the "easel" and turn their attention to designing objects capable of bringing about the utopian transformation of the everyday life of the proletariat (architecture, furnishings, clothing, utensils, and the like). In a seminal article published in *LEF* in 1923, for example, Nikolai Chuzhak declared that the crisis that Russian art had experienced since the end of the nineteenth century had weaned it entirely from the idea that art is mere decoration of life. He accused Soviet artists who now occupied themselves with the "decoration" of labor (i.e., mere depiction) of not going far enough. Art, he insisted, should instead be a method of "life-building" (*zhiznestroenie*) and as such could no longer remain isolated from other means for building life. Why promote the theater as "bio-mechanics in a box" ("kak nekuiu korobochnuiu biomekhaniku"), Chuzhak asked, or music as "condensed hurdy-gurdy noise" ("skondensirovannyi sharmannyi shum"), or verbal art "as some kind of laboratory for hammering out speech" ("laboratoriiu rechekovki"), when thousands of better rhythms and noises pulse through real life? Futurism, with its radical formal experimentation and emphasis on the material quality of art had been a necessary dialectical stage in the development of proletarian art. But a genuine proletarian art must now become one of "production," of "overcoming matter." "Art, as the sole joyous process of rhythmically organized production of good-values (tovaro-tsennostei) in light of the future—this is the programmatic tendency which every communist must follow" ("Pod znakom zhiznestroeniia" 36).

Maxim Gorky, a pre-revolutionary promoter of "workers'" literature and later doyen of Soviet letters (and one of the principal architects of socialist realism), held a similar view of literature and its purpose. Gorky believed that literature exhibits a longstanding interest in depicting the human experience of labor, an orientation he attributed to art and labor being analogous forms of activity. The earliest, oral forms of literature were the means by which ancient workers "organized their experiences," just as the labors of ancient workers represented an attempt to organize their physical existence

("Soviet Literature" 52; there are clear echoes of Bogdanov in this statement). Elsewhere Gorky explicitly compares physical labor, which works raw materials up into finished products such as chairs, tables, needles, and cannons, with literary activity, which works on the more complex "material" of life as a whole ("O literaturnoi tekhnike" 333). Supporting the analogy for Gorky is a notion of creative activity in general (*tvorchestvo*) which precedes the more specific activities of labor and art and arises out of a basic biological drive in humans, namely, the need to "work to change matter, materials, and the conditions of life" ("Ob iskusstve" 444). Language performs the service of "organizing the labor processes of men," and the "thinking in images" in which literature engages is essentially a technique for organizing labor experience in the form of words ("O literaturnoi tekhnike" 336).

What set Platonov apart from the many other adherents of left-wing art in the early Soviet era was the fact that he had actually put the theory of "productionism" into practice by working as a land reclamation engineer. His virtual silence as a writer from 1924–1926 may have been inspired by the example of another "productionist," the proletarian poet Alexei Gastev, who despite the enormous popularity of his poetry pointedly abandoned writing to devote himself to work in the Central Institute for Labor (where among other things the industrial management theories of Henry Ford and Fredrick Taylor were studied; Langerak 32–3, 4). But the idea of productionism was important to Platonov as well. In early 1924, possibly during one of his visits to Moscow, he wrote three reviews for the journal *Oktriabr' mysli* of three other journals representing distinct factions within Soviet literature: *LEF*, which was the organ of the latter-day Futurists; *Na postu*, mouthpiece of politically militant proletarianists; and *Zvezda*, which inclined toward proletarian fellow-travelers. The reviews make it clear that at this point Platonov supported *LEF* and its slogan of productionism, according to which "art is a means of life-building" (see Langerak 39–41). "To organize the emotions," he writes, "means through the emotions to organize human activity, in other words, to *build life*" (*Sochineniia* I–2, 260). In the earlier essay

"Revoliutsiia 'dukha'," published in Voronezh in 1921, he had declared that "the thunder and rhythm of pulsating white-hot machines inspires us more than a thousand of geniuses of sound. The flame of molten ore and the black bodies of caldrons and motors give birth to more colors than any smearing of paint on pieces of canvas" (*Sochineniia* I–2, 173). It is interesing that this passage immediately follows one which seems to anticipate the plot of *The Foundation Pit*, in which Platonov urges the proletariat to "thrust into the clouds structures of rails, concrete, and glass." Gastev's allegory "The Tower" is probably the immediate source here, but Boris Arvatov had also enthused about projected Stalinist skyscrapers as "marvels of glass and steel" (quoted in Dobrenko 159; see also the discussion of this motif in chapter five of this *Companion*).

An essay Platonov wrote a couple of years later, sometime in 1926–1927, offers his most explicit response to the left-aestheticians' calls for a new form of art. Platonov originally sent "The Factory of Literature" ("Fabrika literatury") to the journal *Oktiabr'*, possibly as part of discussion the journal had initiated of Marxist aesthetics and dialectical materialism in wake of a 1925 resolution of the Party's Central Committee, which granted relative freedom to literary factions and thus forced the ever-hegemonizing Russian Association of Proletarian Writers (RAPP), the journal's sponsors, to reconsider its aims. *Oktiabr'* rejected the essay. Platonov then sent it to *Zhurnal krest'ianskoi molodezhi*, which had recently published his story "How Il'ich's Lamp Was Lit" ("Kak zazhglas' lampa Il'icha"), but it remained unpublished until *Oktiabr'*, in a very different incarnation, brought it out in 1991 (Kornienko 31). "The Factory of Literature" is very characteristic of the way in which ideologemes finds their way into Platonov's writings. Platonov begins by deriding Soviet writers who see themselves as enthusiastic portrayers of labor (incidentally, a role urged on writers by no less a figure than Maxim Gorky) but in fact merely wander around factories without understanding anything they see. He then calls on literary critics to play the role of engineers and provide practical blueprints for the writing of novels. He proposes that novelists stop hunting for "raw material" to be

## Chapter Two

worked up in their novels and instead turn to the abundant readymade components—in Russian, *polufabrikaty*—that surround them in the form of human speech. "Myths, historical and contemporary facts and events, everyday activities, the record of a will toward a better fate—all this, uttered by thousands of nameless but living and eloquent mouths...will serve as ready-made components for the writer." He then calls for the establishment of a hierarchy of committees to gather these materials at the level of the factory, the city, the region, and so forth—a vast collective devoted to gathering specimens of everyday Soviet speech, transmitting them to higher and higher levels until the accumulated mass can be sorted into thematic categories and assembled into a grand self-narrative of socialist construction (there are echoes here as well of another LEF notion, that of "factography" or the building of literary art out of unmediated facts themselves).

On the one hand Platonov's scheme reads like a perfectly earnest attempt to apply the LEF precept of productionism, rooting literature directly in the experience of the proletariat, promoting a collective rather than individualistic process of composition. But as a contribution to the doctrine of "productionism" Platonov's article is striking precisely because it undermines the doctrine's very premise by shifting efforts back to the production of literary texts rather than socialist realia. The all-encompassing nature of the scheme, the naïve faith it seems to evince in the possibility of anything aesthetically valuable coming from such a process (unless the *polufabrikaty* are worked over by an artist of Platonov's caliber, which is a very different matter; see the discussion of his language in chapter five on *The Foundation Pit*), and the hierarchical scale of honoraria he appends at the proposal's end (with writer-assemblers getting 50% but critics a mere 5%) all work to insinuate doubts about Platonov's real intentions. In reality it is difficult to judge them definitively and perhaps at our historical distance a text like "The Factory of Literature" seems destined to remain poised between a reading of it as a serious adaptation of LEF ideas (as Langerak essentially sees it, 85–6) and their parody (as in Kornienko's reading, 31).

Another set of utopian ideas, albeit of very different philosophical tenor than those of Bogdanov or LEF, that influenced Platonov in the 1920s were those of Nikolai Fedorov (1829?–1903). Fedorov was an ascetic librarian at the Rumiantsev Museum in Moscow (later absorbed by the Lenin Library, now the Russian State Library). Over several decades he elaborated a philosophical doctrine which he called "supramoralism" and which he eventually set down in a ponderous two-volume work entitled *The Philosophy of the Common Cause*. Although Fedorov was retiring almost to the point of hermitdom, in the later decades of his life he was visited by a series of important figures in Russian culture. Leo Tolstoy was a personal friend, whose ideas about social reform Fedorov freely criticized. The philosopher Vladimir Solov'ev also visited Fedorov; Dostoevsky knew of Feodorov's ideas from his disciple N.P. Peterson; and Leonid Pasternak, the artist and father of the poet Boris, was an acquaintance and drew his portrait (Masing-Delic 104). His ideas enjoyed something of a cult popularity and, in addition to Platonov, in one way or another influenced the thought of such figures as Maxim Gorky, Alexander Bogdanov, Konstantin Tsiolkovsky (the father of Soviet rocketry), and the poets Vladimir Maiakovsky and Nikolai Zabolotsky. At a session of the All-Russian Central Executive Committee (VTsIK), M. I. Kalinin, president of the USSR, even quoted Fedorov on the need to conquer nature as well as reform society (Semenova "N.F. Fedorov i ego filosofskoe nasledie" 6). Platonov had a copy of Fedorov's *Filosofiia obshchego dela* in his library with abudnant notes in the margins; according to his wife, it was one of his favorite works (Malygina 13). He also very likely first came into contact with his ideas through one of the many devotees of his ideas in the Voronezh region, to which Fedorov's most ardent disciple, N.P. Peterson, had moved in the 1890s (see Teskey; Kommentarii 486; Semonova "N.F. Fedorov i ego filosofskoe nasledie" 14; Malygina 72–3; Vasil'ev 43–5).

Fedorov's ideas are a curious mixture of nostalgic Russian Orthodox communalism and industrial-era faith in the powers of science and technology—in a way, an iconic blend of the tensions within Russian culture as a whole on the eve of the twentieth century.

## Chapter Two

For Fedorov the central philosophical and moral dilemma facing mankind was the universality of physical death, the fact that although we live in a material world we also die from material causes ("Why is nature not a mother to us?" he queries in one of the sections of *Philosophy of the Common Cause*). He believed that humanity was locked in a flawed cycle of sexually-driven procreation, which instead of renewing life only perpetuated death, and which furthermore kept people in a state of enmity and disunity. Still worse for Fedorov was the teleological blindness this cycle induced, in which people pursued the chimera of technological progress while neglecting the ancestors of the race. All men are really brothers, Fedorov argued, because they all descend from single "original father" of the race; but subordination to the rule of entropy and to death—the tendency of all things to decay and die, the hurtling toward loss that defines our world—has led them to a tragic forgetting of their ancestors and to estrangement from one another. Society had split into two antagonistic factions, the "learned," who specialized in abstract, theoretical knowledge, and the "unlearned," who were the majority of the people (*narod*, folk) whose domain was mechanical, practical labor. In their present existence, therefore, people live as "wanderers in a crowd, oblivious to their ancestral origins"—a category which in his discussion acquires cosmic rather than merely social significance (*nepomniashchii rodstva*; that Fedorov viewed humans as estranged orphans in search of a father may have had something to do with his own background: he was an illegitimate son of Prince P.I. Gagarin who as a child was suddenly forced, together with his mother, to leave the paternal estate [Masing-Delic 78; see also Seifrid 20-4].

This vision of present reality as a fallen, disunified state had roots in the general worldview toward which Russian Orthodoxy inclined as well as in more specific social doctrines (such as *sobornost'*, an ideal fraternal community of the spirit transcending any purely earthly social arrangements) promoted by Slavophile thinkers in the nineteenth century as well as certain sympathetic doctrines emanating from western Europe (such as the communalism of the French utopian socialist Charles Fourier, which influenced the young

Dostovesky and somewhat later the radical critic Nikolai Chernyshevsky; Semenova "N.F. Fedorov i ego filosofskoe nasledie" 17). Even the element of ancestor worship in Fedorov's thought had its precedents in notions of patriarchy associated with tsarist rule in Russia (where the tsar was popularly considered to be the *batiushka*, the "little father" of his subjects) and, long before that, in the pre-Christian eastern Slavic cult of clan or *rod*.

What made Fedorov's eccentric philosophy appealing to Russian intellectuals in the late nineteenth and early twentieth centuries, though, was the remedy he envisioned for this tragedy, which yoked Orthodox yearnings for santified human community to a strangely literal faith in modern technology. Like Marx, his near contemporary, Fedorov wanted to change the world rather than just analyze it. The first moral task facing humanity, according to Fedorov, was to abstain from the sexual relations that lead to procreation and thus perpetuate the flawed natural cycle. Instead, people must rebel against their slavery to the "blind forces of nature" and become aware of themselves as sons of deceased fathers. The first step in the rebellion against nature was taken, in Fedorov's view, when human beings began to walk upright—an action he declared, in a way consonant with the "productionism" later promoted by the adherents of LEF, to be the first work of art. Fedorov himself insisted on standing as he worked, and lay down horizontally—a posture he identified with death—only for brief periods of 3–4 hours, and that on a bare trunk (Semenova *Nikolai Fedorov. Tvorchestvo zhizni* 32, 312). At this point people would begin to form a communion based on genuine relations of brotherhood and devote themselves to the "common task" of his *opus*'s title, that of harnessing scientific knowledge to make possible nothing less than the physical resurrection of the dead. Fedorov believed that humanity should first master a series of practical tasks aimed at transforming the earth into a truly hospitable home, such as controlling the climate in order to "ventilate and irrigate" the earth (Seifrid 22; one idea involved sending a dirigible into the atmosphere equipped with a lightning rod, to attract thunderclouds, Fedorov 356), harnessing the power of the sun, and even learning to "steer" the

## Chapter Two

"ship" of earth in cosmic space (an aspect of Fedorov's philosophy which particularly appealed to Tsiolkovsky, as well as to Platonov in his early years, especially in his science fiction stories).

The feats of geoengineering Fedorov imagines—which would amount to humanity's seizing control over its own evolution (Semenova "N.F. Fedorov i ego filosofskoe nasledie" 24)—were not the final goal, however, for Fedorov believed that once humanity had attained encyclopedic knowledge of the "metamorphoses of matter" it would be able to engineer a new body by generating prosthetic organs. From here it would proceed to revive those who had recently died and eventually—the grand *telos* of his vision—learn how to gather the dispersed atoms of ancestors who had died long ago and thus to resurrect the entire human race. There was an element of vulgar materialsim, not to say scientific naiveté, in these hopes, since Fedorov assumed that once one had properly reassembled the body, consciousness would return to it automatically. But in late nineteenth and early twentieth century Russia, in a culture very much taken up with apocalyptic and utopian visions, Fedorov's ideas appealingly linked deep-seated Russian moral aspirations with the technological culture of the modern era.

Several of the utopian projects Platonov proposed in his Voronezh journalism (for seeding clouds to produce rain, for blowing up part of the Ural mountain chain to permit warm air to reach Siberia, for harnessing light as a form of energy to power Soviet factories) derive from the engineering schemes mooted in Fedorov's philosophy, as does, in a more general way, the idea which motivates the characters in *The Foundation Pit* of erecting an indestructible shelter for humankind. Fedorov himself remarked that his interest in regulating the climate had been prompted by his awareness of such erratic and destructive phenomena as hailstorms, torrential downpours, and drought—a reason that would have had immediate appeal for Platonov, who was trained and worked as a land reclamation engineeer after seeing the effects of a drought (Malygina 15). Still closer to the "proletarian home" that the characters of *The Foundation Pit* set about building is Fedorov's concept of the museum. Fedorov considered museums an encouraging sign of humanity's attention, however sporadic, to the past rather than the future. In his view the museum is not a passive collection of objects of mere antiquarian interest but a focus point for the cult of ancestor worship in which material objects bearing the imprint of past human lives could be assembled in order to preserve the memory of those lives in tangible form—thus accomplishing a small step on the path toward the future resurrection of the dead (Semenova *Nikolai Fedorov. Tvorchestvo zhizni* 276–80; "N.F. Fedorov i ego filosofskoe nasledie" 38). It is interesting that for Fedorov, in contrast to the later Bogdanov and Soviet ideology in general, progress in the sense of forward motion through time is regarded as a matter of *shame*; the proper effort is to *resurrect*, to return to an ancestral past (Platonov's 1936 story "The Third Son," in which the retiring youngest son shames his boisterous older siblings—both model Soviet selves—into respecting their mother, who lies in her coffin in the next room, is consonant with this sentiment).

The recurring themes of orphanhood, enslavement to a hostile physical world, the somnambulant state in which his starving or fatigued characters so often exist (in the case of "Soul" ["Dzhan"], an entire nation), and of the entropy to which all living things succumb constitute a still more extensive network of Fedorovian references in Platonov's *oeuvre*, as do the schemes his various protagonists devise in response to their plight. In "Satana mysli" (1922), for example, the engineer-hero Vogulev (whose name and profession already seem to anticipate Voshchev and Prushevsky in *The Foundation Pit*) decides that the way to alleviate the proletariat's suffering from the elements is to devise a form of energy called "ultralight," use it to blow up mountain chains, and allow warm air to circulate more freely over the earth, turning it into a garden. In "A Tale About Many Interesting Things" ("Rasskaz o mnogikh interesnykh veshchakh," 1923), a rambling picareque tale which in many ways anticipates the later novel *Chevengur* of how an impoverished peasant named Ivan escapes rural destitution and encounters the world of technology, Ivan at one point encounters something called the "Experimental

Research Institute for Individual Anthropotechnology." Its guiding principles are set forth in a book called "On Building the New Man," which asserts that every civilization represents a form of "organizing matter in the form of machines." The organizational note comes from Bogdanov, but its development within the story is inspired more by Fedorov's "supramoralism": according to Ivan's utopian book, matter will be organized only when mankind undertakes the "chaste" diversion of its energies from procreation to labor. The time has now dawned when mankind will enter a state of "perfect chastity" and conquer not only earth but the planets as well. Ivan later tours a "workshop of immortal flesh," in which "durable flesh" achieved through chastity is finally made immortal through the application of electricity (which has been used to kill microbes in the air). Again in "The Innermost Man" ("Sokrovennyi chelovek," 1927) the itinerant peasant Foma Pukhov, who travels around a Russia devastated by revolution and civil war, wants to complain to "the whole collective of humanity" about their "general defenselessness" before the forces of nature. In particular his sorrow over the death of his wife convinces him of the need for the "scientific resurrection of the dead" (364).

However, already in *Chevengur*, the strange and brilliant novel Platonov completed in 1927, the emphases change and optimism about such schemes diminishes. The novel abounds in Fedorovian themes. Its opening sections portray socially marginal characters—Fedorov's "unlearned"—struggling to survive a severe drought. Its hero, Sasha Dvanov, is orphaned by his father's suicide and now wanders provincial Russia in search of meaning. The motley band of characters who come together in a ludicrously literal effort to create a communist utopia in the remote steppes epitomize the state of abandonment and exposure to hostile nature that for Fedorov constituted the principal human tragedy. The project on which they embark—gathering in a radically egalitarian, chaste community (they decide not to "possess" one another as spouses) whose most immediate purpose is to shelter them from the elements—derives directly from Fedorov's prescriptions for changing the nature of human existence. The fate these ideas encounter in the novel, however, is now noticeably ironic. The Chevengurian experiment fails as winter approaches and the town is invaded by a band of Cossack bandits, and Dvanov "returns" to his father not by resurrecting him but by drowning himself in the same lake in which his father had died. A similar despair over the Fedorovian project haunts the later "Dzhan" (1933–35), in which the hero, Nazar Chagataev, leaves Moscow to return to his central Asian homeland in an effort to locate his nation, collect it, and bring it into the modern age of Stalinist industrialization. Chagataev finds his people wandering in the desert, lost and reduced to a state of near-somnambulance by their struggle to survive. In the original version of the tale Chagataev's efforts fail as the nation disintegrates and its members wander off once again into the desert (in a second, more optimistic version Platonov wrote Chagataev he sets out a second time and manages to reunite them). Fedorov himself had traveled to central Asia and the Pamir range (as it happens, after visiting his student Peterson in Voronezh), a trip which seems to have lent added urgency to his idea that nature, especially the desert, had to be conquered (Semenova "N.F. Fedorov i ego filosofskoe nasledie" 14).

One could even see the sentimental peasant themes of Platonov's early poems and stories as deriving from, or at the very least as being in sympathy with, Fedorov's pronounced anti-urbanism: Fedorov believed that the true struggle against nature would take place not in the technologically-advanced city but in the village, where peasants daily had to contend with physical obstacles to existence (Masing-Delic 93). Whatever its ultimate source, the attraction to an agrarian or peasant utopia—so at odds with Bolshevik industrial urbanism and Proletkul't factory-fetishization which otherwise predominate in his works of the 1920s—forms a distinct minor line within Platonov's thought. The notion of a peasant utopia forms a current within Russian culture that dates back to at least the seventeenth century, when dynastic troubles ignited rumors among the peasants of various regions that a tsar'-redeemer whose rights to the throne had been usurped would return and establish a just order in which fertile lands would be given outright to the peasants. The most famous instance

Chapter Two

in Russian history of peasants acting on this idea is the rebellion led by Emelian Pugachev in the later years of Catherine the Great's reign, and the Dutch scholar Thomas Langerak has pointed out conspicuous parallels between Platonov's "Ivan Zhokh" (1926) and a work published in 1884 called *Pugachev and His Co-conspirators* (*Pugachev i ego soobshchniki*). Langerak also notes that a series of publications on the Pugachev uprising appeared in 1925–6, including a book entitled *The Truth About Pugachev* (*Pravda o Pugacheve*) by the LEF theoretician and proponent of "productionism" in art, Nikolai Chuzhak (112–15). An alternative to the myth of a tsar'-redeemer in Russian peasant utopias is that of a *remote land* of material abundance run by peasants alone (the leading historian of the phenomenon notes many instances in which bands of peasants set off with all their belongings into Siberia in search of such a place; he theorizes that the myth's persistence had to do with the availability of unsettled borderlands in Russia; Chistov 238). The best known of these is the legendary city of Kitezh, which supposedly sank miraculously beneath Lake Svetloyar to escape a Mongol invasion but was destined to rise again from the waves (the Rimsky-Korsakov opera *Tale of the Invisible City of Kitezh* is based on this legend).

Hints of longing for some form of peasant utopia are widespread in Platonov's works, the earliest being, again, the dolorous rural poems in *Golubaia glubina*. In "Ivan Zhokh" the peasants search outright for a Kitezh-like "Eternal-City-on-the-Far-River" (*Vechnyi-Grad-na-Dal'nei reke*); but even those who form a collective in order to bring electricity to their village in "Electricity's Native Land" ("Rodina elektrichestva") or whose self-organized collectives (*arteli*) work better than the Stalinist collective farms in "For Future Use" ("Vprok," the work which so angered Stalin), suggest muted utopian aspirations. The fullest (but also most ironic) expression of these themes is found in *Chevengur*, where a band of semi-literate peasants attempts to establish a radically collective form of existence in an isolated town in the steppes. The Chevengurians shift the houses of the town every Saturday, because they have heard the slogan that communism means constant movement, and they expect the sun on its own to raise crops on their behalf. The fact that their commune is destroyed at the end of the novel by a band of marauding Cossacks may be another detail deriving from the tradition of peasant utopias in Russia: one set of songs about the legendary land of Belovod'e describes its commune being dispersed by Cossacks sent by "the authorities" (*nachalstvo*; Chistov 278). Platonov's peasant utopians also recall the closely related phenomenon of religious sectarianism, which had captured the interest of Russian intellectuals in the early twentieth century (see, for example, Andrei Bely's novel *The Silver Dove*) and it is worth noting that Platonov's native Voronezh region was particularly rich in sectarian movements.

Although the idea of peasant utopianism was tolerated if not encouraged in the years immediately following the revolution—for example, a work by one "Ivan Kremnev" (whose real name was A. V. Chaianov) entitled *My Brother's Journey to the Land of a Peasant Utopia* (*Puteshestvie moego brata v stranu krest'ianskoi utopii*) was popular when it first appeared in 1920 (it is often cited as an influence on Platonov's *Chevengur*)—it soon fell afoul of the strongly urbanist leanings of Marxism (Marx, after all, had referred in *The Communist Manifesto* to the "idiocy of rural life") and of Leninism's aversion to any initiative that did not originate in the Party elite. In Soviet literature of the 1920s peasants seeking to devise their own form of utopia thus increasingly came to be treated with suspicion if not outright hostility. Hence the scandal over the eccentric and romantically utopian *okhlomony* in Boris Pil'niak's 1929 novel *Mahogany* (*Krasnoe derevo*)—which Tolstaia conjectures may have been a response to Platonov's *Chevengur*, with Platonov's *The Foundation Pit* then following as a response to Pil'niak's rewriting of his novel as *The Volga Empties into the Caspian Sea* (*Volga vpadaet v kaspiiskoe more*; see her *Mirposlekontsa* 283, 289). It is symptomatic of both Platonov's leanings and of the disrepute into which the idea of spontaneous peasant collectivism had fallen that in his attack on Platonov's "Vprok" one of the critic Alexander Fadeev's most serious charges was that "the 'holy fool' Andrei Platonov simply reproduces a Chaianov-like *kulak* utopia" by offering a positive portrayal of a peasant commune ("Ob odnoi kulatskoi khronike" 277). Although they are decidedly more tragic, even macabre, than anything preceding them in Platonov's works of the 1920s, the scenes set at the collective farm in *The Foundation Pit* are tinged with an empathy for peasant life which ultimately traces back to this line of Russian social thought—as the possibility of a dialog with Pil'niak on this theme also suggests.

Other esoteric intellectual influences—of which Russia does not suffer any severe shortage—on Platonov's works have been suggested, such as the mystic philosopher G. I. Gurdjieff, some of whose ideas may be echoed in Platonov's theme of the somnambulent state in which so many of his characters seem to exist (Tolstaia "Naturfilosofskie temy u Platonova" 328). Some of the speculative scientific themes in Platonov's science fiction stories suggest that he was familiar with the notion of the "biosphere," that is, of the earth and all its living beings forming a complex organism, promoted by the geologist and philosopher Vladimir Vernadsky (1863–1945; his *Biosphere* appeared in 1926). In "Efirnyi trakt" (also 1926), for example, the engineer-hero Popov realizes that the way to gain mastery over the physical world lies in realizing that electrons are in fact dead organisms which can be brought back to life by applying electromagnetic energy (Kornienko 22). Another possible source for this idea is the early nineteenth-century Russian scientist N.V. Karazin, who theorized about turning the earth into a giant electro-magnet (Malygina *Estetika Andreia Platonova* 23). The nineteenth-century plant physiologist Kliment Timiriazev's ideas about solar energy may also have influenced Platonov, who mentions him several times in articles of the 1920s (Malygina *Estetika Andreia Platonova* 24). Finally, the "anthropotechnology" featured in "Rasskaz o mnogikh interesnykh veshchakh" may have been influenced by Platonov's contemporary, the physicist and philosopher Alexander Chizhevsky, who speculated on the possibility of achieving the "organic exchange" of electrons (Malygina *Estetika Andreia Platonova* 28). In the absence of more specific textual evidence, however, most of these assertions must remain conjectural.

## REFERENCES

Bethea, David. "*Chevengur*: On the Road with the Bolshevik Utopia." Chapter Three in his *The Shape of Apocalypse in Modern Russian Fiction*. Princeton: Princeton University Press, 1989. 145–85.

Blackburn, Simon. *The Oxford Encyclopedia of Philosophy*. Oxford: Oxford University Press, 1994.

Chistov, K.V. *Russkie narodnye sotsial'no-utopicheskie legendy*. Moscow: Nauka, 1967.

Chuzhak, N. "Pod znakom zhiznestroeniia." *LEF: Zhurnal levogo fronta iskusstva*, no. 1 (March 1923): 36 [http://www.ruthenia.ru/moskva/art/statii/chuzhak.htm]

Dobrenko, Evgeny. *The Political Economy of Socialist Realism*. Trans. Jesse M. Savage. New Haven, CT: Yale UP, 2007.

Fadeev, A. "Ob odnoi kulatskoi khronike." *Krasnaia nov'*, no. 506 (1931): 206–9. Reprint: N.V. Kornienko and E.D. Shubina, eds. *Andrei Platonov. Vospominaniia sovremennikov. Materialy k biografii*. Moscow: Sovremennyi pisatel', 1994. 268–78.

Fedorov, N.F. *Sochineniia*. Filosofskoe nasledie. Vol. 85. Moscow: Mysl', 1985.

Gor'kii, M. [M. Gorky] "O literaturnoi tekhnike." In his *Sobranie sochinenii*. Vol. 26. Moscow: Khudozhestvennaia literatura, 1953. 329–336.

———. "Ob iskusstve." In his *Sobranie sochinenii*. Vol. 27. Moscow: Khudozhestvennaia literatura, 1953. 442–8.

Gorky, M. "Soviet Literature." In Vsesoiuznyi s'ezd pisatelei, 1st, Moscow, 1934. *Soviet Writers' Congress 1934. The Debate on Socialist Realism and Modernism in the Soviet Union*. London: Lawrence and Wishart, 1977. 27–69.

Hagemeister, Michael. *Nikolaj Fedorov. Studien zu Leben, Werk und Wirkung*. Munich: Otto Sagner, 1989.

Kornienko, N.V. and E. D. Shubina, eds. *Andrei Platonov. Vospominaniia sovremennikov. Materialy k biografii*. Moscow: Sovremennyi pisatel', 1994.

Langerak, Thomas. *Andrei Platonov. Materialy dlia biografii, 1899–1929 gg.* Amsterdam: Pegasus, 1995.

Lukashevicz, Stephen. *N.F. Fedorov (1828–1903). A Study in Russian Eupsychian and Utopian Thought.* New York: Associated University Presses, 1977.

Malygina, N.M. *Estetika Andreia Platonova.* Irkutsk: Izdatel'stvo Irkutskogo universiteta, 1985.

Masing-Delic, Irene. *Abolishing Death. A Salvation Myth of Russian Twentieth-Century Literature.* Stanford: Stanford University Press, 1992.

McClelland, James C. "Utopianism versus Revolutionary Heroism in Bolshevik Policy: The Proletarian Culture Debate." *Slavic Review* 39:3 (September 1980): 403–25.

Platonov, A. "Sokrevennyi chelovek." In his *Sobranie sochinenii v trekh tomakh.* Vol. 1. Moscow: Sovetskaia Rossiia, 1984. 328–97.

"Proizvodstvennoe iskusstvo." [http://dic.academic.ru/dic.nsf/bse/124165/Производственное] Accessed 7 October 2008.

Rosenthal, Bernice Glatzer. *Nietzsche in Russia.* Princeton: Princeton University Press, 1986.

———. *New Myth, New World: From Nietzsche to Stalinism.* University Park, PA: Pennsylvania State University Press, 2002.

Seifrid, Thomas. *Andrei Platonov. Uncertainties of Spirit.* Cambridge: Cambridge University Press, 1992.

Semenova, S. G. "N.F. Fedorov i ego filosofskoe nasledie." Introduction to N.F. Fedorov. *Sochineniia.* Filosofskoe nasledie. Vol. 85. Moscow: Mysl', 1985. 5–50.

———. *Nikolai Fedorov. Tvorchestvo zhizni.* Moscow: Sovetskii pisatel', 1990.

Shklovskii, Viktor. *Tret'ia fabrika.* Moscow: Krug, 1926.

Teskey, Ayleen. *Platonov and Fedorov. The Influence of Christian Philosophy on a Soviet Writer.* Amersham, U.K: Avebury, 1982.

Tolstaia, Elena. *Mirposlekontsa. Raboty o russkoi literature XX veka.* Moscow: RGGU, 2002.

Chapter 3

# The Literary Context of *The Foundation Pit*

Although his earliest writings, especially some of the poems in the *Golubaia glubina* collection, betray some pre-revolutionary literary influences, Platonov belongs to a group of writers whose real careers began as a response to the Revolution.* He was one of the few Soviet writers who could claim (at any rate, he did claim) that he was proletarian in origin as well as political orientation. *The Foundation Pit* may be unusual if not unique in its grotesqueries of plot, its strange refraction of Stalinist ideology, and its uncanny deformations of the Russian literary language. It remained unpublished in its author's lifetime. Nonetheless it is very much a product of the decade that produced it, the 1920s. The 1920s formed the environment in which Platonov came of age as a writer, the era in which he not only wrote but sought to have what he wrote published, in which he responded to the first reviews of his works in national publications, secured honoraria, appealed to writers and government officials in an effort to arrange housing for himself and his family, and so forth. The literary movements and in particular the fractious literary politics of that first decade of Soviet life are therefore important to the gestation of *The Foundation Pit*. The heated debates and political maneuvering during the 1920s were also the incubator from which "socialist realism," the type of literature (and painting, and music, etc.) that we now think of as distinctly "Soviet" was born—different in tone as that literature is from Platonov's own dystopian tale.

\*   I use the capitalized form "Revolution" to refer exlusively to the Bolshevik Revolution of October 25 (old style) 1917. More general references appear in lower case.

## Chapter Three

The relation between the political and social upheaval of the war years and the revolutions of 1917, on the one hand, and developments in Russian literature, on the other, was not as directly causal as is sometimes assumed. A "revolutionary" art defined by radical formal experimentation, often affiliated with some form of left-wing politics (which in Russia of the pre-Rev era ranged over a broad spectrum, from classical Marxists to anarchists) had already appeared in the early years of the twentieth century and arguably reached its creative apogee in the period immediately *before* the October Revolution of 1917. By the same token, Maxim Gorky's politically tendentious novel *Mother*, later promoted as one of the forerunnners of socialist realism, was written in 1907 (as it happens, while he was on a visit to the United States). Nor did the Bolshevik revolution radically change the literary landscape in any immediate way. Writers who were hostile to its political methods and aims emigrated in large numbers, particularly during the harsh years of civil war that followed 1917 (one thinks of Ivan Bunin, Vladimir Nabokov, Vladislav Khodasevich and others); but those who remained exhibited a wide range of political sympathies and aesthetic leanings, from the ironic disdain of Mikhail Bulgakov (whose "Heart of a Dog" ["Sobach'e serdtse"] of 1925, for example, portrays proletarians as boors or worse) through the poet Alexander Blok, who in his 1918 essay, "The Intelligentsia and the Revolution" ("Intelligentsiia i revoliutsiia") urged intellectuals to "listen to the music of the Revolution," to ardent enthusiasts like the Futurist poet Vladimir Mayakovsky, whose jolting "Left March" ("Levyi marsh," 1918, dedicated to the sailors of the Red Navy) cedes the tribune to "Comrade Mauser" (i.e., the brand of revolver) and urges the proletariat to "tighten its grip on the world's throat."

For most of the 1920s the Party (to give it its full title, the Russian Communist Party [Bolshevik]) was preoccupied with the economic ruin brought on by the recent war and revolution. Faced with the urgent need to consolidate its rule over the fractious remains of the tsarist empire and install an entirely new governmental apparatus, it had little time for involving itself in literary affairs. True, Lenin imposed censorship on the press shortly after the Revolution and the poet Nikolai Gumilev was executed as early as 1921 on a trumped-up charge of "anti-Soviet activity"; but generally speaking, with the exception of open hostility to the new regime, writers were granted fairly wide latitude in the first decade after the Revolution. The border was relatively porous, too, and simultaneous publication of a work in Moscow and Berlin or Paris was fairly common. One of the milestones of literary politics of the decade was, in fact, a decree (on which below) in which the Party stated its refusal to exercise direct control over literary affairs. The "long" 1920s, as we might call them, came to an end with the eventual revocation of this policy in the Party's 1932 decree "On the Restructuring of Literary-Artistic Organizations" ("O perestroike literaturno-khudozhestvennykh organizatsii"), which declared the method of writing called "socialist realism" obligatory for all Sovet writers and which created the Union of Soviet Writers as a mandatory professional organization—together with Glavlit, the state's censorship bureau, whose purpose was to oversee ideological conformity. For those who view the 1930s as a dark age of Stalinist repression, then, the 1920s appear a time of relative tolerance and experimentation.

The comparatively tolerant treatment of literature by the Party in the 1920s did not mean, however, that the decade was tranquil for writers, editors, or publishers. If it was a time of relative creative freedom, it was also one of political tension and fractional dispute. Most writers of note whose careers had begun before the October Revolution of 1917 and who remained in Russia after the Revolution and civil war fell within the category that Leon Trotsky, in his idiosyncratic but influential survey of 1923, *Literature and Revolution*, labelled "fellow travelers" of the revolution (*poputchiki*). The "fellow travelers" were not a coherent faction at all but a loose grouping of writers, most of them members of the pre-revolutionary intelligentsia, who were neither openly supportive of nor hostile toward the Bolshevik regime—though their emotional attitude was often, as Trotsky shrewdly pointed out, one of "internal emigration" (75). Nonetheless the experience of revolution and civil war left a distinct imprint on what most of the fellow travelers wrote in the 1920s. The émigré writer Vladimir Nabokov might have dismissed the October Revolution as "that trite *deus ex machina*" (in his 1937 story "Spring in Fialta") but for most of the writers in this category the upheaval of revolution and civil war was an unavoidable theme. In this sense their works clearly embodied a response to the October Revolution, but it was a response that tended toward ambivalence and irony rather than enthusiastic support of Bolshevik policy (as was the case in more loyalist works like Fedor Gladkov's 1925 *Cement*, a tale of restarting a cement factory, or Dmitrii Furmanov's 1923 *Chapaev*, a tale of a peasant commander in the civil war).

The Symbolist poet Alexander Blok's narrative poem *The Twelve* (*Dvenadtsat'*, 1918), for example, presents a series of flickering images (Boris Gasparov suggests they are intended to allude to the cinema, 8) of a nighttime Petrograd devastated by revolution and civil war, in which a "bourgeois" bundled up against the cold and a stray dog scurry out of the path of a group of Red Army soldiers who emerge out of a blizzard. The soldiers, though, are hardly the conventional heroes of Bolshevik mythology. Marauding as much as marching, at the end of the poem they are transformed into a profane version of the twelve apostles, while a ghostly Christ in a wreath of white roses suddenly appears at their head (Blok's death in 1921 was widely interpreted as marking the end of an era). Boris Pil'niak's 1922 novel *The Naked Year* (*Golyi god*) similarly identifies the revolution with elemental forces (he reinterprets early acronyms used by the Bolshevik government as the sound of the wind off the steppes) and portrays life in a provincial Russian town which is the locus for ruthless action by a handful of Bolsheviks (whom he famously portrayed as men in leather jackets), for the moral and physiological decay of the provincial nobility (they suffer from hereditary syphilis), and for the perpetuation of ancient customs and beliefs predating the westernization of Russia in the eighteenth century (Platonov's 1928 novel *Chevengur* embodies a related view of the revolution as a spontaneous and elemental event, and Platonov briefly collaborated with Pil'niak while working on *The Foundation Pit*).

Isaac Babel's *Red Cavalry* (1926) injected similar ambiguity into an account, based on Babel's actual experience as a correspondent in a Red Army cavalry detachment, of the Bolsheviks' failed attempt to spread revolution westward by invading Poland in 1920. Instead of confidence in the Revolution's historical progress, Babel's tales are laced with irony: his narrator, Lyutov, is an intellectual Jew sent among traditionally antisemitic Cossacks, who, moreoever, have joined the Red Army rather than the Whites, as most of the rest of the Cossacks did (though this much was true of the detachment of Semyon Budyonny in which Babel' himself served). Babel' portrays his Cossacks as elemental beasts and depletes the historical optimism one might expect from a believer in the Bolshevik cause with a constant undertow of pessimism, which casts the Polish campaign as simply one more in a long series of violent and wasteful military endeavors (Tolstoy's *War and Peace* is an important subtext for Babel' in this regard).

In addition to Blok, among poets the category of "fellow traveler" encompassed the Acmeists Anna Akhmatova and Osip Mandelshtam, the erstwhile Futurist Boris Pasternak, whose careers had been established well before October 1917; and so-called "peasant" poets, such as Nikolai Kliuev and Sergei Esenin, who continued to write elegiacally about village life and the rural landscape rather than extol factories. Some of Platonov's early poetry suggests the influence of the Symbolists as well as the "peasant" poets, but that would not have set him apart from other provincial autodidacts of the era.

To the extent that there was any organized faction among the fellow travelers it was a group formed in 1921 calling itself the "Serapion Brothers," after a hermit-monk in a collection of tales by E.T.A. Hoffmann. The Serapions' self-consciously provocative intent, in that era of political score-settling and interorganizational feuding, was to avoid politics altogether. "We are with the Hermit Serapion," they wrote in their manifesto. "We believe that literary chimeras are a special reality, and we will have none of utilitarianism. We do not write for propaganda. Art is real, like life itself. And, like life itself, it has neither goal nor meaning; it exists because it cannot help existing." (quoted in Brown 22–3). Under the tutelage of the older writer Evgenii Zamyatin (author of the dystopian novel *We* [*My*]) and the Formalist literary scholar Viktor Shklovsky the writers Vsevolod Ivanov, Konstantin Fedin, Mikhail Zoshchenko, Mikhail Slonimsky, and Veniamin Kaverin, among others, devoted themselves to the study of literary craftsmanship. Zoshchenko's imitations of semi-literate speech, a style of writing known in Russian as *skaz*, form a particularly important parallel to (if not quite influence on) the narrative manner Platonov himself developed in the mid–1920s.

The literary faction that strode into the midst of these prevaricating fellow travelers and assertively claimed for itself the leading role within post-revolutionary literature was the Futurists. Including such poets and artists as Vladimir Mayakovsky, Alexei Kriuchenykh, Nikolai Aseev, Vasily Kamensky, Sergei Tret'iakov, and, for a time, Boris Pasternak, in the decade preceding the Revolution the Futurists had been the most radical in their approach to artistic experimentation and in the glee with which they offended bourgeois taste. The title of their most important manifesto is "A Slap in the Face of Public Taste." They eagerly printed poems on wallpaper rather than the fine stock preferred by some of their aestheticist contemporaries, declaimed their harsh-sounding poems in brash voices, and wore provocatively strange clothing. Militantly opposed to both traditional realist style and to the aestheticism which had come into vogue with the rise of Russian modernism, the Futurists sought to use formal experiment as a way of creating a new language suited to the new, utopian reality toward which they believed the machine age would lead. In painting such experimentation led to the abstractions of "suprematism," such as Konstantin Malevich's "Black Square," although other painters, such as Mikhail Larionov, found a precedent for the deformation of conventional forms in crude peasant woodcuts, while in poetry such as that of Mayakovsky a similar medium was found in crude (i.e., socially offensive) forms of speech imported from "the street"—both practices analogous in their own way with what Platonov was to do in the language of his works during the 1920s.

## The Literary Context of *The Foundation Pit*

In poetry the signal achievement of Futurism was a style known as "*zaum*" or "trans-sense" language, which ranged from the agrammatical concatenation of neologisms that nonetheless conveyed a certain sense (e.g., Velimir Khlebnikov's "Incantation by Laughter," a poem based almost entirely on permutations of the root for the Russian verb meaning "to laugh") to intentionally abrasive sounds which conveyed no recognizable sense at all (such as Kriuchenkyh's famously nonsensical poetic line "Dyr, bul, shchyl"). Most of the Futurists welcomed the Revolution, which they saw as a guarantor that their plans for a utopian remaking of life would become reality (see Boris Grois's interesting but controversial claim that in this they anticipated Stalinism). They moved rapidly to establish themselves as its rightful artistic embodiment. The artist Nathan Al'tman's startling Cubist designs were chosen to decorate Petrograd for the celebrations marking the first anniversary of the Revolution—and jarringly contrasted with the neoclassical (and recently imperial) buildings from which they were hung. Some sense of how the Futurists saw the Revolution as co-extensive with the radical aesthetic experiments they had cultivated in the preceding decade can be sensed from Vladimir Mayakovsky's "Order to the Army of the Arts," which appeared in the newspaper *The Art of the Commune* in December 1918. The poem brusquely shoves aside the "brigades of old people" and issues a militant call for "comrade" artists to go into the streets and take up positions on "the barricades"; but the "barricades" in question turn out to be not military ones but hearts and minds, and Mayakovsky urges the Futurists to regard the streets as "brushes" and the city squares as "palettes." The poem seems to relish its defiant announcement that "Er, shcha, and sha" (i.e., the Russian letters Р, Щ, Ш) are "beautiful letters, too" as much as it does any moment of political ascendancy.

The vehicle through which the Futurists sought to promote their influence on Soviet artistic affairs was an organization known as the "Left Front of Art," or LEF, which they formed in 1922. The journal the group published from 1923–1925, also called *LEF*, printed works by some of the most significant avant-garde figures of the

Chapter Three

1920s, among them the photographer Alexander Rodchenko, the film director Sergei Eisenstein, and the theater director Vsevolod Meyerhold (Terras 244–6; *LEF* was reformulated in 1927 as *Novyi LEF* or *New LEF*). The Party, however—which held real power—was less enamoured of the Futurists than the Futurists were of power, and vibrant but jarring formal innovation suited the tastes of neither the newly enfranchised proletariat nor of Lenin and most other Party leaders. LEF's influence gradually waned during the 1920s.

Platonov clearly was aware of the Futurists and was particularly attracted to Nikolai Chuzhak's ideas about the supremacy of actual production to art (one Russian scholar even argues that Velimir Khlebnikov's 1913 Futurist opera *Victory over the Sun* was influential on some of his works; Malygina, *Andrei Platonov: Poetika "Vozvrashcheniia"* 37–41); but as a young man from the provinces whose first Soviet career was in land reclamation, he was simply too remote to be a participant of any kind—nor do his works reveal any attraction to the verbal experimentation of Futurism's heyday, even if his unorthodox uses of the Russian language bear some typological resemblance to it.

A belated resurgence of interest in formal experimentation characterized the so-called "Union of Real Art" (in Russian, *Oberiu*), a group which existed in Leningrad from 1927–1930. Consisting mostly of former Futurists, the *Oberiu* sought to perpetuate the writing of trans-sense verse in an effort to arrive at the absolute meanings of words, and, in the strange little texts of Daniil Kharms, to create a genuine literature of the absurd (the absurd elements in Platonov's works, though, have distinctly different—ideological—origin). Despite their ardent leftism (the first spectacle they organized was called "Three Left Hours") the members of the *Oberiu* in reality were closer to free-spirited fellow travelers like the Serapion Brothers than to any of the groups clamoring for the Party's attention as representatives of proletarian literature. They were quickly marginalized.

If some of the formal aspects of the works Platonov wrote in the 1920s bear a convergent resemblance to those of modernists such as Pil'niak, the Serapion Brothers, or some of the Futurists, ideologically he was much closer to a group called the "Proletkul't," or Proletarian Culture movement. The aims of the Proletkul't were superficially similar to those of LEF—with the exception of a minority of beleagured aesthetes, all factions in Soviet literature of the 1920s had to define themselves in response to the question of whether there could already exist a truly "proletarian" culture, and if there could, what it would be like—but Proletkul't pursued them through fundamentally different aesthetic means. Interest in proletarian literature, meaning works written by factory workers, or more accurately, the nurturing of such literary efforts by members of the left intelligentsia, predates the October 1917 revolution. Gorky had been involved at the turn of the century in a publishing venture called *Znanie* ("Knowledge"), whose aim had been the dissemination to a mass readership of works on popular science. He had edited a *First Collection of Proletarian Writers* (*Pervyi sbornik proletarskikh pisatelei*) as early as 1914 (Kasack 130). The Proletkul't itself was founded by Anatoly Lunacharsky, Commissar of Enlightenment, immediately after the February revolution of 1917 which deposed the tsar and estsablished the ill-fated Provisional Government, not the subsequent October Revolution of the same year, which installed the Bolsheviks in power. Its heyday was the years right after the Revolution, 1918–1919.

Proletkul't drew intellectual inspiration from a variety of tendencies, not always consistent with one another, which had appeared in Russian culture in the late nineteenth and early twentieth centuries: social idealism, cosmism (the belief that it was the destiny of the working class to conquer the cosmos as well as earthly society), Marxism, militant atheism, anarchism, and the apocalyptic mood that had so dominated Russian thought at the turn of the century (Kommentarii 470). The "philosophical" ideas about proletarian culture promoted by the leader of Proletkul't's Moscow branch, Alexander Bogdanov, aimed at nothing less than a complete revision of existing scientific knowledge in the name of a future existential utopia. These ideas were enormously influential on the young Platonov and form an important backdrop to *The Foundation Pit* (see the chapter on Platonov's intellectual influences). Lenin, incidentally, stridently opposed Bogdanov and the Proletkul't, and wrote his one would-be philosophical treatise (*Materialism and Empiriocriticism*) as a seething diatribe against Bogdanov's ideas.

The motivating idea behind the proletarian culture movement was the Marxist tenet that literature, art, and other forms of culture comprise the "superstructure" which arises in a society out of the "base" of its fundamental economic relations. According to this view, which in the Russian setting had been reinforced by the writings of the country's leading orthodox Marxist, Georgy Plekhanov, the culture of any given age is determined by the social class that is dominant within it. It therefore followed that once the proletariat had established the "dictatorship" over other classes that Marxist theory predicted as the outcome of the revolution, it would naturally produce its own cultural forms (Brown *Proletarian Episode* 6–7, 26). Whether such culture would arise spontaneously or should be promoted actively was a matter of some debate. Proletkul't in any event saw no reason to refrain from active promotion and established itself as a social-cultural organization intended to serve as a "laboratory of proletarian culture" (Fitzpatrick 104). It organized a series of "studios" in which worker-writers participated as "apprentices" learning to generate literary works as if they were another form of handicraft, if not industrial production (in 1920 there were a hundred provincial branches which between them had enrolled 80,000 workers; Brown 9). It also sponsored journals which published their works, and even, for a time, a "Proletarian University."

The works produced under the sponsorship of Proletkul't, in particular the poetry of such writers as Mikhail Gerasimov and Vladimir Kirillov, inclined toward a manner which came to be known as "cosmism": emotional paeans to physical labor, machines, and the collective of industrial workers (who are always more important than the individual) organized around the image of the universal "Proletarian," who strides forth from the earth to conquer planets and stars. As the poet Pavel Bessal'ko wrote, "We love electrical wires, the railroad, airplanes—these are our muscles, our hands, our nerves. We love factories—they are the sinews of our thoughts, our feelings. This iron head of the collective is the head [in an icon] of the new Redeemer" (quoted in Kommentarii 473). This "proletarian" poetry had more to do with the legacy of Symbolism than with the artistic avant-garde identified with the Futurists and Constructivists (in this it at least avoided what many saw as avant-garde obscurity, however much it tended to veer off into a mysticism of sorts; at a 1919 meeting of Petrograd proletarian writers, the head of the Petrograd Soviet, Grigory Zinoviev, applauded the "proletarian simplicity" of Proletkul't poets, in contrast to "nonsensical futurism"; quoted in Fitzpatrick 100).

After the October Revolution of 1917 the question of whether the Proletkul't should be an autonomous organization perpetuated through worker intitiative or a subordinate organ of the Party or the People's Commissariat of Enlightenment (Narkompros, a branch of the state rather than the Party apparatus) bedeviled it throughout its brief existence. In February 1920 a group of writers dissatisfied with state interference (though not with subsidies from Narkompros) seceded in order to create an organization called the "Smithy" (*Kuznitsa*, located in Moscow; its Petrograd counterpart was called the Cosmists). The most significant influence the proletarian culture movement had on Platonov unquestionably had to do with Bogdanov's utopian ideas about a scientific revolution which would alter the nature of existence, but his organizational ties were with the Smithy group. He helped organize the Voronezh Union of Proletarian Writers in the summer of 1920, and was sent as a delegate to the First All-Russian Congress of Proletarian Writers in Moscow from 18–21 October of that year, an event organized by several members of the Smithy right after their split from the larger Proletkul't movement. One of Platonov's early stories, "Markun," and an article on "Proletarian Poetry" were also published in the Smithy journal *Kuznitsa*. Nonetheless he does not seem to have had any particularly strong commitment to any particular group, including this one. He distanced himself from efforts at the All-Union Congress to steer "proletarian"

## Chapter Three

literature away from the Proletkul't organization, and in response to a question, on a questionnaire distributed at the conference, about which literary group he belonged to, he wrote, "None. I have my own." (Langerak 23–4; Kommentarii 492).

In reaction to this defection by Smithy, which it eventually hounded out of existence, a group of writers calling itself "October" was organized in 1922 on the principle of Party loyalty rather than proletarian origins. Its leading figures—Alexander Bezymensky, Yuri Libedinsky, and Leopold Averbakh, all, incidentally, parodied in their later Stalinist versions in Mikhail Bulgakov's satirical novel *Master and Margarita*—were young and largely uneducated (Struve 78; Brown 31). *On Guard* (*Na postu*), the journal published by the October group from 1923–1925, quickly became infamous for its dogmatism and the intolerance of its attacks on fellow travelers and any one else whose adherence to the Party line its editors deemed questionable (the Party itself, and Lunacharsky in his role as Commissar of Enlightenment, were at this point still reluctant to alienate the fellow travelers, though the question of the Party's role in cultural affairs was widely debated in the Soviet press during 1923–1925). The Proletkul't organization as such went into decline when it lost its Narkompros subsidy in early 1922 (Fitzpatrick 241), but the October group perpetuated a tense awareness of the question of proletarian literature into the early 1930s. In 1923 it managed to take over an organization called the All-Russian Association of Proletarian Writers (known by its Russian initials as VAPP), which had been formed in 1920 under the auspices of the Smithy group and which enjoyed broad representation among proletarian writers (an affiliated hardcore called MAPP, or Moscow Association of Proletarian Writers, was formed at the same time out of the October, Young Guard, and Workers' Spring factions).

The Party finally entered all this organizational and doctrinal squabbling and articulated something in the nature of a policy regarding literature on July 1, 1925, when the Central Committee issued its resolution "On the Policy of the Party in the Field of Artistic Literature." The resolution harbors some ambiguities but was generally welcomed by beleaguered fellow travelers and other non-proletarian writers as a writ granting them at least relative freedom to write without political interference. While insisting on the political dominance of the proletariat in the wake of the October Revolution, the resolution acknowledges that class conflict has not entirely disappeared in the "transitional" period leading to full proletarian dictatorship. In similar manner, while asserting that proletarian dominance must "sooner or later" also become a fact in the realm of literature, it acknowledges the continued existence of fellow-travelers and assorted other non-proletarian writers whose qualifications in "literary technique" should not be ignored. Thus, although the resolution affirms the Party's intention to "aid the development" of proletarian writers and support their organizations "in every way," it nonetheless discourages "communist boastfulness" (*komchvanstvo*) and "sectarianism," and warns against efforts to create a "hot-house" form of proletarian literature (for a full English version of the resolution, see Brown 235–40 or Clark and Dobrenko 40–5).\*

That the October group spoke for all proletarian literature only in its own overheated imagination can be sensed from the existence of a group calling itself "The Pass" ("Pereval," as in mountain pass) which had split off from October and the Young Guard factions in 1923. Led by the moderate Marxist literary theoretician Alexander Voronsky, Pereval emphasized continuity with the traditions of Russian and world literature and promoted such notions as sincerity, intuition, and the reflective cognition of reality as essential to the process of writing. The group's journal *Red Virgin Soil* (*Krasnaia nov'*) in fact became something of a haven for fellow travelers. Because a writer named Alexei Platonov (whose real name was Petr Alekseevich Romanov) belonged to this group, for a while it was once assumed that the signature "A. Platonov" on some Pereval documents referred to Andrei Platonov. This assumption was almost certainly erroneous, though it remains possible that Platonov attended some meetings

\* The Clark and Dobrenko volume, *Soviet Culture and Power. A History in Documents, 1917–1953*, offers an excellent collection in English translation of Soviet cultural documents.

of Pereval in Moscow around 1926. In any event he corresponded a couple of times with Voronsky, who also praised his first collection of stories, the 1927 *Locks of Epiphany* (*Epifanskie shliuzy*), in a letter to Gorky (see Langerak 90–1).\*

Chastened by the Party resolution of 1925, VAPP was once more permitted to publish its theoretical and critical journal, under the modified title *On Literary Guard* (*Na literaturnom postu*; the insertion of "literary" was meant to indicate the new organ's more carefully circumscribed interests). *Na literaturnom postu* abandoned the "nihilistic" attitude toward the culture of the past which had been promoted by its predecessor, and now urged proletarian writers to "learn from the classics" (*Kratkaia literaturnaia entsiklipedia* 6:180). VAPP did not yield on the principle of the need for "proletarian hegemony" in literature, however, and by 1928 it had become evident that the political winds were beginning to blow in the organization's favor. At the 1928 All-Union Congress of Proletarian Writers in Moscow VAPP was merged with RAPP, an umbrella organization which had been set up at the 1925 Congress of Proletarian Writers. Headed by VAPP's leader, Leopold Averbakh, RAPP was now allowed to subsume the confusing welter of proletarian suborganizations that had arisen during the 1920s (in a kind of Darwinian irony, the same fate was to befall RAPP itself when the Union of Soviet Writers was formed). Moreover, luminaries from the Party's Central Committee such as Lunacharsky, who had hitherto tried to balance an endorsement of proletarian literature in principle with a desire to retain the support of non-proletarian writers, now spoke out in favor of RAPP as an organization useful precisely in its eagerness to carry out Party directives (Brown 48–53).

Under Averbakh's direction RAPP now embarked on a campaign of unprecedented viciousness against non-proletarian, or rather, non-Party-orthodox writers of all kinds. Insisting, in a manner later

---

\* Malygina quotes Platonov's widow as stating that he only attended one meeting of Pereval, and after that did not maintain any contact with members of the group. "'Kotlovan' A. Platonova i obshchestvenno-literaturnaia situatsiia na rubezhe 20-x—30-x godov," 59.

discredited as "vulgar sociologism," on class origin as the sole factor determining a writer's worth, RAPP lifted a phrase from an article Lenin had written about Tolstoy in order to insist on the need to "tear off every kind of mask" behind which "bourgeois" writers might try to hide (thus providing something of a parallel in literary politics to the ruthless hunt for *kulaki* and saboteurs which accompanied Stalin's drive to collectivize agriculture and industrialize the country's economy). 1928–1929 saw the decimation of Pereval and the phenomenon (as RAPP critics would have it) of "Voronskyism" as the "Trotskyite" wing in literature, with particularly negative consequences for fellow-travelers. Leading writers such as Leonid Leonov, Mikhail Bulgakov, Alexei Tolstoy, Il'ya Erenburg, Osip Mandelshtam, Boris Pil'niak, and Maximilian Voloshin were now labelled the "bourgeois reaction against the dictatorship of the proletariat" (Kornienko 131). Platonov, a somewhat less well-known writer who had nonetheless been the object of vitriolic attacks by RAPP critics, wrote an essay in which he derided RAPP's fractiousness and implicitly (he does not name names) accused its representatives of being pseudoprofessional writers trying to carve out a "pre-revolutionary" position for themselves as dictators of taste. Instead, he instructs, the writer "must involve himself in construction itself, he must become one of its rank-and-file participants, because at such a time [ca. 1931, i.e., not long after he had finished *The Foundation Pit*, TS] it is hard to write without building the socialist essence itself...it is impossible to acquire the kind of socialist feelings necessary for work by trying to command and observe from the sidelines" ("Velikaia glukhaia" 289–90; the essay was never published).

One reason Platonov may have attracted the attention of RAPP critics may have been his perceived affiliation (which in reality may have been less than it appeared) with Boris Pil'niak. In 1929 Pil'niak had published his novel *Mahogany* (*Krasnoe derevo*) in Berlin before it had cleared the Soviet censors, who then refused to pass it. The most striking element of the novel in the context of the late 1920s is its heavy dose of what had come to be called "revolutionary romanticism," a longing for the days of revolution and civil war when spontaenous action rather than subordination to the Party hierarchy had seemed to embody the revolutionary experience. In *Krasnoe derevo* a group of characters retreats into the countryside to form a primitive commune based on the principle of charity (the resemblance to the utopian revolutionaries in Platonov's *Chevengur* is unmistakeable). Pil'niak was repeatedly attacked in the RAPP-dominated press, and a year later rewrote his novel as *The Volga Flows into the Caspian Sea* (*Volga vpadaet v Kaspiiskoe more*, 1930), in which the eccentric revolutionaries are now displaced by a typical Five-Year-Plan project to construct a giant hydroelecric dam on a river near Moscow. In addition to the scandal surrounding *Krasnoe derevo*, Pil'niak himself may have attracted RAPP's attention because "as Chairman of the Board of the All-Russian Union of Writers, he was the scapegoat used to organize obedience through fear in the literary community as the first Five-Year Plan was initiated" (Terras 339). A similar affair in 1929 involved Evgeny Zamyatin, who resigned from the All-Russian Union of Writers in reaction to the furor caused by the publication of his dystopian novel *We* (*My*) in Prague. He was denied further publication in the Soviet Union and his books were even removed from libraries (Pil'niak had only abjectly had to request that readers destroy volume seven of his recent collected works). In 1931 Zamyatin emigrated from the USSR and did not return.

The Party's provisional endorsement of RAPP at the end of the 1920s proved to be more complex an affair than the RAPP leadership anticipated, however. While RAPP's leadership seemed intent on hunting down doctrinal miscreants among Soviet writers, the Party was more interested in using the organization for its own practical aims connected with the Five-Year Plan. A conference organized by the Party's Central Committee in the summer of 1928 to discuss propaganda and cultural work led to the publication in December of that year of a formal resolution "On the Serving of the Mass Reader with Literature." The document was directed at the press and other forms of mass communication, not just artistic literature, but its implications for writers were nonetheless clear. The purpose of publishing under the Five-Year Plan was to serve as "an instrument for the mobilization of the workers around the tasks of industrialization and agricultural collectivization" (quoted in Brown 89). It was to accomplish this utilitarian aim by putting into the hands of a mass readership accessible and inspiring accounts of just such industrialization and collectivization (a task Platonov's *Foundation Pit* might be said to perform inversely if not perversely). In keeping with this directive *Pravda*, which was the official organ of the Central Committee, began on February 17, 1930 to publish a regular literary page which it filled with sketches, essays, and poems devoted to the topics of construction and collectivization (Brown 90).

As the Five-Year Plan got underway and the Party began to extend its aggressively transformative power into ever more areas of Soviet life, RAPP's bullying dominance over other literary organizations, an independent exercise of power after all, became an anachronism. In 1931 articles critical of RAPP began appearing in *Pravda*, and in 1932 the Party firmly wrested control for itself over all literary and cultural organizations when the Central Committee issued its resolution "On the Reshaping of Literary-Artistic Organizations." Overnight all competing factions were abolished and the Union of Soviet Writers was established as the only legal organization for writers, with "socialist realism," an aesthetic that had yet to be fully defined, as the sole permitted method of writing. Platonov's novel *Happy Moscow* (which was never published in his lifetime) and some of his stories and plays of the 1930s represent his attempt to conform to socialist realism—the aesthetic, visible in works like Fedor Gladkov's *Cement* or Valentin Kataev's *Time, Forward!*, which for many western readers continues to exemplify Soviet literature. *The Foundation Pit* itself, however, belongs to the 1920s, an era in which verbal experimentation in a work of literature still seemed possible and the monolithic ideology of Stalinism, though in the process of enrooting itself, had not yet fully eliminated other perspectives on the meaning of the Revolution.

Another way of assessing *The Foundation Pit* in relation to its Soviet literary context is to consider the other significant events in the fields of literature, publishing, and theater that took place while Platonov was working on his text. Thus, in 1928: book one of Mikhail Sholokhov's novel *The Quiet Don* (*Tikhii Don*) appeared, as did part two of Maxim Gorky's novel *Klim Samgin*. Publication also began of the complete collected works of Leo Tolstoy. In 1929: book one of Alexander Fadeev's novel *The Last of the Udege* (*Poslednii iz udege*) appeared. Vladimir Mayakovsky's play *The Bedbug* (*Klop*) had its premiere in the Meyerhold theater. The first part of Alexei Tolstoy's *Peter the First* (*Petr Pervyi*) was published. In 1930: Mayakovsky's play *The Bathhouse* (*Bania*) had its premiere at the Meyerhold theater. Mayakovsky committed suicide on 14 April, and on 15 April his poem "At the Full Voice" ("Vo ves' golos") was published. In 1931: Boris Pasternak's novel-in-verse *Spektorsky* was published. In 1932: Sholokhov's novel *Virgin Soil Upturned* (*Podniataia tselina*) was published. Gorky's article "With Whom do you Side, 'Masters of Culture'? An Answer to American Correspondents" appeared. Valentin Kataev's *Time, Forward!* (*Vremia, vpered!*) was published (source: Kozhevnikov *et al*. 394–5).

# REFERENCES

Brown, Edward J. *The Proletarian Episode in Russian Literature, 1928–1932*. New York: Columbia University Press, 1953.

Clark, Katerina, Evgeny Dobrenko, Andrei Artizov, and Oleg Naumov, eds. *Soviet Culture and Power. A History in Documents, 1917–1953*. New Haven, CT: Yale University Press, 2007.

Fitzpatrick, Sheila, *The Commissariat of Enlightenment. Soviet Organization of Education and the Arts under Lunacharsky October 1917–1921*. Cambridge: Cambridge University Press, 1970.

Gasparov, Boris. "Tema sviatochnogo karnavala v poeme A. Bloka 'Dvenadtsat'." In his *Literaturnye leitmotivy*. Moscow: Nauka, 1994. 4–27.

Grois, Boris. *The Total Art of Stalinism. Avant-garde, Aesthetic Dictatorship, and Beyond*. Princeton, NJ: Princeton University Press, 1992.

Kasack, Wolfgang. *Dictionary of Russian Literature Since 1917*. Trans. Maria Carlson and Jane T. Hedges. New York: Columbia University Press, 1988.

Kozhevnikov, V.M., P.A. Nikolaev, *et al. Literaturnyi entsiklopedicheskii slovar'*. Moscow: Sovetskaia entsiklopediia, 1987.

*Kratkaia literaturnaia entsiklopediia*. Ed. A.A. Surkov. Vol. 6. Moscow: Sovetskaia entsiklopediia, 1971. "RAPP." 180.

Langerak, Tomas. *Andrei Platonov. Materialy dlia biografii 1899–1929 gg*. Amsterdam: Pegasus, 1995.

Maguire, Robert. *Red Virgin Soil. Soviet Literature in the 1920s*. Princeton, NJ: Princeton University Press, 1968.

Maiakovskii, Vladimir. "Prikaz po armii iskusstv." In his *Sobranie sochinenii v dvenadtsati tomakh*. Vol. 1. Moscow: Pravda, 1978. 176–7.

Malygina, N.M. "'Kotlovan' A. Platonova i obshchestvenno-literaturnaia situatsiia na rubezhe 20-x—30-x godov." In T.A. Nikonova, et al., eds. *Andrei Platonov. Issledovaniia i materialy*. Voronezh: Izdatel'stvo Voronozhskogo universiteta, 1993. 55–61.

———. Andrei Platonov. Poetika "Vozvrashcheniia". Moscow: TEIS, 2005.

Platonov, Andrei. "Velikaia glukhaia." In N.V. Kornienko and E.D. Shubina, eds. *Andrei Platonov. Vospominaniia sovremennikov. Materialy k biografii*. Moscow: Sovremennyi pistatel', 1994. 289–92.

Struve, Gleb. *Russian Literature Under Lenin and Stalin 1917–1953*. Norman, OK: University of Oklahoma Press, 1971.

Terras, Victor, ed. *Handbook of Russian Literature*. New Haven: Yale University Press, 1985.

Trotsky, Leon. *Literature and Revolution*. Ed. William Keach. Trans. Rose Strunsky. Chicago: Haymarket Books, 2005.

Chapter 4

# The Political Context of *The Foundation Pit*

If Platonov is a Soviet writer, in the sense that his works always in some way originate in changes brought about by the October Revolution of 1917, *The Foundation Pit* is a response to a very specific moment in Soviet history: the transition from Leninism (which is to say, roughly, Bolshevik Party rule) in the 1920s to the distinctly different period of Stalinism, which ensued after 1928 when Joseph Stalin consolidated his control over a Party that, though hardly liberal by any definition, in the period since Lenin's death in 1924 had at least had a plurality of powerful figures negotiating policies on its Central Committee. The political life of 1920s Soviet Russia thus parallels (in fact, underlies) the relative tolerance prevailing in its literary life.

The 1920s were also a period of relative economic liberalism in the Soviet Union. In the interests of sheer political survival, during the civil war that followed the October Revolution the Bolsheviks had pursued a policy called "War Communism" which in fact fairly closely followed the measures outlined for the "dictatorship of the proletariat" in Marx's and Engel's *Communist Manifesto*: they nationalized banks and industry, forcibly requisitioned grain from peasants, subjected the populace to the control of a secret police force (the "Cheka," whose Russian initials stood for the "Extraordinary Committee for the Battle Against Counterrevolution and Sabotage"), and imposed a number of radical measures such as (briefly) establishing equal pay for all and abolishing ranks in the military. Within a few years, however, the combined effects of revolution, war, and civil and economic upheaval had reduced the Soviet Union to a dire condition. Realizing that the economy needed to recover, in 1921 Lenin beat a tactical retreat from ruthless state intervention and introduced a series of measures called the New Economic Policy, or NEP. The Soviet state retained control over the "commanding heights" of banks, railways, and heavy industry, but otherwise reintroduced profit as an economic motive and even allowed some forms of private ownership. One result was a distinct improvement in the supply of consumer goods, but NEP also produced a group of beneficiaries, the so-called "NEPmen," who received concessions to run factories, stores, cafés, etc., and were roundly regarded with suspicion, at least by still-ardent supporters of the proletarian revolution. In Fedor Gladkov's 1925 novel *Cement*, for example, the zealously pro-Bolshevik characters are morally affronted by the thought that their beloved cement factory, idle and half-looted after the civil war, might be leased as a concession; and for one character the opening of "cafés-chantants" epitomizes the horrors of this apparent capitulation to the bourgeoisie (though the lesson of the day in Gladkov's novel is that NEP is the product of the Party's higher wisdom, and must be accepted). Even in Yuri Olesha's 1927 *Envy*, a far more ambivalent *cri de coeur* of the old intelligentsia, the object of "envy," both loathed and feared, is a plump NEPman named Andrei Babichev whose greatest achievement is to open a discount cafeteria.

The events in Soviet social and political life on which Platonov draws in *The Foundation Pit*, however, belong not to the NEP era but to the second "revolution"—it was no less than that—undertaken by Stalin and the Party elite when, in an abrupt change from ambiguities of the 1920s, they inaugurated a Five-Year Plan involving an aggressive campaign to industrialize the economy as rapidly as possible, and, simultaneously, to collectivize Soviet agriculture. The motivations for this shift lay partly in Marxist ideology, which saw the fate of the proletariat—in essence, factory workers—as the central political cause of the modern era. Although Marx and Engels wrote harsh critiques of capitalism, they were no pastoralists and in fact admired the technological accomplishments of capitalism, even as they deplored what work in its factories had done to the working class. The *Soviet* perspective on the value of industrialization *per se* is interesting and complex. In their critiques of capitalism Marx and Engels primarily had advanced economies like those of England and the Ruhr valley of Germany in mind. They paid little attention to Russia and other underdeveloped economies, and did not believe that the proletarian revolution would take place in the primitive conditions that prevailed in such places. Soviet ideology usually tried to get around this contradiction between what Marx had said and the claims they wanted to make for their Revolution by citing the "furious pace" of industrialization ("burnyi rost kapitalizma") in the years leading up to World War I rather than its actual level as the Revolution's cause—the pace supposedly having concentrated the forces of capitalism to a greater degree even than that found in far more advanced industrialized economies. Stalin's herculean effort to industrialize the country overnight can thus, in part, be understood as a way of catching up with the Marxist understanding of history, of erasing the embarrassing discrepancy between the Marxist view and Soviet reality.\*

There may, however, have been an even deeper element in the Russian historical consciousness for which orthodox Marxist considerations served simply as a rationalization: the nation's lingering sense of inferiority vis-à-vis "the West," with whose economies (incluuing military) and societies (to a lesser extent) it had been trying to catch up since tsar Peter the Great seized on this idea as the centrepiece of national policy in the early eighteenth century. Something of this anxiety can be sensed in a literary work like Valentin Kataev's *Time, Forward*, which portrays the frenetic efforts to pour the cement foundations for a smelter in the Ural mountains—a significant location, as it turns out, not only because one of the largest Five-Year Plan projects was the construction of a smelter at Magnitogorsk in the Urals but also because the Urals mark the boundary between European and Asian Russia (that is, Siberia and other eastern territories annexed by Russian tsars beginning in the fifteenth century). The novel makes a point of reminding its readers that the site for the smelter lies beyond the Urals, in the "Pugachev steppes"; and when the workers at the plant at last meet the ambitious goal of cement-pouring that they have set themselves, it declares, at once

---

\* See Kotkin's related remark that "The Soviet plan, with its proposals for astronomically large increases in industrial capacity, can be read as both an enraptured paean to industrialism and a terrified acknowledgement of industrial inferiority" (33).

nervously and triumphantly, "We will never again be Asia!" One senses the same complex of emotions in a famous speech by Stalin (which characters in Kataev's novel recite) in which he cautions that "To slow down the tempo [of industrialization] means to lag behind. And those who lag behind are beaten. The history of Old Russia shows...that because of her backwardness she was constantly being defeated. By the Mongol Khans, by the Polish-Lithuanian gentry, by the Anglo-French capitalists...Beaten because of backwardness—military, cultural, political, industrial, and agricultural backwardness...We are behind the leading countries by fifty-one hundred years. We must make up this distance in ten years. Either we do it or we go under" (quoted in Ulam 340). The certain sense of *anxiety* which attends the characters' decisions to make their foundation pit successively larger in Platonov's tale—the sense that their task is undertaken less to realize a utopian opportunity than out of desperation—partakes of a similar complex of emotions.

Whatever the ultimate motivations, industrialization had always been a goal of Soviet policy. In a famous statement Lenin asserted that "electrification plus Soviet power equals communism" (Riasanovsky 485; Platonov's stories of the mid-1920s about efforts to bring electricity to the village are direct responses to Lenin's initiative, as were his work for GOELRO, the state agency created to implement it and his pamphlet *Elektrifikatsiia*). Gosplan, the state planning agency, was created in 1921 in order to co-ordinate industrial policy, and it was the Fourteenth Party Congress in 1925, some four years before Stalin launched his initiative, which first issued the call for mass industrialization. In the struggle for power among leaders of the Communist Party which followed Lenin's death in 1924, however, the proper approach to industrialization was a matter of heated debate. Leon Trotsky and his associates (the "left" wing of the party leadership, which included Lev Kamenev and Grigory Zinoviev) advocated rapid progress toward socialism, but in conjunction with the spread of the revolutionary movement abroad. The opposing "right" faction consisting of Nikolai Bukharin, Alexei Rykov, Mikhail Tomsky and their associates, advocated a gradualist approach to social and economic transformation because they considered Russia to be still unprepared for mass industrialization; they thus defended the continuation of NEP (Cohen 19). Stalin initially sided with the gradualist Right against the Left. Then, as the first Five-Year Plan was set in motion and Stalin consolidated his position at the head of the Party, he turned the arguments of the Left against the Right (or the "rightist deviation," as it now came to be called), lambasting the "Bukharin group" for the heresy of resistance to his program for rapid industrialization (Riasanovsky 477–9). He now injected an unprecedented sense of urgency into the process. Mocking his rival Trotsky's theory of "permanent revolution," which regarded the success of socialsim in other, more advanced countries as a prerequisite for its advance in Russia (a view Lenin had also expressed), Stalin instead promoted the alternative pursuit of "socialism in one country," according to which the Soviet Union would blaze the path on its own (Riasanovsky 481).

The Fifteenth Congress of the Communist Party of the Soviet Union in 1928—not coincidentally, the one at which Stalin consolidated his control over the Party—mandated that a five-year plan for the economy be set up (Riasanovsky 482). The resulting blueprint was officially endorsed at the Sixteenth Party Congress in April 1929 (specifically, at the April Plenum of the Central Committee of the Communist Party)—but in the frenetic atmosphere which accompanied everything having to do with the Plan, the April 1929 document announced that the first Five-Year Plan had actually begun on 1 October 1928, and later the Plan was declared to have been fulfilled ahead of schedule, on 31 December 1932 rather than in 1933 (Ulam 293, 322; Riasanovsky 486). The Plan dictated the creation of large-scale industrial projects employing tens of thousands of workers each and consuming vast amounts of resources. Magnitogorsk, a giant metallurgical factory together with an adjacent town for its workers and engineers in the Ural mountains, was built entirely from scratch (see Kotkin). Kuznetskstroi, another giant smelter was built in western Siberia; Dneprostroi, a massive hydroelectic project, was installed on the Dnepr' river; and the White Sea canal, a massive excavation project, was carried out using prison labor (Shearer 193; see Ruder). The whole endeavor was permeated with an awe of "big steel" and the

Chapter Four

machine age (Kotkin 32), something which the name "Stalin" itself reflected and amplified (the root of the word is *stal'*, the Russian word for "steel"; his real surname was Dzhugashvili)—though as one cultural historian quips, some of this Soviet projection of occult powers onto metal and machines may simply be the awe-struck response "of someone who only yesterday was at the plow" (Vaiskopf 169).

The large-scale activities commanded by the Five-Year Plan brought about genuine economic advances. Under NEP it had taken the Soviet Union until 1928 to reach the level of economic activity that Russia had enjoyed on the eve of World War I (Riasanovsky 485). Under the first three Plans kilowatt hours of energy generated went from 3.2 billion, in 1928, to 31 billion in 1940; coal production went from 10 to 73 million tones per year, iron ore from 1 to 5.5 million tons, steel from 2 to 9 million tons (Shearer 194). Whole new industries were created almost from scratch: in chemicals, automobiles, agricultural machinery, aviation, machine tools, and electrical goods (Riasanovsky 486; for economic details, see also Jasny).

The political atmosphere in which these economic achievements were brought about—in many ways, the subject of *The Foundation Pit*—was, however, an unsettling combination of exuberance and fear. As Kotkin puts it, the rush to industrialize overnight was carried out in an atmosphere of "frenzied Stalinist bacchanalia" (32). If anything, the average Soviet citizen in this era shared an even greater sense of participating in an unprecedented historical epoch and hastening the arrival of a utopian future than had been the case in the disorder which ushered in the October Revolution of 1917. "'When will I finally write my memoirs about the 1930s?' one diarist asked. The fact that this author posed the question in 1932, when the decade had barely begun, illustrates how much of a notion there already existed of the Stalinist industrialization campaign as a distinct epoch in the making." (Hellbeck 55). Hellbeck cites the example of another diarist who sought to organize her personal development in five-year plans (67)—Platonov's characters, with their literal-minded reception of every phrase of Party edicts, are perhaps not as parodic as they first appear. Under the Five-Year Plan workers were encouraged to become "Stakhanovites" by emulating a coal miner from the Donbas region named Alexei Stakhanov, who, it was claimed, had in one remarkable burst of energy overfulfilled his daily quota by a factor of eight. The (nervous) sense of joy which for many accompanied the rush to industrialize can be sensed in such Stalin-era musical comedies (whose very existence might otherwise, in light of the era's tragedies, appear baffling) as *Happy Guys* (*Veselye rebiata*, 1934), *Volga, Volga!* (1938), or *The Swineherdess and Shepherd* (*Svinarka i pastukh*, 1941; for the impact of Stalinism on everyday Soviet lives see also Fitzpatrick).

The Plan also fostered a strange, essentially fantasist attitude toward the "science" under whose auspices it has supposedly been devised. In a key speech entitled "A Year of Great Change" which he delivered on the twelfth anniversary of the Revolution in 1929 Stalin boasted that "all the objections raised by 'science' against the possibility and expediency of organizing large grain factories of 40,000 to 50,000 hectares each have collapsed and crumbled to dust. Practice has refuted the objections of 'science,' and has once again shown that not only has practice to learn from 'science' but that 'science' also would do well to learn from practice" (*Works* 12: 135). In similar spirit a character in Kataev's *Time, Forward* who objects to plans to rush cement production by pointing out that the technical manuals for the German-made mixers they are using caution against overuse is told that the manuals were written by mere "mortals." This was the era in which Trofim Lysenko's belief in the inheritance of acquired characteristics (so that wheat "toughened up" by having been stored in cold conditions could be planted in the far north) was used to suppress early Soviet developments in genetics. It was an age of voluntarism, which encouraged the belief (essentially a Nietzschean one) that the human will could triumph over all obstacles.

It was also, however, a period in which the whole country was subjected to quasi-military mobilization, with the effort to industrialize spoken of in exclusively militaristic terms such as "front," "struggle," and "campaign" (Riasanovsky 488).\* Stalin opens his "Year

\*   Kotkin quotes one pamphleteer who, paraphrasing Clausewitz, writes that "construction in our conditions is a continuation of war, only by different means" (396, n. 19).

of Great Change" speech with the declaration that "the past year was a year of great change on all the *fronts* of socialist construction. The keynote of this change has been, and continues to be, a determined *offensive* of socialism against the capitalist elements in town and country" (*Works* 12: 124). The disciplinary ramifications of this view were palpable and direct. Causing delays in work, or even arriving at work late, could be severely punished. Setbacks in fulfillment of the Plan's overambitious targets were attributed not to the Plan's own unrealistic demands and the resulting haste and chaos-cum-management but to the activities of "wreckers," alleged internal enemies who were sometimes additionally accused of carrying out the bidding of foreign agents. Periodically the efforts of the GPU (the secret police, successors to the Cheka) to unearth such plots took the form of "show trials," such as that involving coal mines of the Shakhty region of the Donets Basin. The police claimed to have uncovered a widespread counterrevolutionary conspiracy but in reality they rounded up a hapless group of engineers and put them on trail for sabotage. Five of them were shot, while fourteen were sentenced to long prison terms. Another such instance involved the so-called "Industrial Party" (*prompartiia*), which was alleged to be a network of saboteurs who had infiltrated the highest reaches of planning agencies at the direction of Raymond Poincaré, the President of France (Ulam 302, 336). In her commentary to some of Platonov's letters his widow lays the blame for his departure from Voronezh on one of the members of this alleged organization, Ramzin, who supposedly wanted to undermine the plans Platonov had submitted to GOELRO, the state electrification agency—but her accusation is impossible to verify (Langerak 74).

The other prong of Stalin's campaign to "modernize" the Soviet Union, the collectivization of its agriculture, was arguably even more ambitious and certainly far more costly in human lives than the drive to industrialize. Like the industrialization campaign, the collectivization of agriculture had a certain precedent in Marxist theory, at least to the extent that private ownership of land—the sadly underrealized goal of post-emancipation reform in the countryside—was at odds with the state's encroachment on other areas of economic life. Again as in the case of industrialization, this moment in theory overlay more deep-seated attitudes and anxieties.

Despite its slogans promising "All Land to the Peasants!" the Bolshevik regime generally regarded the peasantry with a mixture of fear and distrust as a reservoir of conservative, "patriarchal" (i.e., stubbornly feudal) attitudes likely to hinder the Bolsheviks in their efforts to obtain and consolidate power. One plausible explanation for the reasoning behind Stalin's plan to industrialize the country is that he and his officials realized that if NEP succeeded it was likely to entrench a *peasant* economy that would retain control over the food supply and have little interest in large-scale industrialization (Riasanovsky 485). Another is that, faced with a temporary shortage of grain brought about by the unrealistically low prices set by the state, the Party declared an "emergency" which justified violating the terms of NEP and returning to the coercive measures of War Communism (Conquest 88–90).

Still deeper lay the long history of subordination of the Russian peasantry to the governing order in Russia, be it the tsarist officialdom and aristocracy or agencies of the Soviet state. Russian peasants had been serfs, bound to their landlord and forbidden or severely limited in their rights to move off his estate from the sixteenth century until 1861, when they were emancipated but saddled with debts to their former landlords for the land they had received (see Hellie, Field). In fact, in Russia proper (versus in other areas of the Russian empire, such as Ukraine or the Baltic territories) agriculture had traditionally been a communal affair, with strips of land—legally the property of the landowner but regarded by the peasants as theirs ("we are yours, but the land is ours," as the peasants expressed it)—being assigned annually by village elders (gathered in an organization called the *mir*) to families whose responsibility it was to farm them, with part of the proceeds being shared by the village as a whole. This system worked well during famine, when it ensured the survival of a greater number of villagers than would otherwise be the case. But it was woefully ill-adapted to any would-be market system, since there was relatively little incentive to produce beyond a certain minimum; and what surplus produce existed had a hard time reaching markets, given the dire condition of Russia's roads and its almost complete lack, until very late in the nineteenth century, of railroads. Nonetheless there were Russian intellectuals in the nineteenth century such as Alexander Herzen who viewed the peasant *mir* as a native form of socialism and a potential model for social development in both Russia and the West. Views like Herzen's or those of Leo Tolstoy, who admired what he believed to be the moral simplicity of peasant life and took to wearing a peasant blouse himself, were exceptions in a long, post-eighteenth century history of alienation between peasants, who persisted in their largely unchanged medieval culture, and a nobility which had been culturally westernized by Peter the Great's reforms. In works like Ivan Turgenev's *Notes from a Hunter's Album* (1852) one of the central issues is whether peasants and nobility even know how to talk to one another.

    To reform-minded officials in the later nineteenth century, by which point the peasants had been emancipated, the drawbacks to this traditional system of communal farming were painfully evident. In one of the sadly belated efforts in which the reigns of Alexander III and Nicholas II abounded, the minister of transport and then of finance, Sergei Witte, sought to break up peasant communes and redistribute their land in the form of single-family farms along the lines of what prevailed in Ukraine (the *khutor*, roughly, a single-family farm similar to those in western Europe and North America). In an ironic mirror-image anticipation of Stalinist collectivization, Witte wanted to spur a rapid increase in agricultural production in the Russian countryside. The surplus grain could then be dumped on the European market, creating a net inflow of currency to Russia. This inflow of currency would then fund the construction of steel mills, which would produce rails, locomotives, and other essentials of heavy industry (see von Laue). What Witte wanted to do, in other words, was to reverse the "vicious circle" of Russian poverty in which poorly developed agriculture hindered the development of industry, and vice versa (Ulam 292). The extension of railroads into the Russian countryside would then make it easier to bring grain to market, which in a virtuous cycle would then increase exports of grain to Europe. Calling his campaign "the wager on the strong" ("stavka na sil'nykh"), Witte sent armies of surveyors and agricultural advisors into the countryside to redistribute communally held land (followed, only a couple of decades later, by Platonov and his colleagues with their land reclamation schemes). Witte's reasonable estimate was that it would take until ca. 1930 to individualize Russian agricultural holdings—more or less exactly the date at which Stalin began his campaign to collectivize them.

The first Five-Year Plan introduced in 1929 projected five million households in collective farms by 1932–3 (Conquest 107). The means used to bring this about were a throwback to the days of War Communism when a series of forced grain requisitions—then thought to be a temporary if brutal expediency—were carried out in order to supply cities like Moscow and Petrograd with food (Ulam 298). Though there was some resistance to it within the Party (the so-called "rightist" opposition headed by Bukharin, Rykov, and Tomsky, for example, advocated a gradualist approach whereby peasants would be voluntarily drawn into cooperatives; Volkogonov 170, 172), Stalin began ordering the forced requisition of grain at prices set by the state in 1928 (Shearer 194). As in the case of industrialization, the predominant tenor of speeches and directives concerning collectivization was militaristic, with Stalin himself speaking of "reconnaissance," "front," "offensive," "retreat," "calling on reserves," and "total annihilation of the enemy" (Volkogonov 168). The tactics could be military as well, often involving the encirclement of villages or even entire regions by armed detachments (Ulam 347). The herding of peasant families onto collective farms was accomplished by "shock troops" sent into the countryside including members of local party committees, the political police, internal security forces, military units, and volunteer gangs from urban factories (Shearer 194). Describing these troops in his "Year of Great Change" speech, Stalin claimed that collectivization had been "taken in hand by the advanced workers in our country...It must be acknowledged that of all existing and potential propagandists of the collective-farm movement among the peasant masses, the worker propagandists are the best" (*Works* 12: 135). The "activist" who manages affairs on the collective farm in *The Foundation Pit* and the murdered workers Kozlov and Safronov belong to the ranks of these "propagandists." Peasants were organized into either a *kolhkoz*, as in *The Foundation Pit*, a more radically collectivized form whose members worked the land in common and delivered the bulk of what they produced to the state (the Russian abbreviation stands for *kollektivnoe khoziaistvo* or "collective management"); or into a *sovkhoz* (for *sovetskoe khoziaistvo*, or Soviet management), whose members functioned as wage-earning employees of a state-run agricultural enterprise (Riasanovsky 489). Despite the obviously coercive nature of the campaign, Stalin claimed in his "Year of Great Change" speech that without its "Leninist" approach the Party would not have been able "to transform the collective-farm movement into a real mass movement of the peasants themselves" (*Works* 12: 133)—a remark Platonov may very well have had in mind when writing the scene in which the village horses spontaneously "collectivize themselves" by dropping wisps of hay in a common heap.

The frenetic effort to collectivize Russian agriculture in pursuit of economic goals was further fanned by the Marxist notion of class feeling, which in Soviet conditions had come largely to mean class hatred—except that in the Russian village at the end of the 1920s this hatred was not so much incited as invented (Conquest 97).* The emotional focal point for the campaign became the notion of the "kulak," ostensibly a social and economic category comprising rich peasants (the landlords having long been eliminated; "kulak" is the Russian word for "fist," and connotes grasping rather than striking) it grew into something resembling a paranoid obsession with demonic overtones reminiscent of witch-hunts in medieval Europe (with interesting parallels: like witches, kulaks were blamed for poor harvests and the deaths of livestock). One Party document

---

\*  Teddy Uldricks suggests that "Marxism served not so much to introduce sophisticated concepts of economic and social analysis to the worker and peasant as to create a new set of adversary symbols (e.g., the bourgeoisie, the capitalists, the imperialist powers) as the object of their semi-instinctive class hatred" ("The 'Crowd' in the Russian Revolution," quoted in Stites 6).

defined a kulak as a peasant having an income of more than 300 rubles per year, engaging in trade, and leasing out equipment or buildings (Volkogonov 165). Another defined a kulak farm as one which used hired labor or had a mill or engaged in commercial activities—a definition which covered a large segment of the peasantry (Conquest 100). The remaining peasants were categorized as either *bedniaki* or poor peasants, the supposed beneficiaries and most ardent supporters of collectivization, and *seredniaki*, or "middle peasants," who ran the risk of being considered allies of the kulaks (hence in Platonov's tale the fear of the peasant whom Chiklin strikes that if he falls down Chiklin will think something "prosperous" of him, and his desire somehow to earn the rights of a poor peasant through his sufferings; Chandler/Meerson 86, Ginsburg 79–80). The assumption was that "as a class" better-off peasants must by definition be exploiters of poorer peasants and would naturally resist the formation of collective farms. In November 1929 Stalin declared that henceforth the Party would switch from its policy of limiting exploitation by "wealthy" peasants to one of "liquidation of the kulak as a class" (Ulam 325, Volkogonov 165).* Following a Party edict in 1930 kulaks were banned from joining collectives even if they wanted to, a measure which left them destitute (Volkogonov 169). In practice, however, any attempts at fine discrimination in defining the class of kulaks and regulating their behavior were abandoned as directives from Moscow began to insist that the pace of collectivization be accelerated and ever greater numbers of kulaks—who were simply

---

\*   At one point in *The Foundation Pit* the activist is writing a progress report on his efforts to collectivize the village. When he comes to the phrase "liquidation of the kulak as a class" he "could not insert a comma after 'kulak' since there had been none in the original directive" (Chandler/Meerson 110, Ginsburg 97). An ominous ambiguity hung over the presence or absence of a comma in this phrase. In a speech to the Conference of Agrarian Marxists on 27 December 1929 Stalin included a comma and spoke of liquidation "the kulak, as a class"—which implied the removal of a social boundary. In an article "On the Question of Liquidating the Kulaks as a Class" published on 21 January 1930, however, the comma disappears and the phrase now referred to liquidating "the kulaks as a class," which implied mass extermination (Zolotonosov 273–4; also *Kotlovan* 159, n. 79; Chandler/Meerson 173–4, n. 61).

*assumed* to exist in large oppositional numbers—be rounded up. In such conditions the label of "kulak" was often applied to peasants who simply owned a few cows or had once hired workers. As for Stalin, Khrushchev's wry remark during the posthumous denunciation of him at the Party's Twentieth Congress was that he had "studied agriculture only in the cinema" (quoted in Volkogonov 168).

The pace of collectivization and "liquidation" was accelerated in early 1930 but it was already becoming apparent that the Party's coercive measures were resulting in a mass exodus from the recently collectivized farms (Ulam 327, Shearer 196). On 2 March 1930 Stalin published an article in *Pravda* entitled "Dizzy with Success" in which he performed a dizzying rhetorical reversal of his own. He now denounced the motivations of overzealous activists—who in reality had been frantically trying to meet the Party's demands—as "anti-Leninist" and mockingly imitated their reasoning: "Why should we consolidate the successes achieved when, as it is, we can dash to the full victory of socialism 'in a trice': 'We can achieve anything!', 'There's nothing we can't do!'" (*Works* 12: 198–9). In a "Reply to Collective-Farm Comrades" (whose confusion is understandable) published in *Pravda* on 8 April 1930, after grousing that "it is so-called dead souls that are withdrawing from the collective farms...it is not even a withdrawal, but the revelation of a vacuum" (*Works* 12: 224), Stalin nonetheless explained that "as long as the offensive against the kulak was waged in a united front with the middle peasant, all went well. But when some of our comrades became intoxicated with success and began imperceptibly to slip from the path of an offensive against the kulaks on to the path of a struggle against the middle peasant, when, in pursuit of high collectivisation percentages, they began to apply coercion to the middle peasant, depriving him of the suffrage, 'dekulakising' and exprorpriating him, the offensive began to assume a distorted form and the united from with the middle peasant to be undermined, and, naturally, the kulak obtained an opportunity of trying to rise to his feet again" (*Works* 12: 208; the brutal slapstick of the collective farm scenes in *The Foundation Pit*, in which characters repeatedly punch one another and fall over, or fear to fall over, reads like a literalization of the rather crude metaphors filling Stalin's speech).* This explanation came despite the fact that as recently as December 1929, in a speech to agricultural students "Concerning Questions of Agrarian Policy in the U.S.S.R." he had declared the "anti-Marxist" nature of the idea that peasants would spontaneously move toward socialism to be "beyond doubt" (*Works* 12: 154).

These strange reversals of policy notwithstanding, at the Seventeeth Party Congress in 1934 Stalin declared socialism victorious in the USSR (Shearer 205) and by 1937 it could be argued that Stalin, the Party, and the instruments of state security had emerged victorious: nearly all the peasants had been absorbed into collective and state farms (Ulam 352). The costs, however, were staggering. The lurid scene in *The Foundation Pit* in which flies breed in the rotting carcasses of slaughtered cows has its basis in actual events (Platonov in fact had spent much of 1929, when he was already working on *The Foundation Pit*, touring kolkhozes and sovkhozes for Russian Federation's branch of Narkomzem—as a technician rather than as a writer; Kornienko 139). Threatened with collectivization, peasants began slaughtering their livestock on a mass scale in order to consume it or at the very least destroy it so that it would not be given over to the commune (the state even restricted the sale of salt in this period, to prevent the peasants salting their meat to preserve it; Volkogonov 169). By 1934 the number of cattle, sheep, horses, and pigs in the USSR was approximately half what it had been in 1929 when the collectivization campaign began (Shearer 196, Ulam 331–2, Riasanovsky 488). In a country whose agriculture was largely unmechanized, the loss of horses who pulled the plows had a significant collateral effect on production.

Still more tragic were the human costs of the campaign. Famine afflicted the northern Caucasus, Ukraine, and the Volga region—which, as Platonov witnessed, had been hit hard by famine

---

\*   For an excellent study of Stalin's peculiar idiolect and its influence on the Party and governmental rhetoric under his rule, see Vaiskopf, *Pisatel' Stalin*.

as recently as the early 1920s (Volkogonov 170). In addition to those who were shot as kulaks or died of starvation, hundreds of thousands of families had their property confiscated and were transported to remote areas (Volkogonov 166). In 1930 and 1931 the authorities deported 1.8 million peasants as "class enemies" (and in addition to these deportations there were others in these years not directly linked to collectivization, such as the removal of Chechens and Crimean Tatars to Central Asia; Shearer 196, 202). The countryside saw social dislocation on a massive scale, with migrants trying to leave the countryside and orphaned children fleeing the site of their parents' death (Shearer 203). As the leading Russian biographer of Stalin puts it, "It seems unlikely that the exact number of people swept up in this whirlwind of lawlessness will ever be known" (Volkogonov 166). Estimates nonetheless range from one million kulaks (five million, if one counts their families) who disappeared during the collectivization campaign to 8.5–9 million "affected by dekulakization" (Volkogonov 166).

What, then, to make of the Stalinist Five-Year Plan? It undeniably brought about a transformation of Soviet society and the Soviet economy that exceeded anything the Bolshevik regime had accomplished in the years immediately following the Revolution. It achieved nothing less than a transformation of Russia from an agrarian into an industrial power. As "Stalin's revolution drove the USSR headlong into the twentieth century," however, it also "brought into being a peculiarly despotic and militarised form of state socialism" (Shearer 216). One historian calls Stalin's campaign to collectivize Soviet agriculture nothing less than a "war against the nation" (Ulam 289) while another suggests that "collectivism was a euphemism for the systematic annihilation of the traditional peasantry and its forcible transformation into a class of industrialized rural workers" (Hellbeck 146).

 The historiographical legacy of the Five-Year Plan is correspondingly contentious. One tendency has been to regard its architect Stalin as a throwback to ruthless but effective leaders like Timurlane or Genghis Khan (Ulam 289)—or like Ivan the Terrible or Peter the Great, the more immediate models from the Russian tradition whose precedent Stalin more or less openly invoked (Kotkin 282–6). Like Stalin, the hero of Sergei Eisenstein's three-part film *Ivan the Terrible* (1944–46) can be seen either as a cruel tyrant or a strong-willed reformer who must impose his will on a short-sighted and recalcitrant nation. That the precedent of Peter the Great and his similarly abrupt efforts to transform the country was in the air in the late 1920s can be sensed from Platonov's own 1927 tale "Epifanskie shliuzy," in which a grand Petrine scheme for linking the Don and Oka rivers ultimately comes to naught (and, as discussed in the chapter on Platonov's biography, the parallel was not lost on hostile reviewers of the tale); or implicitly from *The Foundation Pit*, in which plans to construct a giant "proletarian home" result only in a large pit. At times Stalin himself seemed consciously to invoke the Petrine parallel. In his "Year of Great Change" speech, for example, he boasts that "we have *accelerated* the development of the production of means of production and have created the prerequisites for transforming our country into a *metal* country" (*Works* 12: 127)—echoing the claim made by Peter the Great's eulogist that the tsar was Russia's "Sampson" who found his nation weak but made it into one of stone ("Zastal on v tebe silu slabuiu i sdelal po imeni svoemu kamennuiu, adamantovu," Prokopovich 53), which in turn is a paraphrase of the Emperor Augustus's claim to have found a Rome built of bricks transformed it into one of marble.

There is yet another, broader historical perspective that one might take on the Five-Year Plan. Viewed in terms of what it at least *claimed* to be doing, the Stalinist plan to industrialize the Soviet economy appealed to a range of progressive ideas that were influential in European thought since the Enlightenment. As Stephen Kotkin remarks,

> The Soviet blueprint for this new society, the "Five-Year Plan for the Development of the National Economy," may have been a calculated piece of propaganda, but much of its propaganda appeal derived from a corresponding commitment to development, the acclaimed universal goal of civilization, and a grounding in science, the supreme language of modernity. The published three-volume text of the plan, with its numerous charts and graphs, proclaimed on every page the reliability

of scientific planning and the seemingly limitless possibilities afforded by modern technology, when combined with the ultimate science of society, Marxism (30).

Stalin's Five-Year Plan therefore constitutes, as Kotkin asserts, not, or not only, a bizarre series of events in a semi-civilized land on the fringe of Europe but "an integral part of the course of European history." Stalinism itself, at least in this propagandistic mode, projects a "quintessential Enlightenment utopia" (363–4). This is essentially the circle of ideas which motivated the young Platonov, who as a journalist in Voronezh confidently predicted that socialism would alleviate physical suffering on earth and who labored as a land reclamation engineer to help bring that vision about.

If true, however, the claim that the Five-Year Plan derived ultimately from the Enlightenment might point to yet another way in which *The Foundation Pit* captures its essence: as an abstract scheme, a product of minds fated to be realized, ultimately, only on paper (just as in Platonov's "Epifanskie shliuzy" the plan for a canal linking the Don and Oka rivers works only on a map in St. Petersburg). If only on the level of the Plan's empirical implementation, Stalin himself was aware of its still-abstract, paper nature. In the "Dizzy with Success" article he complains that in some regions there are only "paper resolutions on the growth of collective farms, organisation of collective farms on paper—collective farms which have as yet no reality, but whose 'existence' is proclaimed in a heap of boastful resolutions" (*Works* 12: 201). It could be argued that the socialist realist literature mandated by the state after 1932 in fact existed primarily *in order* to provide this kind of paper surrogate for the Stalinist utopia. Stalin himself had blurred the boundaries between real and metaphorical construction when, in a meeting with writers on the eve of the first Congress of Soviet Writers, he supposedly called writers "engineers of human souls." There is thus a sense, of which Platonov was keenly aware, that the only real socialism being built was on the pages of novels. If *The Foundation Pit* is strange—which is to say, permeated by unreason—it is because the phenomenon it portrays ultimately was.

# REFERENCES

Cohen, Stephen F. "Friends and Foes of Change." In Stephen F. Cohen, Alexander Rabinowitch, and Robert Sharlet, eds. *The Soviet Union Since Stalin*. Bloomington, IN: Indiana University Press, 1980.

Conquest, Robert. *The Harvest of Sorrow. Soviet Collectivization and the Terror-Famine*. New York: Oxford University Press, 1986.

Field, Daniel. *The End of Serfdom. Nobility and Bureaucracy in Russia 1855–1861*. Cambridge, MA: Harvard University Press, 1976.

Fitzpatrick, Sheila. *Everyday Stalinism: Ordinary Life in Extraordinary Times. Soviet Russia in the 1930s*. Oxford: Oxford University Press, 1999.

Hellbeck, Jochen. *Revolution on my Mind. Writing a Diary Under Stalin*. Cambridge: Harvard University Press, 2006.

Hellie, Richard. *Enserfment and Military Change in Muscovy*. Chicago: University of Chicago Press, 1971.

Jasny, Naum. *Soviet Industrialization 1928–1952*. Chicago: University of Chicago Press, 1961.

Kotkin, Stephen. *Magnetic Mountain. Stalinism as a Civilization*. Berkeley: University of California Press, 1997.

M. Lewin. *Russian Peasants and Soviet Power. A Study of Collectivization*. New York: W.W. Norton and Co., 1968.

Platonov, Andrei. *Kotlovan. Tekst, materialy tvorcheskoi istorii*. Introduction by V. Iu. Viugin. Commentary by V.Iu. Viugin, T.M. Vakhitova, and V.A. Prokof'ev. St. Petersburg: Nauka, 2000. St. Petersburg: Nauka, 2000.

Platt, Kevin M.F. "Rehabilitation and Afterimage. Alexei Tolstoi's Many Returns to Peter the Great." In Kevin M.F. Platt and David Brandenberger, eds., *Epic Revisionism. Russian History and Literature as Stalinist Propaganda*. Madison, WI: University of Wisconsin Press, 2006. 47–68.

Prokopovich, Feofan. "Slovo na pogrebenie Petra Velikogo." In V. A. Zapadov, ed. *Russkaia literatura XVIII veka, 1700–1775*. Moscow: Prosveshchenie, 1979. 53–5.

Riasanovsky, Nicholas V. and Mark D. Steinberg, *A History of Russia*. Seventh edition. New York: Oxford University Press, 2005.

Ruder, Cynthia Ann. *Making History for Stalin. The Story of the Belomor Canal*. Gainesville, Fla.: University Press of Florida, 1998.

Shearer, David R. "Stalinism, 1928–1940." In Ronald Grigor Suny, ed., *The Cambridge History of Russia*. Vol. III. The Twentieth Century. Cambridge: Cambridge University Press, 2006. 192–216.

Stalin, J.V. *Works*. Vol. 12. Moscow: Foreign Languages Publishing House, 1955.

Stites, Richard. "Iconoclastic Currents in the Russian Revolution: Destroying and Preserving the Past." In Abbot Gleason, Peter Kenez, and Richard Stites, eds. *Bolshevik Culture. Experiment and Order in the Russian Revolution*. Bloomington, IN: Indiana University Press, 1985. 1–24.

Ulam, Adam B. *Stalin. The Man and His Era*. New York: Viking, 1973.

Vaiskopf, Mikhail. *Pisatel' Stalin*. Moscow: Novoe literaturnoe obozrenie, 2001.

Volkogonov, Dmitri. *Stalin. Triumph and Tragedy*. Ed. and trans. Harold Shukman. New York: Grove Weidenfeld, 1991.

von Laue, Theodore Hermann. *Sergei Witte and the Industrialization of Russia*. New York: Columbia University Press, 1963.

Zolotonosov, Mihkail. "'Lozhnoe solntse'. ('Chevengur' i 'Kotlovan' v kontekste sovetskoi kul'tury 1920-x godov)." In N.V. Kornienko and E.D. Shubina, eds. *Andrei Platonov. Mir tvorchestva*. Moscow: Sovremennyi pisatel', 1994. 246–83.

Chapter 5

*The Foundation Pit* Itself

A note on Platonov's title: because the word "pit" in some English translations of the Bible appears as a synonym for hell or the underworld (see, for example, Psalms 16:10 and 49:9), the English title *The Foundation Pit* has a more ominous ring to it than does the original Russian, *Kotlovan*. Because it is part of the vocabulary of building, the word "*kotlovan*" has a more prospective ring to it. It denotes the pit or hole in which the foundation for a building is to be laid—and certainly motifs of the pit and the grave come into play in Platonov's tale—but something like "The Building Site" would capture more of its at least provisional air of optimism.

## THE GENERIC CONTEXT OF PLATONOV'S TALE: THE 'PRODUCTION NOVEL'

The events Platonov portrays in *The Foundation Pit* involving the excavation of a foundation pit as part of a plan to construct a "proletarian home" and the formation of a collective farm in the nearby countryside patently mimic the structure and thematic concerns of a type of novel that had become increasingly prominent in Soviet literature over the course of the 1920s: the "production" novel, whose staple theme was industrialization, which it typically represented as efforts of one kind or another to restart a factory idled by the civil war, to increase production dramatically within an existing factory, or heroically to create a vast new factory complex from scratch—all always as part of an effort to meet or

## Chapter Five

still better to exceed the Party's economic plans (after 1928, the Five-Year Plan). The production novel was absorbed as a central component in the "socialist realist" aesthetic that became mandatory for all Soviet writers after the first Congress of Soviet Writers was convened in 1934, but it had in fact existed for several years before that event—as Platonov's own *Foundation Pit*, written in the early 1930s, bears witness.

The 1920s were a period of intense and often acrimonious debate among Soviet literary factions over what Soviet or proletarian literature should actually look like (see the chapter on Platonov's literary context) but one principle which increasingly came to be accepted over the course of the decade was that it should depict labor, especially labor understood to be a part of the larger effort to construct socialism. It was this aim which motivated a series edited by Maxim Gorky called *A History of Factories and Plants*, as well as the *White Sea Canal* collection, produced by a brigade of writers dispatched to the canal's excavation site, and the flood of so-called "production sketches" (*proizvodstvennye ocherki*), accounts by writers of their visits to factories and construction sites, which filled Soviet journals and newspapers during the first Five-Year Plan (the newspaper *Izvestiia*, for example, published production sketches by Maxim Gorky, Vsevolod Ivanov, and Fedor Gladkov; *Literaturnaia gazeta* ran a weekly rubric called "Writers on the Front of Socialist Competition"). Platonov made earnest efforts to contribute to this genre. Sometime in the spring of 1929 he travelled to a paper mill on the Kama river and wrote up his experiences in a sketch called "In search of the future (A journey to the Kama Paper Mill)," which he submitted to a competition for such sketches run by the journal *Smena*. Unfortunately, his submission coincided with the attacks on him in the press for his story "Usomnivshiisia Makar" and it was out of the question for him to receive any kind of award. In a gesture that could be taken as a perfect symbol of his relations with official Soviet literary culture, Platonov then used the *reverse* side of the sketch's typescript to write, in pencil, part of the manuscript of *The Foundation Pit*. In one of the most ironic pairings that resulted, one of the sheets of paper from the latter part of the typescript extols a "lofty model of a working man" and the "fate of the whole proletarian cause" while the pencil manuscript on the reverse narrates the scene in *The Foundation Pit* in which a peasant lies down in a coffin and tries hard to die (Vakhitova 112–16). That the real-life Kama paper mill was rewarded for its competitiveness with radio equipment and 100,000 rubles for the construction of worker's dormitories are also details that seem to have made their way into the tale. Platonov also spent January to April 1930 in Leningrad, at the Stalin Leningrad Metallurgical Factory, and the Russian scholar Natalia Kornienko conjectures that this visit may also have been one of the sources for scenes in *The Foundation Pit* (*Zapisnye knizhki* 7).

Both critics and ideologues of the production novel, however, generally felt that mere factual reportage of present efforts was insufficient; instead, in keeping with Gorky's ideas about the inspirational link between art and labor (on which see the chapter on Platonov's ideological context), the writer was urged to anticipate the utopian future while capturing its emergence in the present moment. The formula arrived at for doing this, which came to be called "socialist realism," was highly codified. As Katerina Clark shows in her influential study of the genre, the Union of Soviet Writers (which also ran a literary institute as a forum in which to train young writers) maintained a list of approved exemplars which writers were told unambiguously to emulate. The novels that were written over several decades of socialist realism's dominance are consequently remarkably repetitious, adhering with relatively little divergence in anything important to what Clark calls a "master plot" populated with recurring character types and stereotypical episodes. Because Soviet writers were often imitating earlier models, a novel such as Fedor Gladkov's *Cement*, the first version of which appeared in 1925, can turn out to bear a close resemblance to a later work, such as Platonov's *The Foundation Pit*—though in Platonov's case this is because his tale is really a self-conscious commentary on the genre as a whole, that is, it is a work that is well aware that it is written in response to a cliché.

## Chapter Five

Even a cursory glance at a couple of socialist realist exemplars reveals a similarity of plot and character type to *The Foundation Pit*. In Gladkov's *Cement* the hero, Gleb Chumalov, is a recently demobilized Red Army soldier—that is, someone like Voshchev released from his previous role in life—who returns to his native town on the Black Sea only to find that he must adjust to the new social conditions of the post-revolutionary era. One depressing discovery he makes is that the local cement factory has fallen into disuse during the Revolution and civil war and now has goats grazing on the weeds that have grown up in its yard (Voshchev, meanwhile, sleeps in a weedy lot that turns out to be a future construction site). Gleb enthusiastically sets out to to organize the local workers and get the factory up and running again (in this Gladkov follows a formula that was to harden into dreary cliché in Soviet literature which held that the principal natural desire of every proletarian was to labor in a factory). The workers' rushed, spontaneous efforts, however, bring no results because (according to the logic of this dominant type of Soviet literature, which as Clark notes was written to illustrate the Bolshevik party's view of itself) the workers need to learn to submit to Party guidance, even when it demands what their naïve but purist political minds regard as shameful compromises (such as postponing the production of cement in order to repair a ropeway so that firewood can be brought over the adjacent mountain range, or accepting the technical advice of the bourgeois foreign engineer who had once run the factory). When two workers are shot by bandits while working on the ropeway their deaths are treated not as unfortunate casualties but as necessary, almost ritual sacrifices to the Bolshevik cause (just as a vigil is held over the murdered Kozlov and Safronov in Platonov's tale). Eventually the Party's managerial wisdom proves itself and the factory is restarted, on the fitting date of the fourth anniversary of the Revolution—an event portrayed by Gladkov, who came from an Old Believer family, with distinctly eschatological overtones, as though the very mountains and air were rejoicing in the event. Gleb has been transformed from a wily loner into a disciplined and subordinate member of the collective.

*The Foundation Pit* Itself

The novel represents the production of cement as a transcendent fulfillment, the filling with substance of what had been a void: the literal emptiness of the abandoned factory as well as the metaphorical wasteland of postrevolutionary economic ruin (in Platonov's tale no one undergoes transformation and nothing is produced except a pit which serves as a grave—pointed inversions of parallel moments in a production novel like *Cement*).

In the 1932 novel *Time, Forward!* by Valentin Kataev—to take just one example written on the eve of socialist realism's formal declaration as the mandatory aesthetic for all Soviet artists, i.e., precisely when Platonov was writing *The Foundation Pit*—the hero, David Margulies, is an engineer like Platonov's Prushevsky who is caught up in a utopian construction project. In this case it is the giant smelter at Magnitogorsk, the factory complex built by the Soviets from scratch in the Ural mountains. As in *The Foundation Pit*, the audacity of the endeavor is underscored by repeated reference to the town and its smelter having been created as if out of nothing, in the middle of a wasteland (bare steppe in the case of *Time, Forward!*, the vacant, weed-covered lot in *The Foundation Pit*; compare the similar motif in Gladkov's *Cement*). One of the signal achievements of the Magnitogorsk project is moreover the five-story building of brick and glass (i.e., in this steppe setting, a tower) which has been erected to house the plant's workers. The central drama of the novel, however, has to do with the characters frenetic efforts to beat a record, recently set by a rival group in Khar'kov, for the amount of concrete poured in a single day. Margulies finds himself torn between two conflicting views of the situation. On the one hand are more cautious engineers and the technical manuals for the cement mixers they have imported from Germany; on the other are enthusiasts, both workers and journalists, who want to race ahead at all costs. Margulies is willing to take a "dialectical" view of science and side with the youthful enthusiasts but he keeps warning that construction cannot be rushed beyond the technical capacity of the machines at their disposal (the calculations Prushevsky must run in order to ensure that the soil on the construction site can support the increasingly monumental edifice the characters dream of building form the parallel moment in Platonov's tale). In the end, though, the view that machines should serve socialism rather than the other way around prevails (abetted by recitations of speeches by Stalin in which he warns Russia against falling behind the technological accomplishments of the west, the penalty for which is to remain an "Asiatic" backwater). The triumphant breaking of the record by the Magnitogorsk workers is presented not just as a feat of labour but as a triumph over nature. Margulies even promises a skeptical American visitor that the Soviet Union will bring a lost paradise back to humanity, surrounding the continents with warm streams to mitigate the effects of winter—precisely the ameliorative dreams nurtured by Platonov's characters but disappointed at his tale's end.

## PLATONOV'S REFRACTION OF THE PRODUCTION NOVEL IN *THE FOUNDATION PIT*

Platonov's tale refracts this formulaic genre of Soviet literature in a parody whose aims are ideological rather than artistic, which is to say that his underlying concern is with what Gary Saul Morson calls the "etiology of utterance" in the production novel, its motivating assumptions about Soviet life, rather than with the production novel's often hackneyed artistic means (Morson 113). In essence Platonov rereads the "Marxist" premises of works like *Cement* and *Time, Forward!* in surpisingly literal ontological terms, as if accepting Marxism's claim to be a materialist philosophy as meaning that it must be a philosophy that deals in the world of matter.

That *The Foundation Pit* might be a "parody" in this sense should not necessarily be taken as meaning that Platonov was in some simple way an opponent of the Stalinist regime and its projects. At a meeting organized in February 1932 by the All-Russian Union

## The Foundation Pit Itself

of Soviet Writers to discuss his situation, he emphatically asserted that he had "always and consciously wanted to be a political writer," repeating the claim a few minutes later when one of his interviewers asks whether he thinks of himself as a satirist ("'...Ia derzhalsia i rabotal'," 102, 104). Parts of *The Foundation Pit* clearly do belong to political parody—the mindlessness of the "radio loudspeaker" at the collective farm blaring idiotic slogans, the Party activist who wonders if the hens on the collective farm are "pro-kulak" because they are not laying any eggs, the sense that the construction project and collectivization are being carried out mostly by half-wit characters who only dimly understand the aims of the Five-Year Plan, and the utter lack of any real accomplishments whatsoever: in the end the grandiose construction project "produces" nothing but an enormous pit filling up with snow, while the drive to collectivize agriculture has resulted in the mass slaughter of livestock and the social disruption of the kulaks' expulsion. Moreover, the political parody undeniably present in *The Foundation Pit* addresses a specific moment in the implementation of the First Five-Year Plan: the period immediately after the publication of Stalin's "Dizzy With Success" article in March 1930, which briefly threw the frenetic race to industrialize into reverse (and this topicality obtains whether the date at the end of the text—December 1929-April 1930—indicates the time when the events portrayed within it take place, or the time when it was written; see also Naiman and Nesbet 624). What *The Foundation Pit* suggests, however, is that Platonov continued to sympathize with what he thought *should* have been the point of the Five-Year Plan—he partly subscribed, in other words, to the aims of the Stalinist utopia—even if he satirized and lamented the manner of its realization. The most accurate statement to make about *The Foundation Pit* might be that it is at once a parody of the genre of the production novel that mocks its worldview—and its apotheosis, a work aimed, in a sense, at being the last production novel that could ever be written.

In *The Foundation Pit* Platonov thus reproduces elements of the plot structure and character types of the production novel while

## Chapter Five

redefining the genre's emphases. One obvious way in which the tale does this is through the development of its characters. The standard production novel of the mid- to late-1920s, like its still more codified socialist realist successors, often portrays people whose subjective states of mind are prey to assorted doubts and petty self-concerns. Over the course of a typical work, however, such characters, unless they are villains, typically learn to subordinate their inner life to the larger project of industrialization or collectivization in which they are involved—which project also emerges as an expression of the unerring will of the Party. Voshchev and Prushevsky, however, the dual heroes of Platonov's tale, are lonely individuals whose intensely personal search for meaning does *not* end with the revelation of the Party's vision of history as higher truth (Voshchev in fact decides that the activist must have "stolen" truth from the rest of them, while Prushevsky contemplates suicide).

Platonov's most significant departure from the ideological framework of the production novel, however, lies in the subtle shift in emphasis his narrative accomplishes from the technical difficulties which must be overcome in order to build the proletarian home (a somewhat artificial display of which fills many a socialist realist work) and the accompanying political work of the Party to the nature of existence itself, in its most immediate sense as existence in the physical world.

The reasons for this shift lie in a combination of philosophical influences and, undoubtedly, an insistent personal vision. One of the most interesting ways in which he accomplished the shift is, in effect, never to take any physical action for granted but simply by reporting them to represent even simple motions or gestures to which we normally devote no conscious thought—and on which narrative generally remains silent (Popkin 55–6)—as if they were full-fledged, dynamic events. For example, at the beginning of the tale, when the weary Voshchev finds a ravine in which to spend the night, instead of simply telling us he fell asleep Platonov states that he "felt the cold on his eyelids *and used them to close his warm eyes*" (Chandler/Meerson 3, Ginsburg 5; emphasis added).* When Voshchev wakes the following morning Platonov again states the seemingly obvious by reporting, as if it were noteworthy, i.e., *not* to be taken for granted, that Voshchev "again faced the task of living and nourishing himself" (Chandler/Meerson 4, Ginsburg 5, "he had to live and eat again"). A few pages later a clock that someone has hung on the wall in the workers' barracks moves "patiently on *due to the momentum of its dead weights*" (Chandler/Meerson 13, Ginsburg 14; emphasis added). The information that weights pulled by gravity operate a pendulum clock is unexceptional, but Platonov's seemingly egregious statement of the fact draws attention to it as if it were a form of toil whose outcome was uncertain, and his description of the weights as "dead," which is true of them as something inertly hanging, introduces an ontological note reminding us that the forms of matter among which we move are lifeless and our own "live" existence among them is vulnerable. Not even the succession of day by night counts as self-evident in this text. "Night continued in the garden," Platonov reports in one scene, as though it might have been otherwise (Chandler/Meerson 35, Ginsburg 37).

Platonov finds the most telling evidence for the nature of human existence in the gaunt and tired workers at the foundation pit, who belong to a recurring type in his fiction which consists of characters who live less at the margins of society than at the very

---

\*   Quotations are from the first translation indicated, followed by reference to the page number of the parallel passage in the second. For purposes of comparison the passage from second translation is sometimes also provided. "Chandler/Meerson" refers to the 2009 translation by Robert and Elizabeth Chandler and Olga Meerson; "Ginsburg," to Mirra Ginsburg's 1994 translation. "*Kotlovan*" refers to the annotated Russian edition of *The Foundation Pit* published in 2000 by Nauka. Chandler's and Meerson's translation usually stays closer to the syntax and word choice of Platonov's text. It therefore often sounds stranger than Ginsburg's, but I place it first in most examples because it provides a better sense of what the underlying Russian is like. Like Chandler's and Meerson's, Thomas A. Whitney's translation of 1973 tends to preserve the oddities of Platonov's language. It is based, however, on the imperfect Russian version published by Ardis in 1973 in which there are some minor omissions and transpositions.

margins of existence itself. An icon-bearing procession the narrator encounters during a drought in "Electricity's Native Land" ("Rodina elektrichestva"), for example, moves over the parched, barren earth led by a priest who is "covered with gray hair, tormented and blackened" while even the face of the Virgin Mary on the icon is wrinkled, "which showed Mary's familiarity with the passions, cares, and evil of everyday life" (*Sobranie sochinenii v trekh tomakh* 1:62–3). At the beginning of *Chevengur* an old woman in the village gives starving infants a drink made from poisonous herbs, to put them out of their misery. "An orphan, a prisoner, the plague, death, the desert—would it be possible to intensify this picture of abandonment and loneliness?" sardonically quipped one reviewer in the 1930s (Gurvich 360). In the case of *The Foundation Pit* the worker-characters' condition can be seen as an extreme version of the theme, well-represented in socialist and communist literature, of the sufferings of the proletariat; but there is a decided irony in the fact that the events Platonov portrays take place a decade *after* the Revolution, when at least some amelioration of workers' sufferings could be expected.\* When Voshchev—who among the characters in the tale most often represents Platonov's concern with how being is faring in the world—enters the barn which serves as a makeshift workers' barracks at the excavation site he finds a group of men sleeping on the floor. "All the sleepers were thin, as if they had died; the cramped space between each man's skin and his bones

---

\* Eric Naiman and Anne Nesbet point out a series of suggestive parallels between *The Foundation Pit* and a novel by Émile Zola called *Travail*, which was published in France in 1901 but appeared in Russian translation in the Soviet Union in 1923. In Zola's novel the characters strive to turn a foundry into a model factory called "Maison commune," i.e., a "communal home" not unlike the "proletarian home" of Platonov's tale. At the beginning of Zola's novel the hero, like Platonov's Voshchev, wanders aimlessly through town until he ends up at the gates of a factory called "L'Abîme" ("The Abyss"). Like Voshchev, he then enters a beer hall, where he finds tired but decent workers. Much of Zola's novel concentrates on the exploitative nature of labor under capitalism, to be replaced by lighter and joyous labor in the "maison commune" ("Mise en Abîme: Platonov, Zolia i poetika truda" 620–2).

was occupied entirely by veins, and it was clear from the thickness of these veins how much blood they must let pass during the tension of labour. The cotton of the shirts conveyed with precision the slow refreshing work being carried out by the heart—there the heart was, beating close by, in the darkness of the devastated body" (Chandler/Meerson 11, Ginsburg 12–13). Later Voshchev watches Kozlov dig and sees that his "trousers had gone bare from movement; his sharp, crooked bones were like jagged knife blades tight against the skin of his shins. The defencelessness of these bones filled Voshchev with anxious nervousness: the bones might tear the flimsy skin and come out through it" (Chandler/Meerson 20, Ginsburg 24). Even a stranger who suddenly appears on the opposite side of the gully is described as having a body which "had wasted inside his clothes and his trousers were swaying on him as if empty" (Chandler/Meerson 47, Ginsburg 48).

If Platonov's portrait of this kind of suffering begins with the proletariat, however, it does not stop there. The peasants subjected to collectivization in the latter part of the tale, too, are generally impoverished and hungry, and even the pampered bureaucrat Pashkin and his wife are merely lucky, and temporary, beneficiaries of their physical circumstances: they live well only because for now they happen to be able to eat meat, butter, and other rich food, i.e., their existence does not escape the harsh laws of the physical world.

That world in *The Foundation Pit* is one which subjects all vital processes to a finite equation which yields no surplus and from which there is no escape. When Platonov remarks that "Chiklin possessed a small stony head, densely overgrown with hair, because all his life he had been either digging with a spade or pounding with a sledgehammer and there had been no time for thinking" (Chandler/Meerson 37, Ginsburg 40) we might take it as satire or even embittered solidarity with a workingman's plight, were the conceit not repeated in still more literal terms elsewhere. As Kozlov hacks away at the ground Platonov tells us that he works "without memory of time or place, discharging the remnants of his own warm strength into the stone he broke up, the stone getting warmer as Kozlov himself grew gradually colder" (Chandler/Meerson 20, Ginsburg 24)—as though Kozlov's mental state were entirely determined by the laws of thermodynamics. "Each was existing without the least surplus of life," Platonov remarks of the workers asleep in the barracks (Chandler/Meerson 12, Ginsburg 13). Thus does the waiter in the beer room Voshchev enters at the beginning of the tale avoid disagreements, because "rather than exhaust his strength at work he preserved it for private life" (Chandler/Meerson 2, Ginsburg 4). So too does Voshchev hold a strangely delimiting, almost material sense of the "meaning" he seeks in life, conjecturing that if there is no truth to be found in life it must be because "there had been once, in some plant or heroic creature, but then a wandering beggar had come by and eaten the plant, or trampled this creature down there on the ground in lowliness, and then the beggar had died in an autumn gully and the wind had blown his body clean into nothing" (Chandler/Meerson 114, Ginsburg 101; in a 1922 newspaper article he published in Voronezh called "Proletarian Poetry" a momentarily ardent materialist Platonov rejected the idea that "truth" [*istina*] is an abstract concept—"my whole body wants *istina*," he wrote, "and what the body wants cannot be immaterial, spiritual, or abstract" *Sochineniia* I–2 164). When the activist dies at the end of the tale, Voshchev decides that he had "sucked" the meaning of life out of Voshchev and everyone else (Chandler/Meerson 155, Ginsburg 135).

  The three brief paragraphs describing the young Pioneer orchestra Voshchev encounters early in the tale exemplify the kind of constant inquiry into the state of existence which Platonov conducts as he narrates the events of his world (the young Pioneers, in this case all girls, are the equivalent of a Party-organized girlscout troop). It is not that the passage denies the pioneers emotion or thought and presents them as mere physical bodies. On the contrary, a "happiness of childhood friendship" shows on their faces, which moreover are lit with nothing less than "the realization of the future world in the play of youth." Yet Platonov tells us that they were born under the desperate conditions of the civil war which followed the Revolution, when "the dead horses of social warfare were lying in the fields" and their pregnant mothers were so starved that in some cases the children were even born without skin (because the "reserves" of the fetus within them were the only nourishment they had—a particularly grim version of Platonov's existential equation). As a result the girls are all thin and the solemn joy on their faces has to substitute for "beauty and homely plumpness." As Voshchev contemplates the spectacle they present, wondering whether these girls passing before him somehow know the meaning of life—and it is characteristic in Platonov for a procession encountered by the hero to serve as this kind of existential tableau, as the icon-bearing procession of starving peasants does in "Rodina elektrichestva"—it is to the condition of their bodies that he pays particular attention. They have frail but "hardening" bodies and legs "covered with the down of youth." Despite the traces of physical deprivation which they still bear, they represent "time coming to maturity in a fresh body." There is an undeniable potential for lust, for an attraction to phsyicality, in their "swarthy legs filled with resolute tenderness" and in particular in the birthmark on the "swelling body" of the "small woman" who breaks ranks to pick a plant from the side of the road. She triggers longing in both Voshchev and the cripple Zhachev, but Voshchev becomes concerned for the "purity and intactness" of these representatives of the future world (in this regard the little girl Nastya who is adopted by the diggers is their younger cousin) and warns Zhachev off (Chandler/Meerson 8, Ginsburg 9–10). As in the philosophy of Nikolai Fedorov, the future world would be threatened by a seizure here and now of its physical embodiment. The mixture of salacious and vaguely pedophilic overtones with utopian ideology in Platonov's passage is actually not unique in Soviet literature of the 1920s. Yuri Olesha's 1927 *Envy* features a teen-age heroine, Valia, who emblemizes the new world. She is both the fiancée of an ideal soccer-playing, future-building Soviet youth and the object of resentful longing by the tale's bohemian, alcoholic anti-hero Nikolai Kavalerov. At one point Kavalerov peers voyeuristically through a hole in a fence as Valia performs gymnastic exercises. She is wearing black trunks which reveal "the whole structure of her legs," which are suntanned and covered with nicks and scars from vigorous outdoor sports. The "cleanliness and tenderness" of her upper body show how "charming" she will be, "maturing and turning into a woman" (Olesha 121).

Sexuality in Platonov is always problematic, and whatever that may or may not tell us about him as a person, in his works it always serves as yet another index to the trials of physical existence. In the early Voronezh journalism sexual desire is denounced, in the spirit of Fedorov's philosophy, as a primitive force opposed to utopian consciousness. In "At the Beginnings of the Kingdom of Consciousness" ("U nachala tsarstva soznaniia"), for example, he declares that the kingdom of consciousness ushered in by the Revolution succeeds one of feeling, which was "chiefly that of sex" (*Sochineniia* I–2:143), while in "On the Culture of Harnessed Light and Comprehended Electricity" ("O kul'ture zapriazhennogo sveta i poznannogo elektrichestva") he declares that the culture of the past, dedicated primarily to the production of gametes, was a dead end; only the nascent culture of thought and technology would transform the cosmos. In Platonov's literary works the characters often seem to avoid sexual relations out of a lack of interest, as in "Coachman's Settlement" ("Iamskaia sloboda," 1927, the name for the suburb of Voronezh where Platonov was born), whose protagonist Filat "did not get excited about girls" ("devitsam ne radovalsia") and who is handy at all sorts of tasks "except marrying" (*Sobranie sochinenii v trekh tomakh* I:256). *Chevengur* in particular envisions utopia as an all-male society (see the discussion in Borenstein 225–63 of this as a general trait of Soviet culture in the 1920s; see also Bullock).

When it is not banished from the world of Platonov's texts altogether, sexuality tends to take on troubled forms, such as the homosexual executioner who puts Bertrand Perry to death in "Epifanskie shliuzy" ("you won't like it, but that's how it has to be," Platonov wrote to his wife; Platonova 165), or Serbinov, the Muscovite who visits Chevengur in the novel of that name, who wants to make love to a girl on his mother's grave—or Zhachev in *The Foundation Pit*, who is often described as "moving his hand in his pocket," or Kozlov, who "caresses himself" at night under the blanket and therefore tires easily when he has to dig the next day.* Later in his career Platonov seems to have reached an accommodation with the need for sexual relations—but with evident reluctance, as in the 1937 "The River Potudan'" ("Reka Potudan'") whose hero at first flees his marriage and only after his wife tries to drown herself does he return to her, and even then dispiritedly (see Naiman "Andrei Platonov and the Inadmissibility of Desire"). As with his theme of existence in general, the theme of sexuality in Platonov is not a purely idiosyncratic concern but echoes topics which exercised Soviet culture as a whole. As Naiman points out, throughout the 1920s Soviet society as a whole wrestled with "the problem of sex." The apogee of the theme's discussion in literature came in 1927 (when Platonov was writing *Chevengur*) and thereafter waned ("Andrei Platonov and the Inadmissibility of Desire" 320).

The existential tragedy in Platonov has to do with sentient being finding itself imprisoned within, and threatened with being reduced to, such states of pure physicality. Platonov speaks of the kinds of human attributes we are used to thinking of as transcending the flesh as if they were entirely contained within it. At the opening of *The Foundation Pit* he remarks that Voshchev sits down at a window to "listen to various sad sounds and feel the anguish of a heart surrounded by hard and stony bones," in effect reducing the metaphoric site of our emotions to the corporeal organ beating in our chest (Chandler/Meerson 2, Ginsburg 4). Similarly, the expiration of the peasant who has lain down in a coffin and willed his own death has more to do with a purely physical process of heat exchange than with the departure of a metaphysical soul: "The peasant's heart had, of its own accord, risen up into his soul, into the cramped space of the throat, and it had clenched tight there, releasing the heat of dangerous life into his outer skin" (Chandler/Meerson 101, Ginsburg 90). In the same episode Voshchev and Chiklin encounter

---

\* Neither Kozlov nor Zhachev is a kulak, but one of Platonov's notebooks from 1929–1930 contains the entry, "The kulak is like an onanist, he does everything on his own, into his fist" (*Zapisnye knizhki* 34).

## Chapter Five

an old peasant pleading with his wife to stuff food inside him so that his body does not fly away, because he believes his soul has departed from his flesh (Chandler/Meerson 99, Ginsburg 88).

What makes this state of affairs tragic is that in Platonov's world nothing escapes the law of entropy, which subjects everything, the mind and soul as well physical objects and the human body, to a relentless process of decay ending in disintegration and death (Zhachev's teeth, "worn down to nothing on food," are a minor grotesque index of this process; Chandler/Meerson 7, Ginsburg 9). One particularly stark example of this theme is the scene in which Chiklin returns to the tile factory where the owner's daughter once gave him a furtive kiss. Chiklin's memory is of a June day when a young girl raised herself on her toes and pressed her plump lips to his cheek, but when he returns the passage of time is evident in the ravages that entropy has wrought. The factory itself has sunk down into the ground and its yard is empty and deserted (in Gladkov's *Cement* similar motifs denote historical tragedy). The staircase on which he was kissed has now become decrepit and turns to "exhausted dust" when Chiklin touches it. In the middle of this desolation, on the bare ground, lies a nearly naked, emaciated woman who is dying. She turns out to be Nastya's mother. Her lower jaw has collapsed "from weakness" and Nastya has tied a string around her head to prevent her "toothless mouth" from gaping open. When Nastya asks her if she is dying because she is bourgeois, the mother replies simply "I got bored...I'm worn out" (Chandler/Meerson 55, Ginsburg 52-4). When Chiklin later returns to check on the corpse it has become covered with "fur," as if it had reverted to an animal state. After the mother's death, her mother's disintegrated skeleton is all Nastya has to console her.

In one of his surprisingly frequent, if necessarily subtle, allusions to a biblical texts, in a scene at the excavation site Platonov reworks the notion of birds as symbols of untroubled existence (as found in Luke 9:58, where Jesus tells his disciples that foxes have holes and birds of the air have nests, but the Son of Man has nowhere to lay his head; or the Sermon on the Mount in Luke 12:24, in which he states that ravens neither sow nor reap "yet God feeds them") into a portrait of entropy's effects on all being. "The sun was still high, and birds were singing plaintively in the illuminated air, not in triumphant celebration but searching for nourishment in space. Over bent, digging people swallows were hurtling low; tiredness stilled their wings, and beneath their down and feathers was the sweat of need; they had been flying since first light, ceaselessly tormenting themselves to fill the stomachs of their chicks and mates. Once Voshchev had picked up a bird that had died in an instant in midair and fallen to earth; the bird was all in sweat, and when Voshchev plucked it, so as to see its body, what remained in his hands was a scant sad creature that had perished from the exhaustion of its own labour" (Chandler/Meerson 19, Ginsburg 23).

The several generalizing statements on the nature of existence which Platonov offers in *The Foundation Pit*, often at moments when the narrative pauses to survey the surrounding landscape, further affix this *endurance of entropy* as a universal condition. "It was hot; the daytime wind was blowing, roosters crowed somewhere in a village. Everything surrendered itself to meek, unquestioning existence," Platonov tells us on the tale's first day (Ginsburg 7–8, Chandler/Meerson 5). The mowed grass and damp earth on the vacant lot that is to become the excavation site bespeak "the general sorrow of life and the vain melancholy of meaningless existence" (Chandler/Meerson 14, Ginsburg 18). And again, later, in the countryside near the collective farm, Platonov states that "endurance dragged on wearily in the world, as if everything living was situated somewhere in the middle of time and its own movement; its beginning had been forgotten by everyone, its end was unknown, and nothing remained but a direction to all sides" (Chandler/Meerson 73, Ginsburg 69–70, which for the last phrase has "nothing was left except direction").

Ultimately in Platonov the question is whether anything other than a body subject to wearying toil and disintegration can survive in this world. This existential theme is one of the fundamental precepts of his worldview and as such transcends any concern—which undeniably registers in the text of *The Foundation Pit*—with more immediate political issues, such as the fact that the exhausting labor workers must perform under the Soviet regime does not appear to differ from that under capitalism (on this see Naiman and Nesbet 631). But Platonov's existential vision turns out to implicate the *ideology* on which the Soviet regime relied, because the state of affairs he depicts represents a kind of primitive or naïvely literal interpretation of Marxist materialism, which holds that matter is all that exists, and that what we might think are spiritual entitities are really only the ephemeral results of material processes. There are moments in *The Foundation Pit* that verge on parody of this kind of philosophical naiveté, of which there are plenty of sincere examples in the journalism Platonov wrote in his Voronezh years. Contemplating the engineering project before him, for example, Prushevsky (who in many respects resembles the young Platonov with his Bogdanovian-Proletkult-ish ideas) wonders, "Could a superstructure develop from any base? Was soul within man an inevitable by-product of the manufacture of vital material?" (Chandler/Meerson 22, Ginsburg 26). The general inclination of *The Foundation Pit*, however, is to extend at least provisional trust to the Five-Year Plan as a possible remedy to the trials of physical existence. The response to the difficulties portrayed in *The Foundation Pit* is thus not at all Leninist, as in the standard production novel—that is, Platonov's tale does not work to show us, as Soviet readers in need of edification, that the Party knows best how to guide the construction of socialism—but a peculiar blend of Platonov's former utopian aspirations and their disappointments.

One clear response to the existential dilemma in *The Foundation Pit* is that of Voshchev, who embodies the empathy toward suffering being central to the philosophy of Nikolai Fedorov and expressed in the desire to collect and preserve its remnants. Lying in the grass beside the road at the beginning of the tale, Voshchev sees a dead leaf which had been brought there by the wind and now "faced humility in the earth." He places the leaf in a special compartment of the bag he carries, in which he gathers "all kind of objects of unhappiness and obscurity." "I shall store and remember you," he tells the leaf, promising to find out why it lived and perished without knowing the meaning of life (Chandler/Meerson 6, Ginsburg 8). A few pages later Platonov refers to Voshchev's bag as one in which he collects things "for memory and vengeance" (Chandler/Meerson 11, Ginsburg 12). The link between Voshchev's habit of collecting discarded objects and the Stalinist project for constructing socialism comes later, in the village scenes, when Platonov remarks that Voshchev gathers up "for socialist vengeance" things which had once belonged to "brotherly, labouring flesh." He delivers them to the activist, who scrupulously draws up a list of the bag's contents. "Now [Voshchev] was presenting these liquidated labourers to the attention of the authorities and the future, in order to achieve vengeance through the organization of eternal human meaning—on behalf of those who are now lying quietly in the earthly depth" (Chandler/Meerson 136, Ginsburg 118). The Fedorovian theme becomes still more evident in a conversation which takes place soon after between Prushevsky, Zhachev, and Nastya. When Zhachev asks Prushevsky whether "science" will be able to resurrect people "after they've rotted," Prushevsky tells him it will not; but Zhachev retorts that Lenin lies in state in Moscow "awaiting Science," and Nastya chimes in that he will "arise and live and be like a dear old grandfather" (Chandler/Meerson 138, Ginsburg 120).

Essentially the same empathetic response underlies the narrator's comments on nature lying in a state of dull meaningless, or "endurance" dragging on wearily in the world. Within Platonov's *oeuvre* these sentiments can be traced back to the elegiac "peasant" poems of the early collection *Golubaia glubina* (themselves perhaps partly inspired by Fedorov) in which wattle fences, ravines, and the stars above serve as dolorous indices to melancholy. The other closely related moment in *The Foundation Pit* is the hints at the idea of a peasant utopia which appear in the collectivization scenes and which manage to suggest—briefly, tentatively, and in the end futilely—that redress for the dire conditions of physical existence might somehow be organized spontaneously among the animals themselves (in nature, in other words) and by extension among the peasants who live among them. The sagacious horses who collectivize themselves, each bringing a mouthful of straw to place in a communal pile in the Organizational Yard, are partly a satire on the "voluntary" nature of collectivization; but also partly a utopian vision of Fedorovian collectivity extending throughout nature. A screenplay Platonov wrote in 1929 entitled "The Machinist" ("Mashinist") contains a similar scene: returning from their watering hole, twenty horses gather grass in their mouths from the side of the road then place it in a common pile in the collective farm's corral and "begin to eat collectively" (235).* An entry in Platonov's notebook for 1929–30 reads: "Left unattended (*ot bezprizornosti*) the livestock in the kolkhoz became conscious by itself: it drinks water, hauls feed, organizes itself, etc." (*Zapisnye knizhki* 33).

In these scenes Platonov may also have been responding to the similarly animist themes informing the long narrative poem "The Triumph of Agriculture" ("Torzhestvo zemledeliia") by his contemporary Nikolai Zabolotsky (1903–1958), parts of which first appeared in the Leningrad journal *Zvezda* (№ 10, 1929) when Platonov was writing *The Foundation Pit*. Although Zabolotsky's poem celebrates mechanized farming in the spirit of the Five-Year Plan (the arrival of a tractor relieves both peasants and animals of physical toil) it idiosyncratically develops its theme in the form of conversations among horses, cattle, peasants, a soldier, and even a wooden plow. Among the details in Zabolotsky's poem which suggest that Platonov may have had it in mind when writing *The Foundation Pit*

---

\*    In the screenplay this is also, however, followed by a more clearly satirical procession of cockroaches voluntarily expelling themselves from the farm. "The Machinist" in many ways appears to anticipate *The Foundation Pit*, in particular its second half, which portrays events on a collective farm also called "The General Line." Many of these—self-collectivizing horses, peasants stacking up coffins for future use, a shouting activist overseeing the activities, the expulsion of *kulak* peasants on a raft—are repeated in *The Foundation Pit*. The 1929 screenplay may well have served as a rough draft for *The Foundation Pit* (Kornienko 140). The screenplay was never filmed and no records of it have been found in the archives of any Soviet film studio. The extant copy was written by Platonov in pencil, in a school notebook.

are a discussion among peasants as to where the soul is situated and whether anything remains of us other than "powder" when we die; an anthropomorphic bear who begs a night storm to relent; a deliberative assembly (*veche*) of cows; a "horses' institute" whose representative laments the physical hardships they endure; and a promise made to the animals by the tractor that literacy will be brought to them along with the destruction of the old world: "We'll raze the old world to its ashes/And together read the letter "A"/Aloud in a huge chorus" (275). Like Platonov's tale, Zabolotsky's poem playfully (or wistfully) recombines elements of the standard Five-Year Plan narrative—without, however, veering into the grotesque, as Platonov does. Both Zabolotsky's poem and Platonov's tale also echo the Futurist poet Velemir Khlebnikov's 1920 "Ladomir," an long narrative poem on the Revolution filled with apocalyptic imagery which at one pantheistic moment declares, "I see equine freedom/ and equality before the law for cows/the years will once again merge into an epic/the [lock] has fallen from human eyes" ("Ia vizhu konskie svobody/I ravnopravie korov/Bylinoi snov' sol'iutsia gody/S glaz cheloveka spal zasov," 15).

The more aggressive and utopian mindset in *The Foundation Pit*, however, is associated with the plans to build a "proletarian home" and in particular with the figure of the engineer Prushevsky. Prushevsky is motivated by an empathy for suffering being similar to Voshchev's—gazing on an empty field he feels sad that "people should have to live and be lost on this mortal earth, where comfort had yet to be arranged" (Chandler/Meerson 44, Ginsburg 46)—but his response is to undertake the reconstruction of physical reality in order to provide shelter from the destructive forces of nature. His plan is to build a "monumental new home" into which all the workers of the town will move, abandoning their individual residences; but this home in turn would be merely the precursor of a much larger edifice some other engineer is destined to build in "ten to twenty years" in the form of a "tower in the middle of the world," in which all the labourers of the world would settle "for a happy eternity" (Chandler/Meerson 21-2, Ginsburg 25). The point of this vision is not, as it had been for many Russian radicals from the nineteenth century onward, the communal social arrangement that would result, but the security of the inhabitants' physical being. Prushevsky painstakingly calculates the soil density of the construction site and the dimensions of the projected building in order to ensure "the indestructibility of the future all-proletarian dwelling" whose purpose is to "protect people who until then had lived on the outside" (Chandler/Meerson 30, Ginsburg 33). What the workers are doing when they exhaust themselves digging in the foundation pit, Platonov tells us, is thus nothing less than installing "an eternal stone root of indestructible architecure" (Chandler/Meerson 48, Ginsburg 49). Safronov, too, urges the workers to finish construction as soon as possible, so that "childhood personnel may be shielded from ill wind and ailment by a stone wall" (Chandler/Meerson 65, Ginsburg 63) and Pashkin, who reports to the head of the local Party organization that the building needs to be much larger than originally planned, argues that otherwise all the children fertile socialist women will bear in the future will "be left outside, amid unorganized nature" (Chandler/Meerson 78, Ginsburg 72).

What the characters hope their utopian structure will provide, in other words, is an indestructible domicile for being that would supersede the too-vulnerable one of the human body. Pashkin's reference to "unorganized nature," which sounds like a satirical barb directed at the belief that Party organization can be extended to the natural world, in fact serves as in index to the ideological influences on the utopian vision outlined in the tale. Some precedent for the "proletarian home" in *The Foundation Pit* can be found in Fedorov's idea of the museum as a means for preserving elements of the past until mankind learns how to resurrect the dead; but its more significant source is Bogdanov's grand notion of "tectology" as a science of sciences uniting all existing knowledge of the physical world and thereby making it possible to change that world's structure. In the article "Proletarskaia poeziia" ("Proletarian Poetry"), which Platonov published in the journal *Kuznitsa* in 1922 at the height of his own utopian-technological fervor, he defines history as "the path toward redemption through humanity's victory over the universe." At the end of history, he states, immortality will be attained by freeing mankind from "the prison-cell of physical laws, the elements, disorganization, randomness, mystery, and horror." For the present, Platonov concedes, the proletariat will have to make do with the "organization of the symbols of reality" in art; but this was intended to be only the first step toward the ultimate task of "organizing and transforming reality itself, matter itself" (*Sochineniia* I–2: 164–5).

In *The Foundation Pit* Prushevsky similarly understands his work as an engineer to involve the application of human mind to the inert substance of the world. As he stands in the middle of the vacant lot contemplating the project he is about to undertake, Platonov tells us that he pictures "the whole world as a dead body, judging it by those parts of it that he had already converted into structures; the world had always yielded to his attentive, imagining mind that was limited only by an awareness of the intertness of nature; if material always gave in to precision and patience, then it must be deserted and dead" (Chandler/Meerson 14, Ginsburg 18). As he develops his plan for the building what Prushevsky tries to apprehend, then, is the "precise construction of the world" which eludes the dolorous, meaning-seeking Voshchev but on whose basis that world might be remade (Chandler/Meerson 5, Ginsburg 7). What *The Foundation Pit* represents is the meeting of this kind of utopian thinking, to which Platonov was so attracted in his Voronezh youth, with the Stalinist Five-Year Plan. The hope it tentatively essays is that the projects for constructing socialism carried out under the auspices of the Plan might somehow incorporate the aim of redeeming humanity from the world of matter. Pashkin's concern about nature being left "unorganized" is therefore only partly satirical; it also reflects an earnest existential desire. Or, another way of putting it which perhaps comes closer to the ideological ambivalence characteristic of Platonov, it is satirical only to the extent that the utopian hope of extending the Five-Year Plan into nature proves false.

That hope is broadly shared by the characters in the tale. When Voshchev tells a member of the trade-union committee that he has

Chapter Five

been fired for thinking about "a plan of life" (Chandler/Meerson 4, Ginsburg "the plan of life," 5) there is no doubt what Party initiative resonates in the word "plan." In a moment of despair Safronov asks Chiklin whether it is true that there is nothing but sorrow in the world and that "only in us" does there exist the Five-Year Plan (Chandler/Meerson 37, Ginsburg 40); and Voshchev, just after he learns that the coffins Chiklin has brought to the village are for the murdered Kozlov and Safronov, gazes up at the "dead, murky mass of the Milky Way" and wonders "when a *resolution* would be passed [up] there to curtail the eternity of time and redeem the wearisomeness of life" (Chandler/Meerson 80, Ginsburg 74; emphasis added). Nor was the projection of political designs onto the natural world (be it hopeful, cynical, or hubristic) limited to Platonov and his esoteric philosophical sources. In Alexander Solzhenitsyn's 1962 reckoning with Stalinism, "One Day in the Life of Ivan Denisovich," the tale's peasant protagonist Shukhov—who may very well be a literary descendent of the simple-minded Pukhov who skeptically tours the beginnings of Stalinism in Platonov's 1927 "Sokrovennyi chelovek"—on being told by a more educated prison-camp inmate that by government decree the sun now reaches its zenith at 1 pm rather than noon asks, "did the sun come under their laws, too?" (74).

The paradox that Prushevsky and the other characters in *The Foundation Pit* must confront is that the existential redemption, the rescue from bodily weakness and death, that they hope to arrange by building their proletarian home is dependent on matter itself. The benefit they desire is spiritual, in that what they hope to do is rescue being from its subordination to matter; but everything in the world around them only serves to underscore being's tragic dependence on matter: the doctrine of materialism may be all too correct, after all. Prushevsky thus wants the building he designs to be filled with people, and the people in it to be filled "with that surplus warmth of life that had been termed the soul" (Chandler/Meerson 22, Ginsburg 25)—as though the phenomenon of "soul" would result automatically from altering the energy equation currently prevailing in life. Again, noticing on the excavated walls of the foundation pit how the topsoil rests on a distinct layer of clay beneath it, he wonders whether a "superstructure can develop from any base" and whether "the soul within man [is] an inevitable by-product of the manufacture of vital material" (Chandler/Meerson 22, Ginsburg 26). There is an obvious ideological parody in this oversimplification of Marxism's precept that the forms of culture are a "superstructure" which arises out of, i.e., is caused by and therefore secondary to, a "material" base of economic relations within society (and the parody repeats itself in such remarks as those by a Party official to Voshchev, that "happiness will originate from materialism, not from meaning," Chandler/Meerson 4, Ginsburg 5). But the parody equally indicts the radical materialism of Platonov's youth, when he brashly declared in one article that "there are no values for us outside of matter" and called "spirit" (*dukh*) nothing more than a "growth" on matter (*narost*; "Revoliutsiia 'dukha'," *Sochineniia* I–2: 171); and together with that youthful radicalism, perhaps, it indicts the ambivalence at the heart of the very utopian doctrines of Fedorov, Bogdanov, and their like in early twentieth-century Russia, all of which confusedly propose the manipulation of matter as a means to a spiritual goal.

The Stalinist Five-Year Plan, again, is involved in this to the extent that its aggressive assault on reality and its totalitarian schemes appear to hold out the promise of remaking physical reality. The tale's real tragedy involves not—or not only—the political events of starving workers pressed to labor on a building project whose escalating grandiosity means that only a pit will ever result, or peasants brutally herded by Party activists into a collective farm. It is signalled, rather, by the onset of winter, which here as in Platonov's earlier novel *Chevengur* makes clear the characters' failure to alter the natural order. It is signalled in particular by the death from cold of Nastya, their little mascot of the future whom they dote on but fail to protect from the elements. The most authentic digging any one does in the novel, then, is when Chiklin spends fifteen hours excavating a "sepulchral bed in eternal stone" for her—an inversion of the utopian "proletarian home" they had hoped to build. Instead of serving as a promise for the bright future, then, as it would have in a standard Soviet production novel, the foundation pit becomes a grave emblemizing the proletariat's continued subordination to the world of matter. That the Five-Year Plan fosters a culture of idiotic directives and overbearing bureaucrats who force the proletariat to toil as much as it ever did under capitalism, that it senselessly strips the peasants of their possessions and in the name of class hatred expels some of them downriver on a raft makes it a form of political evil which Platonov clearly labels as such. But the real tragedy in *The Foundation Pit* is that in causing such grief all around, the Five-Year Plan also fails at what Platonov considers the one truly significant goal it might have attained: the remaking of physical reality. All this haste, he in effect says, all this mobilization of our lives to build gigantic smelters and factories, all this radical re-organization of our rural life into collective farms, and yet we still die.

## PRINCIPAL CHARACTERS

### The activist

His name is capitalized as "the Activist" in the Ginsburg translation, which captures the sense of particularity attending Platonov's consistent use of only a simple noun to refer to him. He is thus the quintessential "activist," a satirical version of an over-zealous Party worker sent out to the village to organize a collective farm and oversee its political activities. A character called "the activist" also figures prominently in Platonov's screenplay "The Machinist." He barks orders, forces the peasants to dance in time with music blaring from the radio (which he pretends to direct) but in the end is hoisted by the shovel of the excavator operated by the machinist-hero of the title—and dropped into the river. In *The Foundation Pit* the activist spends his evenings obsessively studying directives sent down from the provincial office of the Party, zealously implementing any instructions sent his way but also worrying lest he behave overzealously (a reference to Stalin's cynically moderating article "Dizzy with Success," which accused the very Party activists he had only recently sent into the countryside to carry out his radical program of collectivization of having overdone it). In Russian, as several commentators have pointed out, *aktivist* closely resembles *antikhrist*, "Antichrist," though whether Platonov intentionally meant to suggest this parallel is a matter of conjecture.

## The bear

Bears appear often in Russian folklore, where they are typically endowed with human traits and given the name "Misha" or "Mikhail Medvedev" (*medved'* is Russian for "bear"). The trait most often assigned to them is industriousness. The folkloric bear is often referred to as "trudoliubivyi medved'"—"industrious," or more literally, "labor-loving bear"—and wooden toys featuring a bear who hammers at an anvil when a string is pulled were a typical item of woodworking sold at Russian fairs. Platonov's brother, Semen Platonovich Klimentov, recalled there being a bear who "worked" as a hammerer in a smithy in Iamskaia sloboda, where Platonov grew up (*Zapisnye knizhki* 328 n.59). Hence the bear's tongue-in-cheek deployment in *The Foundation Pit* as "the most oppressed hired worker." If understood, on the other hand, as a human who has been *reduced* to a state of animality, Platonov's bear becomes a symbol of extreme enslavement (see Malygina, who further finds a parallel with the character Sharikov, a dog who is turned into a proletarian in Mikhail Bulgakov's story "Heart of a Dog," 28). Compare also Nastya's mother, who in her state of extreme debility grows "fur" before she dies. In general the idea that oppressive labor reduces workers to a bestial state is part of the ideology of labor (see Naiman and Nesbet, who note a parallel between Platonov's bear and the furnace operator Morfain in Émile Zola's *Travail*, 627). In *The Foundation Pit* the bear becomes an avenging agent of death as he goes through the village finding out and killing its kulak inhabitants.

## Chapter Five

### Chiklin

In Platonov's notebooks he was originally called "Klimentov," which was Platonov's true surname (*Zapisnye knizhki* 39, 44). An entry dated 1930 in the third of Platonov's extant notebooks reads: "Chiklin is a primitive, fresh person" (*Zapisnye knizhki* 36). Not only is he the most prominent among the characters digging the foundation pit, Platonov describes him as having spent his life hacking away at something ("vsiu zhizn' bil baldoi"). Platonov often gives his characters semantically suggestive names. In Russian Chiklin's surname appropriately echoes verbs associated with striking, beating, hammering one's way through to something (*chikat'*, *chkat'*, *prochknut'*; Kharitonov 155).

### The diggers

Malygina notes that one can think of Platonov's characters as arranged on a scale of increasing "humanization," with the lowest position being occupied by those reduced to a near-animal existence, barely subsisting on the boundary between life and death and having no "excess of life" available to them for higher mental functions. Thus the diggers at the foundation pit "sleep like the dead" (26–7) and in their waking hours descend into a pit to work. An entry in Platonov's 1930 notebook reads, "A typical person of our time is naked—without soul or possessions, in the bath-house dressing room (*predbannik*) of history, ready for everything except the past" (*Zapisnye knizhki* 42; bathhouses in Russian culture are sometimes associated with death and the underworld—as is playfully represented, for example, in Mikhail Zoshchenko's 1924 story "The Bathhouse," whose narrator-hero is stripped to a state of nakedness and robbed of his meager possessions when he visits an average Leningrad bathhouse). A similar character appears in the 1929 screenplay "Mashinist." Platonov calls him simply "the *seredniak*" (a peasant of middling wealth, supposedly between a kulak and a poor peasant or *bedniak*) and describes him as "barefoot and poorly dressed. He gazes into the distance with empty eyes drained of color, barely comprehending anything" (234). Later, when this character is running from an approaching train but in his confusion fails to get off the tracks, Platonov notes that "his face does not express fright—he runs automatically and observes with empty, clear eyes the sunlit world around him" (236). In the screenplay it is another poor peasant named Kuz'ma, rather than a violent Zhachev-like figure, who regularly meets out proletarian "justice" by striking people with his fist—except that Kuz'ma is so weak that he is the one who collapses from the blow.

## Kozlov

An entry in Platonov's notebook for 1930 reads: "Kozlov is a lover of conflict. Illness, so devoted to liberation that it's funny" (*Zapisnye knizhki* 39). The root of his surname in Russian is "*kozel*," or "goat," which in prison slang of the time also meant "sexual pervert" (Kharitonov 157). Kozlov indeed continues the thematic line of troubled sexuality begun in the tale by Zhachev: he "caresses himself at night under the blanket" and then has insufficient strength to work during the day. Considering that it is Kozlov together with Safronov who is murdered at the collective farm, another possible association with the root of his surname is "kozel otpushcheniia," "scapegoat," which would sardonically reverse the motif of sacrifice ordinarily attending such deaths in Soviet novels. The commentators to Platonov's notebooks also point out that there was a Kozlov area (*okrug*) in the Central Black-Earth Region (known by its initials as TsChO, or Che-Che-O in the local pronunciation—this was the region about which Platonov and Pil'niak wrote the satirical sketch that got them into trouble with the critics of RAPP in 1929) and that it became famous in 1930 for attaining one of the highest percentages in the country—94%—of "total collectivization" of its agriculture (*Zapisnye knizhki* 333 n. 92).

Chapter Five

## Nastya

In mainstream Soviet literature children and young people are typically represented as embodiments of the communist future (not least in Alexander Fadeev's wartime novel *The Young Guard*, about an underground antifascist youth movement; *Young Guard* was also the name of a journal for young people which began publication in 1922, and a publishing house). At times Soviet literature suggests that children must be sacrificed, however. In Gladkov's *Cement* Gleb and Dasha's daughter Nyurka, who bears some resemblance to Nastya, is given up to an orphanage so that her mother can devote herself to Party work. She dies in the orphanage's impoverished and unsanitary conditions (there is also an eerie scene toward the end of the novel in which an infant corpse is found bobbing in the Black Sea surf). Naiman and Nesbet also point out a parallel between Nastya as an embodiment of the communist future and Zola's *Travail*, where children are destined to transcend class boundaries (625). That Nastya so readily accepts the ideology of the Five-Year Plan, agreeing to forget her bourgeois mother (until she falls ill and asks for her mother's bones), mindlessly reciting political slogans, and goading the bear on his "dekulakizing" raids suggests that she is in part a satire on this Soviet stereotype. That she has "come to love the Soviet government and now collects objects for recycling," as Prushevsky reports in his letter, does so as well—but a drive to collect recyclable items was a real part of the campaign to collectivize (specifically, to help fund the purchase of tractors) and was often carried out by bands of girl Pioneers (*Zapisnye knizhki* 332 n. 91). Nastya's existential fate, however—her death at the end of the tale from illness brought on by being left unprotected before the elements—lends her figure another meaning and suggests another lineage. Deaths of innocent children occur throughout the works of Fedor Dostoevsky, where they always sentimentally signal lost possibilities for human happiness (Nelli in *The Insulted and the Injured*, who is probably one of Nastya's prototypes, or Ilyusha in *The Brothers Karamazov*) or serve as a litmus test for utopia (as, again, in *The Brothers Karamazov*, where Ivan asks his brother Alyosha whether he would be willing to arrange eternal happiness for all of humanity if the price to be paid for it were the death of an innocent child). Behind Dostoevsky's dying innocents, certainly behind Nelli in *The Insulted and the Injured*, very likely stands little Nell, whose melodramatic death is the culmination of Dickens's *The Old Curiosity Shop*. The fact that Nastya sleeps in a painted coffin (and keeps her toys in another) already marks her as a macabre ironization of Fedorovian hopes for redemption from physical suffering in *The Foundation Pit*. Her orphanhood, a common tragic state for characters in Platonov (e.g., Sasha Dvanov in *Chevengur*), is another such marker. Platonov's notebook for 1930 contains an entry which would appear to refer to Nastya and which reads, "The word 'mama' has been repealed" (*Zapisnye knizhki* 43). That Nastya dies and is buried in the pit is the pre-eminent symbol of utopia's failure in the tale. At the same time, the name "Nastya" comes from "Anastasiia," which in Greek means "resurrection" (Kharitonov 167). Platonov appended a note to his manuscript of *The Foundation Pit* which appears in *Kotlovan* and in the Chandler/Meerson translation, but not in Ginsburg or some other Russian versions: "Will the USSR [*esesersha*] perish like Nastya, or will it grow up to be a complete human being, into a historically new society? This was the concern which formed the theme of the work as the author was writing it. The author may have erred in having portrayed in the girl's death the demise of the socialist generation, but this error resulted from excessive concern for something beloved, whose loss would be equivalent to the destruction not only of the past but of the future as well" (Kornienko 150; *Kotlovan* 116). An entry in Platonov's 1930 notebook suggests something similar: "The dead in the foundation pit are the seed of the future in the earth's aperture. <u>The bath house dressing room</u>" (*Zapisnye knizhki* 43; underlining his). If Platonov intended these notes earnestly, Nastya's death at the end of *The Foundation Pit* may be more ambivalent than somber; but if he was simply looking for some kind of optimistic turn in the hopes that it might make his tale publishable, the mood remains tragic.

Chapter Five _____

## Lev Il'ich Pashkin

Pashkin is a government official who enjoys excessive privileges, a stock figure in Soviet literature of the 1920s, which from time to time mounted campaigns against the bureaucracy. In his notebook of 1930 Platonov identifies him as "a bourgeois functionary" (*Zapisnye knizhki* 39). In some mainstream Soviet works, such as *Cement*, the point about such figures is to teach readers (in their ideal form, innocent workers eager to follow Party instruction) that *even when* Party officials appear to be obstructionist bureaucrats who enjoy unfair privileges, the Party line is still correct. In others, such as Mayakovsky's satire "The Ones Who Held Their Meeting for Too Long" ("Prozasedavshiesia"), recalcitrant bureaucrats are the object of romantic revolutionary ire, obstacles in the path of a more immediate realization of communist goals (not to mention Bulgakov's *Master and Margarita*, like *The Foundation Pit* never published in its author's lifetime, in which corrupt bureaucrats are punished by the devil). Stalin even announced a "sharpening of the battle against bureaucracy" as one of the "slogans" of the First Five-Year Plan in his speech delivered at the April 1929 Plenum of the Party's Central Committee (*Works* 12: 14; see also Vakhitova 115). The roots of this negative type lie deep in Russian satirical literature of the nineteenth century (especially the works of Nikolai Gogol and Mikhail Saltykov-Shchedrin—on whose "Story of a Town" ["Istoriia odnogo goroda"] Platonov's "City of Gradov" ["Gorod Gradov"] is heavily reliant) if not indeed earlier still, e.g., the sixteenth-century "Shemiaka's Judgment"). Pashkin is questioned about his first name and patronymic because they sound like a conspicuous reference to *Lev* (Leo) Trotsky and Vladimir *Il'ich* Lenin, whose conjunction in the Stalin era would be bizarre indeed. The surname "Pashkin" most readily suggests the verb "pakhat'," "to plow," and thus peasant background; but the—in ending is evocative of Slavonicized Jewish surnames common in the tsaristera "pale of settlement" (present-day western Russia and eastern Ukraine and Belorus'): Nakhamkin, Abramkin, Raikin, Rivkin (Kharitonov 162). "Pashkin" the well-off bureaucrat thus would seem to draw on the widespread conviction among native Russians in the 1920s and 1930s that the Soviet bureaucracy was dominated by Jews.

## Prushevsky

An engineer, and member of the pre- as well as post-revolutionary intelligentsia (see, for example, the reference to his childhood memory of servants cleaning the house before holidays). Both the root and suffix of "Prushevsky" suggest ultimate origins in the Polish nobility and point to the inevitable failure of his plans for manipulating matter: *proszek* in Polish means "(something which has been ground to) powder" (Kharitonov 163); and in Russian the cognate *prakh* means "dust," specifically in the biblical sense of what remains of us after we die. Prushevsky's status explains his certain aloofness from the other characters in the tale (*Zapisnye knizhki* 330 n.73), though the activist is glad when he arrives at the collective farm because he believes Prushevsky will bring learning to the ignorant masses. Prushevsky is also, subtly, Voshchev's close parallel, even twin: in one passage, he looks at Voshchev and wonders whether "they" (i.e., the proletariat), too, will become the intelligentsia. Prushevsky also represents a stock character in Soviet novels of the 1920s: a member of the technological intelligentsia (a closely related variant is the foreign, especially German or American, engineer) whose class origins should mark him as an enemy but who is tolerated or even accepted, sometimes even welcomed into the socialist family, to the extent that he contributes his vitally needed expertise to the construction of socialism. The *doubts* Prushevsky experiences also belong to this stock type, save that in the standard Soviet novel they are either circumscribed (the doubting, inwardly resisting specialist is handled by Party members who see through him and know how to deploy his skills) or transcended (by the *intelligent* undergoing an inward conversion to the Party's cause). A tension between this kind of character's personal life and his public role as engineer on an important construction project was a topos of

## Chapter Five

Soviet literature, but Platonov inverts the topos by emphasizing Prushevsky's unalleviated feelings of oppression and thoughts of suicide. Within Platonov's *oeuvre* Prushevsky belongs to a series of "supermen" heroes who embody their author's most aggressive utopian schemes (in broader terms their origins lie in Nietzsche as well as in such "Napoleonic" heroes of nineteenth-century Russian literature as Raskolnikov, in Dostoevsky's *Crime and Punishment*, or Hermann in Pushkin's "Queen of Spades"). These characters are always intent on the complete transformation of the earth through the voluntarist-rationalist imposition of a "project for saving humanity" (examples are Vogulov in "A Satan of Thought" ["Satana mysli"]; Mikhail Kirpichnikov in "The Ethereal Path" ["Efirnyi trakt"]; Prokofy Dvanov in *Chevengur*; and Bertrand Perry in "The Locks of Epiphany" ["Epifanskie shliuzy"]; Malygina 30–2). They are also related to less ambitious "technological" heroes, such as the narrator of "Electricity's Native Land" ("Rodina elektrichestva"), whose links with Platonov's own career in land reclamation are still more evident (Malygina 33). Malygina also points out the parallels between Prushevsky, who sacrifices himself to build the proletarian home, and a description of Lenin Platonov wrote in a 1920 article on the occasion of Lenin's 50th birthday: "All his soul and his uncommonly wonderful heart burn and are consumed in the creation of a bright and joyful temple of humanity on the site of the stinking crypt where our primitive oppressed fathers lived—rather, not lived, but died all their lives, every day, rotting in deathly grief" (36; quotation from *Sobranie sochinenii* I–2: 17). Unlike Prushevsky, the otherwise closely-related machinist in Platonov's 1929 screenplay "Mashinist" does not specifically *project* any redemptive structures. Rather, in closer conformity with the production novel as well as with Platonov's land reclamation stories of the 1920s, he is shown at the more immediate tasks of toiling to keep an electrical generator running, then working the controls of an excavator which dredges a river for the collective farm. A notebook entry for 1930, however, reads "Voshchev—on the excavator" (*Zapisnye knizhki* 40), so it is possible that the character in "Mashinist" evolved into two closely related characters in *The Foundation Pit*. The notes of personal loneliness are also lacking in the screenplay: the machinist eagerly gives up his fiancée to another worker so that he can keep on dredging rivers.

## Safronov

A "socialist," an ideological conformist who is also an ideologically alert (*bditel'nyi*) writer of denunciations of other people (Malygina 35). He parrots official slogans. His name alters by one letter its evident root in the Greek name "Sophronius" ("Sofronii" in Russian), which means "clear-thinking" (Sophronius of Jerusalem, 560–638 a.d., was a teacher of rhetoric). Kharitonov suggests that the letter alteration, which mimics semi-literate spelling, is meant to negate any allusion to the character's prescience (157).

## Voshchev

Arguably the most significant character in the tale, and the one closest to its author's point of view. In Russian his surname suggests *vosk*, "wax," perhaps significant as a common substance of natural origins which sometimes also, via its association with candles placed before icons, symbolizes gentleness or meekness (Tolstaia 259–60; a related example in Russian literature occurs when Marmeladov in Dostoevsky's *Crime and Punishment* says of his kindly superior, "He is—wax...wax before the face of the Lord; melting as wax!" 15). "Voshchev" also clearly echoes *votshche*, a biblicism (and actually an Old Church Slavic word rather than Russian) which means "in vain." Another associative line is invoked through *voobshche*, meaning "in general," especially as used in the colloquial phrase "nu, voobshche" (often shortened to "nu vashche"), which means approximately, "that takes the cake, that does it, there's nothing left to be said about this" (Kharitonov 169 n. 4). Voshchev resembles the hero of an existential novel (e.g., Sartre's *La Nausée*: dispossessed, dislodged from the safe, accepted routine of life but for that reason awakened to the tragedy of existence). The notes in *Kotlovan* point out that Voshchev's age, 30, suggests a parallel with Christ, who was baptized and begin his ministry then; it was also Platonov's age when he began working on *The Foundation Pit* (140). Voshchev's expulsion from his workplace would also seem to reflect Platonov's own difficulties in finding a permanent arrangement for himself and his family in Moscow. Platonov's notebook for 1930 has an entry which reads: "Voshchev—a vision. Dies from [unclear]. Felt everything" (*Zapisnye knizhki* 39). Another reads "Voshchev hadn't noticed how he had lived without the sense of life" (*Zapisnye knizhki* 43). The reverse side of the tenth page of Platonov's manuscript of *The Foundation Pit* (which was written in pencil on thin, cheap paper) has the following note, crossed out by Platonov, for a novella to be called "The Meaning of Life." It was apparently to have had an epigraph which read "The plot is not new, the suffering repeats itself. N. Voshchikov. 1867" (Vakhitova 112). In an unfinished draft for a story called "The Young One" ("Maloletnii") the hero Voshchev is endowed with a family life. He leaves work (dismissed by an "automatic bell" brought back by the factory director from a business trip to America) but hesitates to enter his house, and once inside hesitates to let himself be seen, because he fears his wife will stop loving him (*Zapisnye knizhki* 329–30 n. 70, Kornienko 122). Within Platonov's oeuvre, Kornienko notes that the "doubting protagonist" who figures in the cycle of "true tales" (*byli*) Platonov wrote in 1929 becomes the "esthetic dominant" of *The Foundation Pit* (140). Malygina assigns Voshchev to the type of meek wanderers, devoted to preserving the "soul" and in search of something other than mere biological existence, who appear in Platonov's works of the 1920s: e.g. Foma Pukhov in "Sokrovennyi chelovek," Zakhar Pavlovich in *Chevengur*. Often these characters in Platonov are peasants, but Voshchev is a worker. In *The Foundation Pit* the "wanderer" also finally becomes a participant in and chronicler of a socialist construction project and the collectivization of a nearby village. Voshchev is an implicit protest against "unconscious, mechanical existence" (the tale's first sentence states that he was released from his job in a "mechanical" factory) and suspects that "professional leaders" like the activist may have hidden the meaning of life from him (Malygina 41–3). Passages which were present in an earlier draft but omitted in the final version provide more psychological motivation for Voshchev's search for the "meaning of life" and "truth" (*istina*). Voshchev speaks more volubly in them, wondering out loud whether any one might discover the "arrangement" (*ustroistvo*) of the cosmos, promising to figure out the meaning of life in the future but lamenting that he cannot yet do so. A labor union official welcomes his speculations as signs of the rising cultural level of the proletariat and arranges a salary for him of 38 roubles per month (Vakhitova and Filippova 95–7). Platonov's deletion of such passages in the final version renders Voshchev far more taciturn and despondent, and the poetics of the tale more opaque and allusive.

## Zhachev

Primarily a caricature, a political joke in the form of a literalized metaphor: in Russian Platonov calls him "urod imperializma," which Ginsburg more literally translates as "cripple of imperialism" (because he lost his legs in World War I, the "Imperial" war) and Chandler and Meerson translate more connotatively as "freak of imperialism." Zhachev is a satirical embodiment of the idea of class hatred (for an earnest version of which one need go no further than Averbakh's hostile review of Platonov's "Usomnivshiisia Makar"). He is a "cripple" in another way, too: his injuries reduce him to a grossly physical existence, so that his primary concerns are eating (especially food he extorts from the well-off Pashkin) and lusting after the young Pioneer girls (though he does become a chaste custodian of Nastya). In Russian his name echoes two homonyms: the verb *zhat'*, meaning both "to reap, to mow" and "to press, to squeeze." It also almost certainly is meant to suggest *rvach*, "a greedy/grasping person" and possibly also a south Russian dialect verb, *zhachit'*, meaning "to work a great deal"

Chapter Five

(Kharitonov 155). One of Platonov's notebooks from 1930 contains the entry, "<u>The cripple</u> ruins everything" (*Zapisnye knizhki* 41).

## IMPORTANT SYMBOLS

### The proletarian home/tower

References to a utopian edifice—a house, home, tower, cathedral—appear in several of Platonov's works of the 1920s, and one Russian scholar notes that images such as "tower" and "home" (the Russian *dom* can mean either "house" or "home") should be seen as belonging to a broader series of imagined means for saving humanity from the physical world that appear in Platonov's works almost from the very beginning (for example, the idea that a *motor* could be devised that would do this appears in "In the Starry Wasteland" ["V zvezdnoi pustyne"] and "Markun"; Malygina 76). In the screenplay "Mashinist," which appears to have been an early version of *The Foundation Pit*, the characters build only an electrical station and a locomotive. *The Foundation Pit* magnifies these projects into a utopian scheme.

In an article he published in the Voronezh newspaper *Zheleznyi put'* in 1919 entitled "To Beginning Proletarian Poets and Writers" ("K nachinaiushchim proletarskim poetam i pisateliam") Platonov urges his "brothers and comrades" among the railway workers to organize a collective creative writing studio "in order to begin building on earth a unified cathedral of human creativity, a unified residence for the human spirit." "We will explode this pit (*iamu*) for corpses which is the universe," he vows in a moment of Nietzschean rage a few paragraphs later, "with the shards of the chains we have torn off we will kill its blind, decrepit master, God, and with the stumps of our bloodied hands we will finish building what we have only now begun to build" (*Sochineniia* I-2, 11-2). Two years later in the Voronezh newspaper *Ogni* he argues in the spirit of the left-wing avant-garde that proletarian art would appear automatically, as the result of technological changes brought about by the Revolution. "Thrust structures made of rails, concrete, and glass up into the clouds, fill them with machines more intelligent than people, let the earth crumble under the weight of a working humanity which is happy for the first time" ("Revoliutsiia 'dukha'," *Sochineniia* I–2, 173).

Dreams of arranging utopian asylum in the form of a house also appear in Platonov's early fiction. In the post-apocalyptic fantasy "Descendants of the Sun" ("Potomki solntsa," 1922) a narrator from the future recounts how environmental disaster nearly destroyed the earth in 1924 (the magnetic poles shifted, the Mediterranean froze solid) but mankind declared war on nature and managed to win. "Machines labored and molded out of the clumsy, formless, and cruel earth a home for humanity. And that was socialism," he reports (*Sochineniia* I–1, 224). "A Satan of Thought" ("Satana mysli"), written in the same year, is the tale of an engineer named Vogulov who attempts to transform the geography of the planet to human benefit. It was an era, the narrator informs us, when "the thunder of labor shook the earth and it had been a long time since any one looked at the sky—every one's gaze was lowered toward the ground, all hands were busy." Under Vogulov's command are "million-strong armies of workers, who tore into the earth with machines and altered its form (*obraz*), making of it a home for humanity" (*Sochineniia* I–1 197–8). In "A Story about Many Interesting Things" ("Rasskaz o mnogikh interesnykh veshchakh," 1923), a meandering picaresque tale Platonov co-wrote with his Voronezh friend Mikhail Bakhmetev, the hero Ivan Kopchikov gathers a group of poor peasants together to form a "bolshevik nation." One of their first communal projects is to build a windmill in the form of a wooden *tower* ("And there rose up against the sun a wooden tower under the hot hands of people who were alone in the hostile world, bonded together by misfortune and the threat of the sun"). Then they construct a "big house for every one" which Platonov describes at a level of detail suggetive of an architectural plan. The house is built in the form of a ring, with a garden in its middle and a garden surrounding it; each room is equipped with a ventilator activated by body heat whenever any one enters; the house has invisible central heating, while its boards are all soaked in a special flame-retardant liquid Ivan has derived from plants. Next to this "miraculous" house stands a similar structure for livestock. The utopian theme continues later in the story when Ivan comes upon a "workshop" devoted to achieving human immortality (through the application of electricity) and while there reads a pamphlet on "The Construction of the New Man" which is a condensation of Fedorovian ideas (in particular, that chastity is the necessary prerequisite to immortality; *Sochineniia* I-1, 259-65).

The building theme in "Doubting Makar" ("Usomnivshiisia Makar," 1929), one of the stories which got Platonov into trouble with the zealots of the Russian Association of Proletarian Writers (RAPP), is particularly close to that in *The Foundation Pit*. Having decided to make his way to Moscow, "to the center of the state," in order to see what technological accomplishments the Revolution has brought about, the simple peasant Makar finds himself, like Voshchev, at a construction site. When Makar asks what they are building, a passerby tells him it will be "an eternal home made of iron, concrete, steel, and bright glass" (like Voshchev, Makar is hired by the construction crew but becomes disenchanted with the bureaucrats in charge and eventually ends up in a mental asylum, where at the story's end he reads out words from a speech in which Lenin complained "our institutions are crap"; *Gosudarstvennyi zhitel'* 98, 106). That Leopold Averbakh, the leader of RAPP, singled out the motif of the building in one of the more heated parts of his attack on Platonov suggests the image had currency in Soviet discourse beyond Platonov's story—that Platonov had struck an ideological nerve: "And they come to us preaching humanism, as if there were something more genuinely human in the world than the proletariat's class hatred, as if you really could show love for the 'Makars' of this world other than *by building in the ranks of the Makars those new houses in which the heart of socialist man will beat*, as if you could really be a person other than by sensing yourself to be a mere part of that whole which realizes our idea" (12; emphasis added). The "surplus warmth of life that had been termed the soul" (Chandler/ Meerson 22, Ginsburg 25) which Prushevsky hopes to arrange for in the proletarian home of *The Foundation Pit* may well be Platonov's riposte to Averbakh's attempt to appropriate this key image.

The images of utopian buildings which recur in Platonov's works descend ultimately from a complex of ideas in Russian social and political thought of the later nineteenth and early twentieth centuries. Perhaps the most famous example of utopian architecture in Russian literature of the nineteenth century is the crystal palace seen in one of the heroine's prophetic dreams in Nikolai Chernyshevsky's 1863 *What Is To Be Done?* A blend of the actual Crystal Palace built in Hyde Park to house the Great Exhibition of British industrial achievements in 1851 and the kind of communal living arrangements envisioned by the French utopian socialist Charles Fourier (Günther 145), Chernyshevsky's image and its attendant idea that happiness could result from a purely physical arrangement goaded an infuriated Fedor Dostoevsky (who had seen the real prototype in London) to respond with his *Notes from Underground* (1864) and its willfully irrational hero, who longs to stick his tongue out at the marvelous edifice. Dostoevsky also went on to link the idea of a false, i.e., earthly, utopia with the biblical tower of Babel—*ur*-source for all this imagery—in the "Legend of the Grand Inquisitor" section of *The Brothers Karamazov* (Günther 149). Nikolai Fedorov, whose *Philosophy of the Common Cause* was one of Platonov's favorite books, shared Dostoevsky's moral urgency but reverted to Chernyshevsky's postivist faith in science. He considered architecture the most "projective" form of art because of its ability to lift heavy mass upward (Fedorov had a fear of horizontal positions) and wrote about transforming the entire earth from "something elemental and self-propelled into an earthmobile [*zemlokhod*] with the entire human race as its helmsman" (quoted in Malygina 76). Ultimately this terrestrial vehicle was to be superseded by a celestial "cathedral" composed of planets and stars (Masing-Delic 101).

Another, more direct influence on Platonov's image of the "proletarian home" is a brief allegorical sketch entitled "The Tower" ("Bashnia") written in 1913 and included in the widely-read 1918 collection *The Poetry of the Worker's Blow* (*Poeziia rabochego udara*)

## Chapter Five

by the proletarian poet Alexei Gastev, whose decision to abandon poetry in favor of real-world labor had inspired Platonov in the early 1920s. Gastev portrays the construction of an enormous structure reminiscent of Paris's Eiffel tower (Gastev refers to it as consisting of "labyrinths of iron" and topped by a spire). Something of the arduous toil Platonov's own workers perform and their eventual burial in the foundation pit seems anticipated in Gastev's description of how "hands and legs were broken in desperate sufferings, people fell into pits, the earth mercilessly consumed them" as they constructed their "monstrous tower" (chudovishche-bashniu). Gastev describes the massive tower as a burden to the earth itself, whose depths contain "boundless subterranean workers' graves" which continually emit "groans" (121). Incidentally, the combined motifs of *workers buried* beneath the very structure they erect and the *spire* completing the tower also suggest a Russian-historical subtext, that of Peter the Great, whose magnificent capital of St. Petersburg is said to rest on the bones of its peasant builders, and two of whose most characteristic monuments are the Admiralty and the fortress of Saints Peter and Paul, both of which are topped by distinctly unRussian golden spires. Even when the tower in Gastev's sketch has been completed and workers climb up to its spire, they are seized with the apprehension that "perhaps there is no tower, this is just a mirage, a fantasy of metal, granite, concrete; this is dreams...beneath us lies the same endless abyss as before, the grave" (123). Yet the sketch ends on a note of "Prometheanism," the belief, popular among proletarian poets, that the working class was destined like the ancient Greek hero Prometheus to defy the heavens and seize control of nature itself, whatever the costs (Günther 148). "No one will shatter, destroy, or remove this forged tower where the workers of the world have merged into one soul," Gastev declaims, "where their tears and blood have long since transformed themselves into iron!" May there be even more catastrophes and graves, Gastev urges, then he shifts into four lines of poetry calling on "our bold tower-world (derzostnyi bashennyi mir)" to "pierce the heights" with its spire (123; Platonov's call for the proletariat to "thrust structures made of rails, concrete, and glass up into the clouds" in his 1921 article "Revoliutsiia 'dukha'" would seem to be a virtual quotation from this passage). Gastev's version of the tower-myth thus self-consciously reverses the biblical tale of the tower of Babel (perhaps drawing on a similar embrace of the "luciferian" rebelliousness symbolized by the tower in the 1908 *Religion and Socialism* by Anatoly Lunacharsky, the Soviet Union's first Commissar of Enlightenment; Günther 148)—and on the Russian side of things covertly endorses Petrine projects for reshaping physical reality, another important thematic link with Platonov.

There was also, finally, a series of plans in the Soviet era to build utopian edifices to commemorate the Revolution or, later, monumentalize Stalinism. Platonov's notebooks contain no specific mention of these projects, but it is likely that he was aware of them. In 1919 the Constructivist artist and architect Vladimir Tatlin proposed a metal and steel monument to the Third Communist International. Also known as "Tatlin's Tower," it was composed of two airy metal spirals (vaguely reminiscent, in fact, of the Eiffel Tower) placed on top of each other, each containing its own building and each rotating on an axis. It was to have been placed in the middle of the Neva River in Petrograd (later Leningrad) but was never built, though a model was:

Chapter Five

Platonov may also have been aware when writing *The Foundation Pit*—and if he was not explicitly aware, he was attuned enough to the utopianism at the heart of Stalinist ideology to intimate something like them—of plans the Soviet authorities were making for a competition, formally announced in 1931, to design a monumental Palace of the Soviets. The edifice was to be erected on the former site of Moscow's Cathedral of Christ the Savior, which had been dynamited in the autumn of 1931. Unlike the airy and dynamic structure of Tatlin's project all of the finalists in the competition were designs, in the spirit of the new, Stalinist era, for gargantuanly imposing, neobabylonian structures, some of them to be crowned by a giant rotating statue of Lenin (on the differences between these two "cultures," avant-garde and Stalinist, see Paperny):

Yet in one of life's ironic imitations of art (as Vladimir Nabokov would have put it), none of the proposed structures was ever built. For years the site of the former cathedral remained an empty pit, until in the 1960s it was converted into a huge open-air municipal swimming pool. Eventually in 1994–1997 the Russian Orthodox Church and the city of Moscow under mayor Yuri Luzhkov rebuilt the Cathedral of Christ the Savior as an exact copy of the original.

## Excavation

The *digging* in which Platonov's characters are engaged, and which is their only real accomplishment, is also a symbol with considerable resonance in the Russian cultural context. In Platonov's own life its most obvious connection was with his work as a land reclamation engineer in the mid–1920s, when digging wells and dredging rivers was one of his main responsibilities. Related episodes occur in several stories of the 1920s, where they often have sinister overtones suggestive at once of Platonov's growing disenchantment with the Soviet state's ability to transform the countryside and deeper cultural myths. In "A Satan of Thought" ("Satana mysli," 1921), one of Platonov's early science fiction tales, work on a vast project for remaking the earth principally involves "digging into the earth with machines to change its form," and the "satanic" element is the scientist-hero's invention of an enormously powerful explosive device (*Sochineniia* I–1 198). "The Sink-Hole" ("Buchilo," 1922) is mostly a tale about an eccentric peasant and his encounter with the Revolution, until it suddenly deploys the physical term of its title as a metaphor for death: as the hero dies, "the earth beneath him dropped away, like the bottom in the sink-hole of a dried-up Tatar river" (*Sochineniia* I–1 25). In "Rasskaz o mnogikh interesnykh veshchakh" the peasant hero Ivan, lamenting that ravines deprive peasants of arable land, hypothesizes that the Russian word for "ravine," *ovrag*, comes from the expression "O, vrag!" ("Oh, enemy!"). One Russian scholar notes that in Russian folklore ravines are usually regarded as hiding places of the devil

## Chapter Five

(Malygina 44). In "Masters of the Meadow" ("Lugovye mastera," 1927), the peasants must dredge a river which routinely floods their fields but the task is daunting because the river has a sink-hole in it which can swallow objects as large as trees. Even in the generally upbeat and, for all its oddities, more conformist, screenplay "Mashinist" the digging scenes have macabre overtones. The machinist arrives in the village with a steam excavator and begins to dredge the river; but while he is doing this the peasants must remove silt and river weeds by hand. Platonov emphasizes their immersion in the river's filth: the men shovel soil into baskets carried by the women, who then empty the baskets on the shore. "Immobile clouds of millions of moquitoes and flies hover over the laborers. The women carry their baskets to the shore and return to the river. The members of the collective farm dig. Even in the water they sweat: greasy spots of sweat glisten on their naked bodies" (240).

Such episodes in Platonov's stories of the 1920s never just describe his technical experiences; they also illustrate the premise in Fedorov's philosophy that the earth is a hostile domain in need of transformation. But in "The Locks of Epiphany" ("Epifanskie shliuzy," 1927), one of the most significant works published when he left land reclamation to become a writer in Moscow, Platonov further links a utopian-tinged episode of digging with the historical theme of Peter the Great and the vast construction projects he undertook in his efforts to transform Russia into a European state. Bertrand Perry, the hero of the tale, is an English engineer who has been invited to Russia by Peter the Great to oversee the excavation of a canal between the Don and Oka rivers.* Like the digging in *The Foundation Pit*, however, Perry's efforts result not in the installation of a technological marvel but an empty space. The work is arduous, the peasants conscripted to carry it out die in droves or run away,

---

\*   Eric Naiman makes the interesting suggestion that the first name of Platonov's protagonist, Bertrand, is intended as a covert reference to Bertrand Russell and the British labor movement (Perry's middle name is "Ramsey," suggestive of Ramsey MacDonald, British Prime Minister and leader of the Labour Party; "V zhopu prorubit' okno" 68).

local officials hinder the work, and over the whole enterprise hangs the threat of retribution from the tsar. When, despite these obstacles, the canal bed has finally been excavated, it turns out that the supply of water is too meager for navigation.

There was authentic historical background to Platonov's tale (in 1696 Peter the Great commissioned an Englishman named John Perry to construct a similar canal, Langerak 120) as well as a broad discussion in the Soviet press in 1926 of plans to build a Volga-Don canal (Langerak 111). Platonov himself had published articles in a Tambov newspaper in which he proposed installing a hydroelectic plant in structures remaining from the Petrine epoch (Kornienko 58). But as the critic Strel'nikova's attack on "Epifanskie shliuzy" demonstrates, it was impossible in this era of socialist construction to write about Peter the Great in a purely historical vein. What she takes Platonov to task for is the implication she sees in his story that Soviet construction projects parallel the wrecklessly overambitious ones of the Petrine era. In fact Peter and his reign were widely discussed throughout the 1920s, from a variety of viewpoints, as a precedent for the dramatic changes of the Soviet era (as also, in a somewhat different way, was the absolutist reign of Ivan the Terrible—the best-known example of which is Sergei Eisenstein's film *Ivan the Terrible*). Boris Pil'niak, author of an important early novel about the Revolution entitled *The Naked Year* (*Golyi god*, 1922) saw the Petrine reforms as the imposition of a rationalist and statist model borrowed from the west on the utterly unreceptive "eurasian" identity of traditional Russia. The historical writer Alexei Tolstoy, who had portrayed Peter as an uncouth tyrant in works written just after the Revolution (such as "St. Peter's Day" ["Den' Petra"] and "Rearing Up" ["Na dybe"]) went on to heroize him as a visionary leader who created order and progress out of the Byzantine sloth of medieval Russia in his three-volume novel *Peter I*, which won the Stalin Prize for literature in 1941. The novel's first volume was written in 1929, at the inception of the first Five-Year Plan, when the historical parallels between Peter the Great and Stalin's own re-engineering of Soviet society were just coming to the fore (Kornienko 55–7).

## Chapter Five

Platonov's "Epifanskie shliuzy" clearly belongs on the pessimistic end of the interpretive scale, its historical allusion working to suggest is that the Soviet—and more specifically, the Stalinist—project to transform reality might meet the same fate as Peter the Great's failed scheme for a canal connecting the Don and Oka rivers.

What *The Foundation Pit* may capture, then, as a tale of ruinously unproductive digging, is a persistent historical anxiety in Russia that a threatening *nothingness* may be the inevitable outcome of the audacious effort by a powerful ruler to *create* by command. Already in the eighteenth century official pronouncements represented Peter the Great as a potentate who had created modern Russia out of nothing and established its solidity where there had been frailty. At the eulogy delivered at Peter's funeral, Feofan Prokopovich, head of the Russian church, declared Peter to be Russia's Sampson, who found his nation weak but made it into one of stone ("Zastal on v tebe silu slabuiu i sdelal po imeni svoemu kamennuiu, adamantovu," a paraphrase of the Emperor Augustus's claim to have found a Rome built of bricks and left one of marble) and who transformed what had been an unstable power on land into a powerful force on the seas ("vlast' zhe tvoeia derzhavy, prezhde i na zemli zybliushchuiusia, nyne i na more krepkuiu i postoiannuiu sotvoril").\* By the early nineteenth century, however, the polarities in this image began to fluctuate. The opening stanzas of Alexander Pushkin's narrative poem, "The Bronze Horseman" (1825) poise ambivalently between horror and awe as they portray Peter standing

---

\* These remarks draw on my "Excavating the Stone: Some Expansive Notes on a Passage in Dostoevsky," in *Word. Music. History. A Festschrift for Caryl Emerson*, eds. Lazar Fleishman, Gabriella Safran, Michael Wachtel, Stanford Slavic Studies, vols. 29–30 (Stanford, 2005), pp. 399–415. On the parallel with Augustus and the idea that Peter had created Russia out of nothing, see Ju. M. Lotman and B. A. Uspenskij, "Echoes of the Notion 'Moscow as the Third Rome' in Peter the Great's Ideology," in their *The Semiotics of Russian Culture*, Michigan Slavic Contributions, no. 11 (Ann Arbor, MI: University of Michigan, 1984), 62–63. I quote Prokopovich from Feofan Prokopovich, "Slovo na pogrebenie Petra Velikogo," in V. A. Zapadov, ed., *Russkaia literatura XVIII veka, 1700–1775* (Moscow: Prosveshchenie, 1979), 53.

godlike before the "void" of the Gulf of Finland (compare the "void" earth over which the spirit of God hovers just prior to creation in the Book of Genesis), commanding the city of St. Petersburg to appear out of the surrounding bogs. But Pushkin also calls Peter an "idol" (*kumir*, a word with distinctly pagan overtones), and the result of his audacity is a devastating flood as the natural elements he sought to subdue wreak their revenge. Similarly, the bronze horseman of Pushkin's title—Maurice Etienne Falconet's equestrian monument to Peter the Great, which in Pushkin's poem eerily comes to life and pursues the terrified hero, a poor clerk, through the streets of a city—was celebrated as a feat of solidity and presence when it was installed by Catherine the Great. Its base was fashioned from a granite monolith weighing 1,800 metric tons whose transportation from a Karelian forest to the center of Petersburg was an engineering feat in itself. Yet the popular culture of the nineteenth century, and three stories by Vladimir Dal' (an ethnographer, writer, and author of the most important Russian dictionary of the nineteenth century), Fedor Dostoevsky, and Lev Tolstoy, all celebrate the cunning of a peasant who manages to remove an enormous stone obstructing traffic in the capital by *burying* it, in effect reducing its imposing presence to nothing. In a different but related vein, in the first of his "Philosophical Letters" the nineteenth-century westernizer Peter Chaadayev famously castigated Russia for being an *empty* spot on the cultural map that had contributed *nothing* to human civilization.

That a similar complex of historical ambitions and anxieties exercised minds in the Soviet era is suggested by its presence in works by several authors besides Platonov. There is a distinct tension between the idea of *filling* vs. emptiness in Gladkov's *Cement*, a work with which *The Foundation Pit* is obviously in dialog, where a distinct layer of religious imagery—Gladkov was from an Old-Believer family—imputes the meaning of an *empty tomb* to the idle factory and correspondingly celebrates its restarting as *fulfillment*, advent, and resurrection. Even Yuri Tynianov's "Lieutenant Kijé" ("Podporuchik Kizhe," 1928), a whimsical and seemingly unrelated historical anecdote written just before Platonov wrote *The*

Chapter Five _____

*Foundation Pit* can be read as expressing anxiety over an emptiness which supplants presence. In Tynianov's tale a scribal error creates a spectral Lieutenant "Kijé" (in Russian his French-sounding name results from the plural ending of the noun for "lieutenants," "pod-poruchiki," being grafted onto the emphatic particle "zhe") while another removes an otherwise still-living Siniukhaev from offical existence. The eerie humor of the piece has to do with the solemnity with which the cipher that is Lieutenant Kijé is first escorted to Siberia (by officials who fear to tell the emperor that his scapegoat does not exist), then pardoned by the emperor and returned to St. Petersburg, where he marries, fathers children, rises to the rank of general, and finally receives a state funeral. Siniukhaev, meanwhile, wastes away. At the close of the tale Tynianov ironically eulogises, "thus was General Kijé buried, having *fulfilled* all that could be in life, and *filled* with all these things: youth and amorous adventures, punishment and exile, years of service, family life, the sudden favor of the emperor and the jealousy of his courtiers" (350).

On the grander level of state-sponsored ideology the Stalin era promoted itself as the aggressive creator of a new reality on the ruins of the old world, a builder of factories, prodigious producer of industrial goods, thruster of towers into the heavens, even provider to its citizens of a "magic tablecloth" of abundant consumer goods (Fitzpatrick 89–114). The most unsettling implication of *The Foundation Pit* is not just that this image was hollow but that it might also provoke existential tragedy, its Tower of Babel revealing itself, as on other occasions in Russian history, to be a grave.

## THE LANGUAGE OF PLATONOV'S TEXT

The language of the works Platonov wrote at the height of his career in the late 1920s, especially *The Foundation Pit*, is decidedly strange, in Russian as well as in translation; but in its strangeness it reflects a very real historical phenomenon: the linguistic turmoil which accompanied the social, political, and economic upheavals of the Revolution, civil war, and construction of a new, Soviet state and society in the 1920s (on which see Gorham). Because it led to the creation of entirely new institutions of state, the Revolution ushered in a whole new set of terms to denote them and their functionaries (e.g., "Party," "soviet," "commissar," "militiaman," "Red Army soldier") even as it rendered obsolete the corresponding terms of tsarism (not least "tsar" itself but also "minister," "Senate," "Holy Synod", etc.; Gorham 24). To matters of social policy and everyday life the Soviet authorities also aggressively applied a vocabulary derived from Bolshevik political discourse which was initially alien to much of the population. This new "Soviet speak" was disseminated through public speeches, newspapers (witness Platonov's own involvement in this process in his Voronezh years), posters (such as those placed in the windows of ROSTA, the telegraph agency), and, eventually, cinema and radio. It consisted mostly in terms for the entities central to the Marxist-Leninst conception of history, such as "proletariat," "bourgoisie," "strike," "agitator," etc., as well as a rich stock of metaphors, constituting almost a folklore unto itself, for describing the international situation (populated, as one contemporary observer put it, by "avengers of the downtrodden, images of iron and blood, predatory beasts, hydras, hydras with millions of tentacles, images of the enormous flame sweeping over the world like a whirlwind," Selishchev 133). A significant number of the terms in this new political discourse were foreign borrowings (*demonstratsiia*/demonstration, *lozung*/slogan, *shtreikhbrekher*/strikebreaker, *boikot*/boycott). To these were added a welter of new acronyms (USSR, TsK [for "Tsentral'nyi Komitet" or Central Committee], ChK [for "Chrezvychainaia komissiia po bor'be s kontrrevoliutsiei, sabbotazhem i spekuliatsiei" or the Extraordinary Committee for the Struggle Against Counterrevolution, Sabotage, and Speculation—the initial label for the Soviet secret police) and spliced hybrid words such as "Komintern" (for "Kommunisticheskii internatsional," or Communist international), "Glavbum" (for "Glavnoe upravlenie bumazhnoi promyshlennosti," or Main Directorate for the Paper Industry), and

## Chapter Five

"Ispolkom" (for "Ispolnitel'nyi komitet" or Executive Committee; Gorham 24). The "OrgYard" on the collective farm in *The Foundation Pit* mimics this widespread Soviet denotational habit, which literature of the 1920s often portrayed ironically as form of disorienting strangeness (in his novel *The Naked Year*, for example, Boris Pil'niak stretches *Glavbum* out into a sound like the howling wind, while in Mikhail Bulgakov's "The Heart of a Dog" the strange first word of the protagonist, a dog who has been transformed into a proletarian human being, is "abyrvalg," which turns out to be *Glavryba* [for something like "Glavnoe upravlenie rybnoi promyshlennosti" or Main Directorate for the Fish Industry] in reverse).

What made the advent of this markedly new but also newly mandatory discourse so tumultuous in Soviet Russia was the fact that the Revolution had enfranchised, at least nominally, a vast population of formerly oppressed citizens who were predominantly peasant in origin, including large numbers of "proletarians" who had only recently migrated from the village to the city to work in factories. They were overwhelmingly illiterate, or at best semi-literate, and thus ill-prepared to comprehend the terms in which the Soviet government spoke to them about virtually every aspect of their lives, from the international situation to personal hygiene, and in which it ultimately strove to legitimate its rule (Gorham 10). As a result peasant and worker audiences often had a hard time understanding the oratory delivered to them by Party activists and, as they themselves perforce began to absorb the new vocabulary, they often garbled its unfamiliar, bookish terms or reconfigured them as something more comprehensible, however absurd (e.g., *deistvuiushchaia armiia*, "acting army," became *devstvuiushchaia armiia* or "virginal army"; *militsioner*, "militiaman," became *litsimer*, a folk corruption of "hypocrite"; *revoliutsiia*, revolution, became *levorutsiia*, which through the word for "left," *levyi*, suggests something like an illicit revolution; Gorham 26). At the same time the large-scale literacy campaign mounted by the Soviet government, whose success was one of its indisputable achievements, both filled an urgent social need and provided an unprecedented opportunity for the Soviet government to shape the worldview of its citizens (as in the only slightly exaggerated instance of Platonov's activist, who teaches the women on the collective farm how to read by having them rehearse a political lexicon for each letter of the alphabet: "A" is for "avant-garde, activist committee, alleluia-monger, advance, arch-lefist, anti-Fascist", etc.; Chandler/Meerson 102, Ginsburg 91).

The language of *The Foundation Pit* also developed out of one of the principal responses to this linguistic change which registered itself in the literature of post-revolutionary Russia, a manner of writing called *skaz* which consisted in the imitation of markedly non-standard oral speech (an equivalent in American letters would be the southern black dialect imitated in the Uncle Remus stories of Joel Chandler Harris). The vogue for *skaz* in the 1920s had much to do with the political motivation of ceding the narrative tribunal, as it were, to the newly enfranchised peasant and worker classes (though the works in question were far more often written by educated urban writers who were approximating or inventing an "authentic" folk voice). Unlike the nineteenth-century precedents (in works by writers like Gogol, Leskov, and Dal') on which it drew, however, whose leanings were Romantic and nationalist, the 1920s vogue followed a decade of aesthetic experimentation by the literary avant-garde and often sought to use unusual, semi-literate speech as a means to formal innovation. It was this experimentalist aspect of *skaz* which also attracted the attention of Formalist theoreticians of literature, such as Boris Eikhenbaum, who defined it as the displacement of mere description by the implicitly oral mimcry of narrative performance (especially in the works of Gogol; see his 1924 "How Gogol's 'Overcoat' Was Made") and the philosopher-philologist Mikhail Bakhtin, who in his *Problems of Dostoevsky's Poetics* redefined *skaz* as an emphasis on the speech or voice of an Other ("chuzhaia rech'," "chuzhoi golos," *Problemy poetiki Dostoevskogo* 222; *Problems of Dostoevsky's Poetics* 192). In practice *skaz* narrative ranged from the episodic use of "folk" dialog to entire narratives given over to an "authentic" worker's or peasant's voice (such as Alexander Serafimovich's *The Iron Flood*, a novel recounting the long march of a Red Army detachment, the whole of which is related in a mixture of Russian and Ukrainian). At times the effect was pointedly ironic rather than laudatory, as in Pil'niak's *The Naked Year*, where unlettered garblings are treated as avant-garde neologisms; or in Isaac Babel's story "Salt," a part of his civil-war cycle *Red Cavalry*, where the linguistically crude authenticity of a Red Army soldier's account of how he shot a woman who smuggled salt aboard a military train by pretending it was an infant only seems to mask the horror of what he relates. At its complex and sophisticated end the ceding of narrative prerogative to a semi-literate voice could also yield subtly unsettling shifts in the perception of reality. Mikhail Zoshchenko, who wrote comic stories with hidden depths in the narrative voice of an uncultured proletarian, claimed that he was merely the temporary replacement for an "imaginary but genuine proletarian writer" who would someday appear (10; and one scholar has suggested that Platonov was that very writer, Chudakova 117).

Some of Platonov's early stories are clearly meant to be exercises in *skaz* in which a "folk" voice is used to relate the tale of how a simple peasant encounters the Revolution (e.g., the 1920 "Chul'dik and Epishka" or the 1922 "Buchilo"). In a somewhat different vein, the influence of Pil'niak's more modernist-oriented verbal experimentation can be detected in the protracted imitation of the language of an advertising brochure in the 1925–6 "Antiseksus" and in the incorporation in the text of graphic realia such as signs, labels, and letters in some of the stories in the *Locks of Epiphany* collection (1927) as well as in the protracted imitation of Petrine-era speech in the story "The Locks of Epiphany" itself (Langerak 143–4). Platonov also appears actively to have collected examples of the everyday Soviet speech around him. At the February 1932 meeting organized by the All-Russian Union of Soviet Writers to discuss his situation, he comments that, "in our everyday life there exists extremely rewarding material which simplifies the writer's work. In our society the separation between art and reality has decreased. Art lies on the surface of reality in an already half-prepared form, because our reality is so unusual that the distance between art and reality is already close" ("'... Ia derzhalsia i rabotal'" 102). A sketch called "The Factory of Literature" ("Fabrika literatury") which Platonov wrote in 1926 but never published in his lifetime provides some insight into what this "half-prepared" material may have been. In it he comments that he buys leatherbound notebooks in which to collect "half-finished products" for his literary works (in Russian, *polufabrikat*, which denotes any partly-processed good requiring some additional preparation by the purchaser but especially food items requiring only cooking). He then explains that these verbal *polufabrikaty* consist in "myths, historical and contemporary facts and events, everyday doings, the affixation of a will toward a better fate—all this set down by thousands of nameless but living and eloquent mouths, by hundreds of 'dry' official documents which are incomparable in their density and style" ("Fabrika literatury" 197–9). It is likely that this passage and the entire sketch containing it were meant ironically (not least the leatherbound notebooks, since Platonov is known to have used cheap notebooks meant for schoolchildren) but it nonetheless reveals a writer alert to the unusual forms of speech surrounding him.

*The Foundation Pit* itself is not only written in a style which grew out of the linguistic turmoil and literary experimentation of the 1920s, it makes the collision of semi-literate consciousness with the bookish discourse of Soviet ideology one of its primary themes. Like so many other areas of life in Soviet Russia, however, the linguistic culture had changed with the advent of Stalinism in the late 1920s. The cultivation of folk and dialect forms of Russian, or at the very least the welcoming tolerance of them, that had been typical in the years immediately following the Revolution had given way to impatience and even dismissiveness. By the beginning of the 1930s the untutored voice of the peasant and working classes was no longer in vogue. Instead, it was being vigorously repressed in favor of the "correct," literate language of the Party-state (Gorham 132). What *The Foundation Pit* in effect shows is the imposition of this language of the Party-state as a mandatory form of speech on the half-comprehending diggers at the excavation site and peasants

## Chapter Five

on the collective farm. The language of the Party-state invades their world from all sides. The activist teaches peasant women how to read by using a politicized alphabet. Safronov wants to install a radio at the excavation site so that the workers, whom he calls the "backward masses" can experience a cultural revolution by listening to "achievements and directives" (Chandler/Meerson 49, Ginsburg 50)—and once the "radio loudspeaker" is installed it pours forth an incessant stream of words "like a blizzard," urging absurd campaigns such as the clipping of horses manes and tails and the "mobilization" of stinging nettles "on the Front of Socialist Construction" (Chandler/Meerson 57, Ginsburg 55–6). Later the activist sets up another radio on the collective farm, where it blares a "campaign march" to which the peasants all "[stamp] joyfully on the spot" (Chandler/Meerson 129, Ginsburg 113). Party directives, which are regarded as a kind of holy writ, are another important vessel for the language of the state. The activist sits up all night at the collective farm, poring over the latest dispatches from the regional Party headquarters and even tearing up at the sight of the official stamp.

The irony with which Platonov relates such behavior is evident, but in the world of *The Foundation Pit* no one really resists the Party's way of speaking. If anything, they eagerly absorb it. "Let me organize myself close to you," Pashkin tells his overfed wife (Chandler/Meerson 35, Ginsburg 37). If at times this absorption of Party-speak seems ironic, the irony nonetheless reveals an underlying logic according to which political rhetoric can be applied directly to life. Safronov, who is an ideological zealot, tries to use "logical and scientific words" because he knows that socialism is supposed to be scientific (though the fact that he "equips" his words with two meanings, "one fundamental and one reserve" suggests that this discourse is far from straightforward; Chandler/Meerson 36, Ginsburg 38). Kozlov, who develops "an intense love for the proletarian masses," also on waking every morning reads in bed, memorizing "formulations, slogans, lines of poetry, precepts, all kinds of words of wisdom, the theses of various reports, resolutions, verses from songs, and so on" (Chandler/Meerson 75, Ginsburg 70)—an omnivorousness reminiscent of the feckless valet Petrushka in Nikolai Gogol's 1842 *Dead Souls*, who reads any book which comes his way, amazed at how in them words keep forming themselves out of letters. Even little Nastya spout slogans left and right ("Liquidate the kulaks as a class! Long live Lenin, Kozlov, and Safronov!" Chandler/Meerson 94, Ginsburg 84), essentially cancelling the innocence her figure imports from its antecedents in Dostoevsky. Less thematically evident, but still more potent for any contemporary who would have read Platonov's text, are the several passages which paraphrase well-known phrases from speeches by Stalin (on the "dialog" which *The Foundation Pit* conducts with Stalin's speeches of 1929–1930, see Zolotonosov 270–5).

The directive the activist receives toward the end of the tale accusing him and the General Line collective farm of "overzealousness, reckless opportunism and all kinds of sliding away, down left and right slopes" and of "rushing forward into the leftist quagmire of rightist opportunism" (Chandler/Meerson 149, Ginsburg 128–9) mimics key phrases in speeches Stalin made in the context of collectivization, in one of which ("An Answer to Comrades on the Collective Farm," given on 3 April 1930) he explains that "The chief danger now for us is the right-wing one. The right-wing danger has been and remains the chief one for us...Therefore, in order to battle successfully with right-wing opportunism we must overcome 'left-wing' opportunists. 'Left-wing' overzealots are now the objective allies of the right-wing deviationists" (quoted in *Zapisnye knizhki* 324 n. 29). Platonov's notebook for 1929–1930 contains the entry, "A Sketch. The Battle with the Non-chief Danger (the Left one)" and in the sketch "For Future Use" ("Vprok") which so angered Stalin the narrator asks a companion which danger is the chief one and is told that the nonchief danger fuels the chief one (*Zapisnye knizhki* 3, 324 n. 29).

What makes *The Foundation Pit* so unusual is that the narrator as well as the characters—in other words, the text itself—appears to have absorbed the language of the Stalinist Five-Year Plan as though it were the inevitable way to speak about the world. One minor but telling index of this is the way the narrative begins in the second half of the tale to speak of the members of the collective farm using, in Russian, only the single noun "kolkhoz" (collective farm): e.g., "the kolkhoz, carried away by the dance, paid no mind to his word" (Ginsburg 116; Chandler/Meerson 133, though Chandler and Meerson opt for the fuller "collective farm"); "outside the kolkhoz sat down by the fence" (Ginsburg 127, Chandler/Meerson 147). Properly speaking, a kolkhoz is an institution; but by speaking of it as if it were a singular person, Platonov treats the ideology of collectivization as if it were reified truth. This suspension of corrective irony (that is, of a narrative consciousness whose presence implicitly reassures us that the characters' manner of speech is indeed peculiar) resembles some of the stories by Platonov's contemporary Zoshchenko—save that in Zoshchenko the narrative is always a socially-marked oral *performance*, a tale by a racounteur. In Platonov, at least in the works he wrote from the mid–1920s to the early 1930s, no such persona comes to the fore. Instead, the linguistic impulse of Party ideology is allowed to penetrate to the level of grammar itself, triggering unexpected combinations of words that initially appear erroneous but an instant later, on another semantic plane, suddenly resonate as though they were strangely apt. As one Russian scholar describes it, Platonov "thinks within grammar, transmitting a multidimensional view, a paradoxical and antinomial logic; with his unexpected selection and combination of words, of lexical and syntactic constructions which explode the norm but then strike one with their sense, he conveys a vision which transcends thought" (Semenova 365). Or as the poet Joseph Brodsky puts it in an oft-quoted passage, "[Platonov] is a millenarian writer if only because he attacks the very carrier of millenarian sensibility in Russian society: the language itself—or, to put it in a more graspable fashion, the revolutionary eschatology embedded in the language...[Platonov's] every sentence drives the Russian language into a semantic dead end or, more precisely, reveals a proclivity for dead ends, a blind-alley mentality in the language itself" (283, 286).

Ultimately, the verbal events which take place in *The Foundation Pit* are constituted by, and therefore inseparable from, properties of the Russian language (not just its grammar but its network of connotative meanings as well)—and even more specifically, by the peculiar form of that language that began to be deployed in support of state ideology in the Stalin era. It is therefore very difficult to convey a full sense of how his style works when discussing Platonov in translation. But it is not impossible to approximate that sense by describing some of what takes place within the language of his text.*

One way in which Platonov refracts the language of Stalinism in the text of *The Foundation Pit* is simply through the ironic recitation of some of its characteristic phrases (significantly, in the speech of the narrator as much as in that of the characters). In one of the scenes at the collective farm Chiklin lies down to sleep next to Voshchev and the narrator tells us that he then "calmed down until a brighter morning" (Chandler/Meerson 95; "and rested till the brighter morning," Ginsburg 85; "i uspokoilsia do bolee svetlogo utra," *Kotlovan* 75). The morning will obviously be "brighter" than the night, but the "bright morning" (svetloe utro) that was to dawn with the advent of communism also ironically invokes one of the regime's utopian clichés. A similar irony resonates when the narrator reports that "that morning Kozlov had liquidated as a feeling his love for a certain middling lady" (Chandler/Meerson 74; "for a certain middle-class lady," Ginsburg 70; "Segodnia utrom Kozlov likvidiroval kak chuvstvo svoiu liubov' k odnoi srednei dame," *Kotlovan* 63). *Likvidirovat'*, "to liquidate" is a conspicuously foreign term whose only association is with the language of political retribution (as in the slogan that the kulaks needed to be *liquidated* as a class). The irony of (mis)using it as a synomym for "terminate" lies in suggesting that political liquidation extends to all of life's events.

A related instance involving the seemingly inadvertent citation of a phrase from another context has to do not with Stalinism but with the philosopher Friedrich Nietzsche. Of some young girls and adolescents on the collective farm, Platonov's narrator remarks that

---

\*   On language in Platonov see also, *inter alia*, my *Andrei Platonov* 160–75; Tolstaia; Tsvetkov; Dhooge.

Chapter Five

"For the main part they were indifferent to the alarm of their fathers...they lived in the village like strangers, as if pining with love towards something far distant" (Chandler/Meerson 144; Ginsburg curiously omits this phrase, leaping directly from "In general they were indifferent to the anxiety of their fathers" to the following sentence, "and they endured the poverty at home...," 125; devushki i podrostki "v obshchem ravnodushno otnosilis' k trevoge ottsov...oni zhili, kak chuzhie v derevne, slovno tomilis' liubov'iu k chemu-to dal'nemu," *Kotlovan* 104). In Russian the phrase "liubov' k dal'nemu" (love for something—or more likely some*one*, since its opposite, "liubov' k blizhnemu" is the biblical "love for one's neighbor"—distant) has distinct Nietzschean connotations. In *Thus Spake Zarathustra*, in the section entitled "Neighbor Love," Nietzsche promotes "love for the furthest and future ones...and phantoms" over effeminizing love for one's neighbor (see Zholkovsky 289). One of the stories marking Platonov's re-entry into Soviet letters after the critical attacks on him in the late 1920s was the 1934 "The Love of the Distant" ("Liubov' k dal'nemu"). The deployment of the phraseologism in this passage, which initially appears to be just a geographical reference, raises it to the plane of utopian thought on which Platonov's characters seem instinctively to exist.

The more significant of Platonov's verbal effects in *The Foundation Pit*, however, tend to involve grammatically or lexically incorrect usage which turns out to sound apt because it introduces or reinforces an existential theme. One way in which this happens is through the narrative's habit of explicitly recounting events or processes that are normally taken for granted and therefore not remarked—the refusal to take existence for granted discussed earlier. "His heart was beating as usual," Platonov reports as Chiklin begins to dig in the foundation pit (Chandler/Meerson 16). Ginsburg has "his heart beat at its customary pace" (19), in keeping with the general tendency of her translation to smooth over some of Platonov's oddities; but Platonov's "Serdtse ego privychno bilos'" (*Kotlovan* 29) in fact poises ambivalently *between* these two interpretations of the adverb *privychno* (which could mean either "in its usual manner" or "as it was wont to do"). In fact what Platonov does is to use an apparent statement that Chiklin's heartbeat does not increase to make the egregiously obvious, but here highly significant, comment that existence is a task which can never be taken for granted (hence if Chiklin's heart is still beating, that is a noteworthy event). An odder effect occurs when Voshchev leaves the Trade Union committee at the beginning of the tale. Platonov remarks that he walks past the beer room on the outskirts of town and "then Voshchev found himself in space" (Chandler/Meerson 5, Ginsburg 6, "i Voshchev ochutilsia v prostranstve," *Kotlovan* 23). This is a truism, since everywhere Voshchev moves within his world is within "space"; but Platonov's unexpected conjunction of the concrete verb "found himself" (*ochutilsia*) with the abstract noun "space" makes Voshchev the immediate experiencer of a philosophical category. Something similar takes place later in the tale when a group of poor and middling peasants wanders off "and disappeared far off, in outside space" (Ginsburg 85; "and disappeared far away, in space that was strange," Chandler/Meerson 96; "i skrylis' vdaleke, v postoronnem prostranstve," *Kotlovan* 76). The relevant adjective here, *postoronnyi*, means "outside" in the sense of "extraneous" (as in the phrase, "postoronnym vkhod vospreshchen," which prohibits entry to "extraneous," i.e., unauthorized persons). To translate Platonov's phrase as "and they disappeared into unauthorized space" would capture some of the odd literalness with which they appear to depart the ideologically privileged area of the collective farm for the alien terrain surrounding it. A couple of sentences later, "from a large cloud that stopped over some far and remote fields, rain came down like a wall and wrapped the walkers in the midst of moisture" (Chandler/Meerson 96–7; "A wall of rain came down from the huge cloud which stopped over deserted distant fields and covered the vanished marchers with moisture," Ginsburg 86; "Iz bol'shogo oblaka, ostanovivshegosia nad glukhimi dal'nimi pashniami, stenoi poshel dozhd' i ukryl ushedshykh v srede vlagi," *Kotlovan* 76). The noun *sreda*, translated by Chandler and Meerson as "midst" and indirectly absorbed within Ginsburg's "covered" means "element," in the sense of the domain or substance within which something takes place (as in "prirodnaia sreda," literally "natural medium/element," which idiomatically means "environment"). What the rain cloud does, then, is literally to hide the departed peasants behind the very *element* of water (or moisture, *vlaga*).

A more frequent, and ultimately more striking, way in which Platonov's text unexpectedly foregrounds existential themes is through sentences in which incompatible grammatical or lexical elements collide—as though the speaker did not understand they came from different registers of speech. In the scene in which the Chiklin and others stand guard at the collective farm over the murdered Kozlov and Safronov, Platonov states that "current time went on quietly passing in the midnight gloom of the collective farm" (Chandler/Meerson 83; "the flowing time moved slowly in the midnight darkness of the kolkhoz," Ginsburg 76; "tekushchee vremia tikho shlo v polnochnom mrake kolkhoza," *Kotlovan* 68). The Russian phrase "tekushchee vremia" means "current time" as Chandler and Meerson have it, but in the bureaucratic sense of "the present time" (appropriate to economic plans, for instance); its literal meaning is "flowing time," which is what the latinate "current" also means. But it is an abstract flowing. To say—in the kind of semi-literate error that any schoolteacher would have corrected—that such time *was going* in the gloom of the collective farm is to reify it as a physical process and remind us of the frictive way the self experiences the world in Platonov. When Prushevsky, who views engineering as a struggle between sentient being and dead matter, stands looking across the foundation pit toward a distant industrial complex and Platonov remarks that the engineer knew that "there was nothing there except dead building material and tired unthinking people" (Chandler/Meerson 21; "there was nothing there but inanimate building materials and tired, unthinking men," Ginsburg 25; "tam net nichego, krome mertvogo stroitel'nogo materiala i ustalykh, ne-dumaiushchikh liudei," *Kotlovan* 32). The phrase "mertyi material" is literally "dead material," but it means simply "objects and tools used in production." Platonov's use of the phrase in the context of Prushevsky's thoughts about his profession, however, awakens the adjective's existential meaning and underscores the theme of being's struggle against matter and death. This is, in fact, one of Platonov's favorite puns and its repetition in the text sustains a discourse about ontological death. In one of the scenes at the collective farm Platonov tells us that "Chiklin and Voshchev left the OrgYard and went to look for dead inventory, in order to judge its fitness" (Ginsburg 87; "Chiklin and Voshchev left the Yard to go and look for the dead stock, in order to glimpse its fitness," Chandler/Meerson 98; "Chiklin i Voshchev vyshli s Orgdvora i otpravilis' iskat' mertyvi inventar', chtoby uvidet' ego godnost'," *Kotlovan* 77). The phrase's antonym appears with macabre irony as snow begins to fall on the collective farm and the peasants, "having liquidated the last of their steaming live inventory [...] began to eat meat: (Ginsburg 100; "after liquidating all their last breathing livestock, the peasants had begun to eat beef," Chandler/Meerson 113; "lividirovav ves' poslednii dyshashchii zhivoi inventar', muzhiki stali est' goviadinu," *Kotlovan* 86). "Zhivoi inventar'," which is literally, "living inventory" but idiomatically means "cattle," is, in fact, the dominant phrase in Russia's traditionally agrarian economy, and assigns "mertvyi inventar'" its contrasting meaning as equipment and tools. In Platonov's use of it, however, the unexpected conjunction of it with the adjective *dyshashchii* ("breathing") once again highlights the literal meaning of *living* and intensifies the tragic sense of what has taken place.

Most characteristic of Platonov's play on the language of Stalin's would-be utopia, however, are the instances in which he uncovers existential meanings in the phraseology of the Soviet government and its Five-Year Plan, or political meanings characteristic of Stalinism within the lexicon of everyday events.

When Voshchev delivers the sack of discarded objects he has been gathering to the activist, the latter makes a list of its contents. "Instead of people, the activist listed tokens of existence: a bast sandal of a bygone century, a tin ring from the ear of a shepherd, a homespun trouser-leg, and sundry other accoutrements of a labouring but

## Chapter Five

dispossessed body" (Chandler/Meerson 136; "Instead of people, the activist entered evidences of existence: a bast shoe from the last century, a leaden earring from a shepherd's ear, a trouserleg of homespun cloth, and a variety of other equipment of a laboring but propertyless body," Ginsburg 118; "Vmesto liudei aktivist zapisyval priznaki sushchestvovan'ia: lapot' proshedshego veka, oloviannuiu ser'gu ot pastush'ego ukha, shtaninu iz riadna i raznoe drugoe snariazhenie trudiashchegosia, no neimushchego tela," *Kotlovan* 99). The word *trudiashchiisia*, used to modify "body" at the end of Platonov's phrase normally functions as a noun meaning "laborer" or "worker" (as in, "po pros'be trudiashchikhsia," "at the workers' request," the usual rationalization given by Soviet authorities for price hikes). By coupling it with the noun *telo*, "body," however, Platonov awakens its literal meaning: together with the ideological concept of the workers to whom the objects belonged there appears the image of a *body* which *labors* but has nothing—an existential rereading of Marxist terminology which is entirely in keeping with Platonov's philosophical response to the Soviet regime.

When Chiklin strikes a peasant at the collective farm who says he continues living "without meaning to" while Kozlov and Safronov have been murdered, "the peasant staggered but was careful not to lean over too far in case Chiklin thought he had kulak inclinations himself, and so he stood even closer before him, wishing to get himself maimed more powerfully and then petition for himself, by means of suffering, the right to life of a poor peasant" (Chandler/Meerson 86; "The peasant fell, but he was afraid to move back too far, or Chiklin might think something prosperous about him, and he stood up even closer to him, hoping to get maimed still worse, and earn by his suffering the right to life as a poor man," Ginsburg 79–80; "Muzhik bylo upal, no poboialsia daleko uklonit'sia, daby Chiklin ne podumal pro nego chego-nibud' zazhitochnogo, i eshche blizhe predstal pered nim, zhelaia posil'nee izuvechit'sia, a zatem iskhodataistvovat' sebe, posredstvom muchen'ia, pravo zhizni bedniaka," *Kotlovan* 70). The scene most immediately suggests the literal meaning of the action the peasant tries to avoid, *uklonit'sia*, "to lean over"; but in the language of Stalinism and its metaphors of journey on the road to utopia this same verb means "to deviate (politically)." The act of falling when Chiklin hits him (Chandler and Meerson accurately have him stagger, not fall) would thus be a politically deviant admission of guilt as a prosperous peasant—and the world in which Platonov's characters move thus ironically becomes one in which every physical action is directly linked with a political meaning. A related, sinister example occurs early in the tale when the workers in the barracks tell Voshchev that he can stay there for the night, "Go and sleep there till morning—then they'll sort out who you are" (Chandler/Meerson 11; "Go there and sleep till morning, then we'll see about you," Ginsburg 12; "Stupai tuda i spi do utra, a utrom ty vyiasnish'sia," *Kotlovan* 27). Both Chandler/Meerson and Ginsburg in this instance go directly to the implied meaning of the phrase but omit the seemingly innocent remark beneath which it is buried: the verb *vyiasnit'sia*, especially in the reflexive form used here, more generally means something like "to clear up" (like a sky after rain). The political meaning (which in Russian would more correctly be conveyed by the transitive form of the verb: "utrom tebia vyiasniat," "in the morning they will sort you out") that the authorities are going to *clear up* the question of Voshchev's class identity, and with that his social standing, is thus overlaid ominously on what first appears to be a simple statement that in the morning things will be brighter or clearer for him.

The Russian-American scholar Olga Meerson has identified a characteristic narrative strategy in Platonov's works—a principle of his poetics—which while not exclusively involving language as such, as the above examples do, nonetheless works toward similar ends. Meerson sees Platonov's works as dominated by a device she terms "non-estrangement" (*neostranenie*). Her term consciously negates that of "estrangement" (*ostranenie*) which Russian Formalist critics in the early 1920s applied to what they saw as the defining trait of art, its ability to render strikingly new and "strange" our otherwise automatized perception of life (see for example Viktor Shklovsky's celebrated essay "Iskusstvo, kak priem" ["Art as Technique"]). What Platonov's texts do, rather, is to render ordinary and *un*noticeable

## Chapter Five

what should be outrageous, fantastic, or tragic—thus, according to Meerson, making the reader morally complicit in the acceptance of such phenomena. Often enough this involves subtle linguistic shifts of the kind discussed above. When the blacksmith-bear first appears, for example, Platonov's word-order is unexpectedly strange—or rather, *un*strange. The Russian text reads, "kuznets kachal mekhom vozdukh v gorn, a medved' bil cheloveschecki molotom..." (*Kotlovan* 89). As Meerson points out, up to this moment not a word has been said about a bear. All the text prepares us to encounter is "the most oppressed hired hand of all" (in fact the only exceptional thing about him which the narrator remarks is that he is not a member of the collective farm but a hired worker). Normal Russian word order dictates that new information—such as the fact that this hired hand is, in fact, a bear—be placed at the *end* of the phrase, i.e., one would expect the text to read "a na koval'ne bil medved'" ("while at the forge there hammered *a bear*"). The difference is close to that in English between saying "*the* bear" and "*a* bear" (Meerson 22–3). It is interesting that Chandler's and Meerson's translation faithfully follows Platonov's "non-estrangement" and says that "*the* bear was hammering humanly at a strip on incandescent iron on the anvil" (46), while Ginsburg, who in general tends to normalize, has "*a* bear was striking a red-hot iron bar across the anvil with a hammer" (105; emphasis added in both cases). What Platonov's original Russian text does is to introduce the figure of the bear *as if* it were not out of the ordinary, indeed, as if it were something already known and therefore not deserving of commentary.

In *The Foundation Pit* not only the fantastic (and ultimately perhaps satirical) elements such as the anthropomorphic bear and the self-collectivizing horses are subjected to this treatment; death itself is as well. The matter-of-fact way in which the horse being eaten alive by a dog merely "move[s] her legs a step forward, not yet forgetting to live because of the pain" (Chandler/Meerson 113, Ginsburg 100, *Kotlovan* 85) is characteristic, as are Meerson's examples of Prushevsky, who, matter-of-factly "having decided to pass away...lay down on his bed and fell asleep" (Chandler/Meerson 24,

Ginsburg 27, *Kotlovan* 34) and the deaths of Kozlov and Safronov, which are not reported by the narrator at all but only relayed in dialog by Nastya, who explains to Prushevsky why the coffin she used to sleep in is being taken away (Meerson 101, 106).

As Meerson points out, the (Russian) reader's encounter of these characteristic Platonovian passages usually involves an unsettling double-take. "If one carefully rereads Platonov's texts one often discovers a meaning which either runs counter to what one initially perceived or contradicts it altogether" (35). Reading Platonov is a matter of learning to set aside expected clichés and perceive what is truly there. "The reader automatically corrects the 'deformed' variant of these clichés which are anticipated but in fact absent from the actual text, driving off into his subconscious the literal message of the text which is written in black and white and does not appear to be hidden by anything" (36). It was for this reason that the typists who had to prepare Platonov's manuscripts for publication would request triple the normal rate of pay—not because of his handwriting, which was clear enough; but because it was impossible with his texts, as it was possible for other writers, to remember an entire phrase by looking at its first few words. Every word had to be checked painstakingly to make sure the typescript followed what Platonov had written (Taratuta 101). It is for this reason, too, that the label "anti-utopia" is problematic in the case of *The Foundation Pit*—appropriate as it ultimately may be. Everything that ought to carry shock value if this were a straightforwardly anti-utopian work, from flawed Stalinist ideology with its amoral class hatred to the half-witted agents of its imposition and its tragic effects, is buried beneath a mask of ordinariness, as though it scarcely merited narrative comment. What the text instead thrusts to the foreground is such otherwise unnoteworthy existential processes as being, the beating of the heart, and breathing. It is as though, from a referential perspective, the text were inverted.

The cumulative effect of these various verbal and narrative oddities in Platonov's text is to create an idiom in which the lexicon of ideology, of the Stalinist Five-Year Plan with all its utopian implications,

Chapter Five

appears to merge unproblematically with the language of everyday life—and in which therefore neither utopian nor tragic events any longer call particular attention to themselves. Platonov's characters and narrator alike speak as though they did not understand the difference between metaphoric and literal speech: the clichéd and sometimes lurid metaphors that abound in the language of the Party-state thus appear to refer immediately to the physical world, while everyday turns of phrase yield up chiliastic connotations. Platonov's language thus works something like a sustained pun. Puns, a type of verbal behavior known as paranomasia, sound funny to us precisely because for a moment they imply an essential relation between the word and its referent that on further (nearly instantaneous) reflection we realize to be absurd. But this response may in part be culturally determined, because in certain periods of human history and in certain cultures the semantic coincidence would have been taken seriously and would even have been viewed as theologically justified. In the New Testament, for example, there is a passage (Matthew 16:18) in which Jesus says to his disciple Peter (in the King James Version): "And I say also unto thee, That thou art Peter (*Petros*, in the koine Greek in which the text was written—T.S.), and upon this rock (*petra*) I will build my church; and the gates of hell shall not prevail against it." It is unlikely in this instance that Jesus was trying to be funny; rather, he meant to suggest an essential—rather than accidental or random—relationship between the two terms. The moment when Platonov's paronomastic turns of phrase seem strangely apt is precisely one in which the utopian motivations we sense behind this kind of speech appear justified. It is a way in which, in a sense, one—or Platonov—*wishes* one could speak about the world. The moment our sense of linguistic propriety reasserts itself, however—that subsequent instant in which we realize that you cannot really talk about the world this way—is precisely when the designs for utopia begin to unravel. It is the tension between these two impulses which defines the verbal atmosphere of Platonov's tale.

The language of *The Foundation Pit* resists convenient categorization. Because it appears to be anchored in a linguistic consciousness which is at best semi-literate, it seems to affiliate itself naturally with the *skaz* tendency in Soviet literature of the 1920s, whose hallmark was unvarnished verbal naturalism; but the sudden and dislocating semantic effects it produces seem to align it instead with the kind of self-conscious modernist experimentation with language that culminated in the "trans-sense" poetry of the Futurists. As the critic Nikolai Zamoshkin aptly put it at the February 1932 meeting organized by the All-Russian Union of Soviet Writers to discuss Platonov's situation, "all Platonov's works are infected with purely literary anachronisms which come across sounding modernist" ("'...Ia derzhalsia i rabotal'," 110). If there is a parallel to Platonov's language in Russian modernism, perhaps it is to be found not in literature but in the visual arts—in the distorted figures populating the "primitive" peasant woodcuts of Mikhail Larionov, for example; or, still closer, in the childishly crude figures in the paintings of Pavel Filonov, whose contorted expressions and postures somehow cumulatively lend the landscapes in which they are placed an air of apocalyptic sorrow.

## SELECTED ANNOTATIONS OF EVENTS AND SITUATIONS IN *THE FOUNDATION PIT*

The following comments on Platonov's text are meant to provide political and historical background that may be unfamiliar to most non-Russian readers. For fuller annotations, see *Kotlovan* (in Russian) and Chandler/Meerson.

"There was only a beer room for seasonal workers and low-paid categories" (Chandler/Meerson 1; "low-paid trades," Ginsburg 3): in 1921–22 the Fourth All-Russian Conference of Trade Unions developed a 17-tier system of pay categories, with fairly significant differences between skilled and unskilled labor. It was revised in 1927–28, but the revision was criticized by Stalin for its "levelling" tendences. A new, more hierarchical system was developed in 1931–32 (*Kotlovan* 142 n. 5).

"If you mean a plan of your private life, you could already have worked that out in the club or else in the Red Corner" (Chandler/Meerson 4; "the Red Reading Room," Ginsburg 5): "Red Corners" or "Lenin Corners" were first organized at the All-Russian Agricultural and Crafts Exhibition in 1923, and spread throughout the country following Lenin's death in 1924. They were intended to replace the "red corner" traditional in peasant huts, in which an icon was placed (*Kotlovan* 144 n. 13). "Red" in old Russian means beautiful as well as red, and may also have referred to the light of the candle kept burning in front of the icon. "Red Corners" were stocked with political reading matter.

"The state, Voshchev, has given you an extra hour for this thoughtfulness of yours" (Chandler/Meerson 5, Ginsburg 6): on the tenth anniversary of the Revolution in 1927 the Central Executive Committee of the Party issued a manifesto calling for a shift to a seven-hour working day. In October 1929 *Pravda* forecast that by 1930 a million workers would have had their workday reduced by an hour (*Kotlovan* 144 n. 15).

"Voshchev stopped beside the cripple; from the depths of the town a column of Pioneer children was advancing along the street" (Chandler/Meerson 6, Ginsburg 8): the first All-Union Convention of Pioneers was held in August 1929. Preparations for it, including military marches and "Spartakiads" (athletic competitions), were held throughout the country (*Kotlovan* 144 n. 17).

"You should reinforce yourself with physical culture" (Chandler/Meerson 27; "You ought to take up sports to strengthen yourself," Ginsburg 29): "physical culture" (*fizkul'tura* in its Soviet lexical hybrid) or sports was declared a priority of the state in a 1930 declaration of the Party's Central Executive Committee. Its purpose was to "bring the broad masses of the workers and peasants together," and it was overtly politicized. One slogan of the campaign was "Sport Without Class Content is a Dangerous Activity" (*Kotlovan* 149 n. 32).

"Pashkin's wife remembered the time Zhachev had denounced her husband in a letter to the Provincial Party Committee" (Chandler/Meerson 34; "Regional Party Committee," Ginsburg 36): in Russian, *OblKK* or "Oblastnaia kontrol'naia kommissiia." An "oblast'" was a regional geopolitical designation in the Soviet Union and now in post-Soviet Russia. The regional "control committee" was the chief party organ in a region charged with carrying out "purges" of the Party, which reached a peak in 1929 (*Kotlovan* n. 34). These are not to be confused with the far more sweeping and deadly purges carried out under Stalin in the Great Terror of 1936–8.

"But since the line is now directed toward technical specialists, please lie down across from me so that you can constantly see my face and go ahead and sleep boldly" (Chandler/Meerson 41; "But since we have a clear line concerning specialists," Ginsburg 43): the attitude toward non-Party technical specialists in the 1920s and early 1930s ranged from ambivalent to downright hostile. It intensified in particular after the 1928 trial of the supposed "Shakhtinsky wrecker organization" and relented little even when Stalin made statements affirming the Party's interest in attracting engineers and other specialists to Five-Year Plan projects (*Kotlovan* 150 n. 37).

"Should we not install a radio so we can duly listen to achievements and directives?" (Chandler/Meerson 49; Ginsburg 50): the first radio station started broadcasting in the USSR in 1922, and by 1928 there were 23 transmitters (*Kotlovan* 151 n. 41). One of Platonov's notebooks for 1929–1930 has an entry which reads, "The collective farms get by stimulating themselves with radio music; if the loudspeaker breaks, that's the end of it" (*Zapisnye knizhki* 35). The screenplay "Mashinist" is less ambiguous than *The Foundation Pit* about the coercive nature of the music coming from the radio. In it,

175

Chapter Five

the activist sets up a radio and orders the peasants to dance. When they slowly begin to do so he tells them that he will "dekulakize" them, too, if they do not pick up the tempo and orders them to wipe the tears that are streaming down their faces (238). At the end of the screenplay a procession of villagers marches, in a parody of an Orthodox religious procession bearing icons (see also "Rodina elektrichestva"), to the river's shore bearing on poles a loudspeaker, radio equipment, and a large antenna. When they turn the radio on, it plays music and the excavator blows its whistle in time with it.

"Which is better—the ice-breaker 'Krasin' or the Kremlin?" (Chandler/Meerson 60; Ginsburg 58): a ship in the Soviet arctic fleet. In 1928 it participated in the rescue of an expedition led by Umberto Nobile, an Italian arctic explorer (*Kotlovan* 151 n. 43).

"Stalin's most important of all—and then Budyonny" (Chandler/Meerson 64; "The chief one is Lenin [sic], and the one after him, Budenny," Ginsburg 62): Semyon Mikhailovich Budyonny (1883–1973) was a military commander who during the Polish campaign led the First Cavalry in which the writer Isaac Babel served as a correspondent. It was also his First Cavalry which reclaimed Voronezh, where Platonov was then working for the railroad, for the Reds in 1919. In November 1928 in *Pravda* Budyonny had also published his "Open Letter to Maxim Gorky" in which he severely criticized Babel's portrayal of his division in *Red Cavalry* (*Kotlovan* 151 n. 44).

"Prushevsky looked quietly into all of nature's misty old age and saw at its end some peaceful white buildings that gave off more light than was in the air around them" (Chandler/Meerson 67; Ginsburg 65): the buildings are clearly new structures that have gone up as part of the Five-Year Plan. As Yuri Shcheglov has pointed out, one way in which the poetics of the Soviet novel negotiated the distance between an imperfect present and the utopian future was through the manipulation of narrative focus. The "actual" plane of events, shown in effect in close-up and often situated in a relatively intimate space like a communal apartment or government office, might reveal negative phenomena; but the "ideal" plane of the historically-significant construction of socialism, typically identified with large-scale industrial projects, always stood in the wings, ready to be deployed in order to restore the proper perspective. As Shcheglov puts it, in the case of Ilya Il'f and Evgeny Petrov's 1931 satirical novel *The Little Golden Calf* (*Zolotoi telenok*), "the main form in which the ideal plane exists in the novel, influencing its scale and emotional tone, is that of a constant presence on the horizon, like some distant chain of mountain peaks" (87).

"We stacked those wooden coffins into the cave for future use— and now you're digging up the whole gully" (Chandler/Meerson 69; Ginsburg 66): in the original Russian it is clearer that the peasants have not only stacked the coffins but acquired them and then began paying for them in installments, an arrangment known in Russian as *samooblozhenie* (*Kotlovan* 152 n.48). There is an economic-ontological pun of sorts here: the root of the Russian term, *oblozhenie*, connotes "covering oneself over with something," and thus suggests burial (or in a manner characteristic of Platonov, fuses the economic and the physical meanings). A close English equivalent would be "we got those coffins on the lay-away plan." That the peasants have also been sleeping in their coffins is a macabre literalization of an idea in Fedorov's philosophy, namely, that until humanity unites in the "common task" of resurrecting its ancestors, people live a form of death-in-life, subject to the destructive laws of the natural world. This motif is developed even more extensively in Platonov's screenplay "Mashinist," where the entire village occupies itself making coffins and the activist dispatches the kulaks who are to be sent off on the raft in a coffin pulled by a horse. He and the middle-peasant (*Seredniak*) then ride in a horse-drawn coffin themselves to the Organizational Yard, where he whistles for the peasants to gather and forces them to dance to radio music. The rite of preparing one's coffin and lying in it in advance was widespread among Russia's

## Chapter Five

Old Believers (schismatics who left the Orthodox Church in the seventeenth century) between 1669 and 1702, when the end of the world was expected (*Kotlovan* 153 n. 49).

"Once the table groaned with fare/Now there's just a coffin there" (Chandler/Meerson 74; "Where formerly a laden table stood/There stands a coffin now,: Ginsburg 70): Kozlov slightly garbles two lines from a 1779 ode by Gavriila Derzhavin entitled "On the Death of Prince Meshchersky." Kozlov adds the adverb "formerly" (*Kotlovan* 154 n. 53).

"Well and good, well and splendid, but what you have here, as the saying says, is clearly a Rochdale cooperative rather than a Soviet cooperative!" (Chandler/Meerson 75; Ginsburg 71): in 1844 a workers' cooperative was organized in the Engish town of that name (*Kotlovan* 154 n. 54). Its organizers were disciples of Robert Owen, the "father of English socialism" (Chandler/Meerson 169 n. 37).

"The womb matrix for the house of future life was already complete" (Chandler/Meerson 78; "The site for the building that would house future life was ready," Ginsburg 72): Ginsburg's version conveys the proper technical meaning of the term "matochnoe mesto" while Chandler's and Meerson's more literal rendition captures its maternal connotations. On the uterine associations of utopia in Platonov, see Naiman, "Andrei Platonov and the Inadmissibility of Desire" 321.

"The notice states that this was Socialized Property No. 7 of the General Line Collective Farm" (Chandler/Meerson 80; Ginsburg 75): "General Line" may simply refer to a phrase which was often used in the 1920s and 1930s to denote the current policy of the Communist Party; but one of Platonov's Russian commentators, Natalia Kornienko, suggests that it also alludes to a more specific event in Soviet cultural life of 1929—the release of Sergei Eisenstein's film "The Old and the New," work on which had been reported in the press since 1926 using the title "The General Line." Kornienko also suggests that the sudden, unmotivated shifts between scenes in *The Foundation Pit* may be intended as a literary approximation of Eisenstein's technique of montage ("Mashinist" 230; also *Kotlovan* 156 n. 63).

"Out in the fresh air again, Chiklin and Voshchev met the activist— he was on his way to the reading hut on matters concerning the cultural revolution" (Chandler/Meerson 101; Ginsburg 90): a 1929 resolution of the Communist Party's Central Committee had proposed the creation of "councils of reading huts" in which courses would be offered by cultural workers from various organizations (*Kotlovan* 157 n. 68).

"The women and girls diligently bent closer towards the floor and began insistently writing letters, using the scratchy plaster" (Chandler/Meerson 102; Ginsburg 90): in 1929 the Communist Party's Central Committee passed a resolution "On the Liquidation of Illiteracy" and in 1930 made elementary education mandatory for all Soviet citizens. The link between teaching literacy and political education was an intentional part of these policies (*Kotlovan* 157 n. 69).

"Around the church grew the old forgotten grass of oblivion and there were no paths or other signs of human passing—people had evidently not been praying in the church for a long time" (Chandler/Meerson 103; Ginsburg 92): the closure of churches was a cardinal event of Stalin's "Year of Great Change." From November 1929 to April 1930 there was a nationwide antireligious campaign during which churches and monasteries were closed, bells were removed from church belfries (Metropolitan Sergii, head of the Orthodox Church, announced in *Pravda* on 19 February 1930 that the bells were being removed "at the request of the workers"), priests and believers were put on trial, and antireligious departments were opened in Soviet universities (Kornienko introduction to *Zapisnye knizhki*, 13; also 322, n. 19 and 333 n. 93) The women writing in chalk on "boards" under the activist's instruction in the anti-illiteracy scene are probably writing on the backs of icons (*Zapisnye knizhki* 328 n. 56);

Chapter Five ─────────────────────────────────────────

one of Platonov's notebooks for 1929–30 has an entry which reads, "From the icons of the saints (s likov sviatykh) the peasants write on the floor with chalk" (*Zapisnye knizhki* 34). Another entry contains an outline for a dialog: "'Where are your bells?' the Jewish worker asks the Russian worker. 'They took them down, the parasites.' 'Well then, come over to my place, I'll give you communion.' 'Ekh, I'll kill you, you parasite!' 'I know how to do it. I'll place it in your mouth with a little spoon'" (*Zapisnye knizhki* 27). The "circle of atheism" (Chandler/Meerson 104; "Godless circle," Ginsburg 93) refers to the Union of Militant Atheists which existed in the Soviet Union from 1925–1947. By 1930 it had some two million members (*Kotlovan* 158 n. 73).

"A raft's being organized for tomorrow, so that the kulak sector can travel down river and into the sea, and so further and so on" (Chandler/Meerson 109; Ginsburg 96): expulsions downriver of peasants accused of being kulaks actually took place in Russia during the collectivization campaign (*Kotlovan* 159 n. 77). In the screenplay "Mashinist" the kulaks are similarly placed on a raft and pushed down river—by the excavator that has cleared the river of silt, no less. Chapter Eleven of Gladkov's *Cement* portrays a similar expulsion by river of former members of the bourgeoisie, in the era of NEP rather than the Five-Year Plan.

"After liquidating all their last breathing livestock, the peasants had begun to eat beef and had instructed all the members of their households to do the same" (Chandler/Meerson 113; Ginsburg 100): the campaign to collectivize Soviet agriculture led to widespread slaughter of livestock to prevent it being taken over as collective property. As a result there was a brief glut of meat on the market—followed by famine in 1931–32. In 1930 severe fines were imposed for such slaughter (*Kotlovan* 159–60 n. 82).

"'Why are there flies when it's winter,' asked Nastya" (Chandler/Meerson 122; Ginsburg 107): the flies have bred in the rotting carcasses of the livestock slaughtered by the peasants. One of Platonov's notebooks for 1930 contains an entry which reads, "Flies in a blizzard." (*Zapisnye knizhki* 43). There may be a remote literary reminiscence in this image of a passage which occurs in the fourth book of Virgil's *Georgics*, which is entirely dedicated to bees and their cultivation. Virgil proposes the ancient (and entirely fanciful) remedy of *bugonia* ("generated by an ox or bull") as a means to replace a lost swarm: "it's high time to tell of the Arcadian master's memorable/discovery and the way in which, often in those days,/the rotting blood of a slaughtered ox has brought forth bees" (Virgil 69, 102). The positive tenor of Virgil's reference, together with his use of bees to symbolize ideal communal existence ("They alone hold their offspring in common, share the houses/of their city, and live out their lives under grand laws," 65), suggest that Platonov's portrayal of collectivization negates the whole of this idyllic conceit.

"no matter what, he would remain aware of the vanity of friendship founded on dominance rather than on carnal love—and of the boredom of the most distant stars, in whose depths lay the same copper ores and which would need the same Supreme National Economic Soviet" (Chandler/Meerson 145; Ginsburg 126): in Russian, *Vysshii sovet narodnogo khoziastva* (known by its initials as VSNKh) was the administrative agency given responsibility in a 5 December 1929 resolution by the Communist Party's Central Committee for drawing up economic, financial, and technical plans for the industrialization campaign (*Kotlovan* 161 n. 88).

## REFERENCES

Averbakh, L. "O tselostnykh masshtabakh i chastnykh Makarakh." *Na literaturnom postu* Nos. 21–22 (1929): 10–17. Reprint: N.V. Kornienko and E.D. Shubina, eds. *Andrei Platonov. Vospominaniia sovremennikov. Materialy k biografii*. Moscow: Sovremennyi pisatel', 1994. 256–67.

Bakhtin, M.M. *Problemy poetiki Dostoevskogo*. Moscow: Sovetskaia Rossiia, 1979. Translated by Caryl Emerson under the title *Problems of Dostoevsky's Poetics*. Theory and History of Literature, Volume 8. Minneapolis: University of Minnesota Press, 1984

Borenstein, Eliot. *Men Without Women. Masculinity and Revolution in Russian Fiction, 1917–1929*. Durham, NC: Duke University Press, 2000.

Brodsky, Joseph. "Catastrophes in the Air." In his *Less Than One. Selected Essays*. New York: Farrar Straus Giroux, 1986. 268–303.

Bullock, Philip. *The Feminine in the Prose of Andrey Platonov*. London: Legenda, 2005.

Chaadayev, Peter Yakovlevich. *Philosophical Letters and Apology of a Madman*. Translated and introduction by Mary-Barbara Zeldin. Knoxville: University of Tennessee Press, 1969.

Chudakova, M.O. *Poetika Mikhaila Zoshchenko*. Moscow: Nauka, 1979.

Clark, Katerina. *The Soviet Novel. History as Ritual*. Chicago: University of Chicago Press, 1981.

Dhooge, Ben. *Tvorcheskoe preobrazovanie iazyka i avtorskaia kontseptualizatsiia mira u A. P. Platonova. Opyt lingvopoeticheskogo issledovaniia iazyka romanov* Chevengur *i* Schastlivaia Moskva *i povesti* Kotlovan. Diss. Universiteit Gent 2007.

Dostoevsky, Feodor. *Crime and Punishment*. Ed. George Gibian. Norton Critical Edition. 3rd edition. New York: W.W. Norton & Co., 1989.

Eikhenbaum, Boris. "Kak sdelana 'Shinel'" Gogolia." In his *O proze. O poezii. Sbornik statei*. Leningrad: Khudozhestvennaia literatura, 1986. 45–63.

Fitzpatrick, Sheila. *Everyday Stalinism: Ordinary Life in Extraordinary Times. Soviet Russia in the 1930s*. Oxford: Oxford University Press, 1999.

Gastev, A. *Poeziia rabochego udara*. Moscow: Khudozhestvennaia literatura, 1971.

Gorham, Michael S. *Speaking in Soviet Tongues. Language Culture and the Politics of Voice in Revolutionary Russia*. Dekalb, IL: Northern Illinois University Press, 2003.

Günther, Hans [Kh. Giunter]. "Kotlovan i vavilonskaia bashnia." In N.V. Kornienko, ed., *'Strana filosofov' Andreia Platonova: Problemy tvorchestva*. Vypusk 2. Moscow: Nasledie, 1995. 145-51.

Gurvich, A. "Andrei Platonov." *Krasnaia nov'*, no. 10 (1937). Reprint: N.V. Kornienko and E.D. Shubina, eds. *Andrei Platonov. Vospominaniia sovremennikov. Materialy k biografii*. Moscow: Sovremennyi pisatel', 1994. 358-413.

Kharitonov, A. "Sistema imen personazhei v poetike povesti 'Kotlovan'." In Kornienko, N.V., ed. *"Strana filosofov" Andreia Platonova: problemy tvorchestva*. Vypusk 2. Moscow: Nasledia, 1995. 152-72.

Khlebnikov, Velemir. *Ladomir*. Moscow: Sovremennik, 1985.

Kornienko, N.V. *Istoriia teksta i biografiia A. P. Platonova (1926-1946). Zdes' i teper'*, no. 1 (1993).

Langerak, Thomas. "Kommentarii k sborniku A.P. Platonova 'Epifanskie shliuzy'." In *Dutch Contributions to the Tenth International Congress of Slavists. Sofia, September 14-22, 1988. Literature*. Ed. André van Holk. Amsterdam: Rodopi, 1988. 139-68.

Malygina, N.M. *Khudozhestvennyi mir Andreia Platonova*. Moscow: Moskovskii pedagogicheskii universitet, 1995.

Meerson, Ol'ga. *"Svobodnaia veshch'". Poetika neostranenia u Andreia Platonova*. Berkeley, CA: Berkeley Slavic Specialties, 1997.

Morson, Gary Saul. *The Boundaires of Genre. Dostoevsky's Diary of a Writer and the Traditions of Literary Utopia*. Austin, TX: University of Texas Press, 1981.

Naiman, Eric. "Andrei Platonov and the Inadmissibility of Desire." *Russian Literature* XXIII (1988). 319-66.

_____. "V zhopu prorubit' okno: Seksual'naia patalogiia kak ideologicheskii kalambur u Andreia Platonova." *Novoe literaturnoe obozrenie* 4, no. 32 (1998): 60-76.

Naiman, Eric and Anne Nesbet. "Mise en Abîme: Platonov, Zolia i Poetika Truda." *Revue des Études slaves* 4, LXIV (1992): 619-33.

Olesha, Iurii. *Zavist'*. Moscow-Leningrad: Zemlia i fabrika, 1927. Ardis reprint 1977.

Paperny, Vladimir. *Architecture in the Age of Stalin: Culture Two*. Cambridge: Cambridge University Press, 2002.

Platonov, Andrei. "Fabrika literatury." *Oktiabr'*, no. 10 (1991): 195-202.

———. *Kotlovan. Tekst. Materialy tvorcheskoi istorii.* Introduction by V.Iu. Viugin. Commentary by V.Iu. Viugin, T.M. Vakhitova, and V.A. Prokof'ev. St. Petersburg: Nauka, 2000.

———. "Mashinist. Libretto." Commentary and notes by N.V. Kornienko. In N.V. Kornienko and E.D. Shubina, *Andrei Platnov. Vospominaniia sovremennikov. Materialy k biografii*. Moscow: Sovremennyi pisatel', 1994. 229-43.

———. *Sochineniia*. Vol. 1, 1918-1927. Book One, *Rasskazy, Stikhotvorenia*. Ed. N.V. Kornienko. Moscow: IMLI RAN, 2004.

———. *Sochineniia*. Vol. 1, 1918-1927. Book Two, *Stat'i*. Ed. N.V. Kornienko. Moscow: IMLI RAN, 2004.

———. "Usomnivshiisia Makar." In his *Gosudarstvennyi zhitel'*. Moscow: Sovetskii pisatel', 1988. 93-107.

———. *Zapisnye knizhki. Materialy k biografii*. Moscow: IMLI RAN, 2006.

Platonova, M. "...Zhivia glavnoi zhiz'niu (A. Platonov v pis'makh k zhene, dokumentakh i ocherkah)." *Volga*, no. 9 (1975): 160-78.

Prokopovich, Feofan. "Slovo na pogrebenie Petra Velikogo." In V.A. Zapadov, ed. *Russkaia literatura XVIII veka, 1700-1775*. Moscow: Prosveshchenie, 1979. 53-5.

Selishchev, A.M. *Iazyk revoliutsionnoi epokhi*. Moscow: Rabotnik prosveshcheniia, 1928. Reprint: Leipzig: Zentralantiquariat der Deutschen Demokratischen Republik, 1974.

Semenova, Svetlana. *Nikolai Fedorov. Tvorchestvo zhizni*. Moscow: Sovetskii pisatel', 1990.

Shcheglov, Iu.K. "Tri fragmenta poetiki Il'fa i Petrova." In A.K. Zholkovskii and Iu. K. Shcheglov, *Mir avtora i struktura teksta. Stat'i o russkoi literature*. Tenafly, NJ: Ermitazh, 1986.

Shklovskii, Viktor [Victor Shklovsky]. "Iskusstvo, kak priem." In his *O teorii prozy*. Moscow: Federatsiia, 1929. 7-23. Reprint: Ann Arbor, MI: Ardis, n.d. Translated by Lee T. Lemon and Marion J. Reis under the title "Art as Technique." In *Russian Formalist Criticism. Four Essays*. Lincoln, Nebraska: University of Nebraska Press, 1965. 3-24.

Solzhenitsyn, Alexander. *One Day in the Life of Ivan Denisovich*. Trans. Max Hayward and Ronald Hingley. New York: Bantam Books, 1981.

Stalin, J.V. *Works*. Vol. 12. Moscow: Foreign Languages Publishing House, 1955.

Taratuta, E. "Povyshennoe soderzhanie sovesti." In N.V. Kornienko and E.D. Shubina, eds. *Andrei Platonov. Vospominaniia sovremennikov. Materialy k biografii*. Moscow: Sovremennyi pisatel', 1994. 100-4.

Tolstaia, Elena. "O sviazi nizshikh urovnei teksta s vysshimi." In her *Mir-poslekontsa. Raboty o russkoi literature XX veka*. Moscow: Rossiiskii gosudarstvennyi gumanitarnyi universitet, 2002. 227–71.

*Tvorchestvo Andreia Platonova. Issledovaniia i materialy. Bibliografiia.* St. Petersburg: Nauka, 1995.

Tsvetkov, A.P. *Iazyk A.P. Platonova*. Diss. Univ. of Michigan 1983.

Tynianov, Iu.N. "Podporuchik Kizhe." In *Sovetskii rasskaz 20-kh godov*. Ed. E.B. Skorospelova. Moscow: Izdatel'stvo Moskovskogo universiteta, 1990. 329–50.

Vakhitova, T.M. and G.V. Filippova. "K tvorcheskoi istorii povesti Andreia Platonova *Kotlovan* (Fragmenty chernovogo avtografa)." In *Tvorchestvo Andreia Platonova. Issledovaniia i materialy. Bibliografiia.* St. Petersburg: Nauka, 1995. 91–111.

Vakhitova, T.M. "Oborotnaia storona *Koltovana*. Ocherk Andreia Platonova 'V poiskakh budushchego (puteshestvie na Kamenskuiu pischebumazhnuiu fabriku)'." In *Tvorchestvo Andreia Platonova. Issledovaniia i materialy. Bibliografiia.* St. Petersburg: Nauka, 1995. 112–27.

Virgil. *Virgil's Georgics*. Trans. Janet Lembke. New Haven: Yale University Press, 2005.

Zabolotskii, N.A. *Stikhotvoreniia i poemy*. Moscow-Leningrad: Sovetskii pisatel', 1965.

Zholkovsky, Alexander. *Text Counter Text. Rereadings in Russian Literary History*. Stanford: Stanford University Press, 1994.

Zoshchenko, Mikhail. "O sebe, o kritikakh i o svoei rabote." In B.V. Kazanskii and Iu. N. Tynianov, eds. *Mikhail Zoshchenko: Stat'i i materialy* Leningrad: Academia, 1928. 7–11.

Zolotonosov, Mikhail. "'Lozhnoe solntse'. ('Chevengur' i 'Kotlovan' v kontekste sovetskoi kul'tury 1920-kh godov)." In N.V. Kornienko and E.D. Shubina, eds. *Andrei Platonov. Mir tvorchestva*. Moscow: Sovremennyi pisatel', 1994. 246–83.

# INDEX

## A
Akhmatova, Anna 65
Alexander III, Tsar 92
All-Russian Congress of Proletarian Writers 71
All-Russian Union of Soviet Writers 24, 76, 110–1, 158, 173
All-Union Congress of Proletarian Writers 74
Al'tman, Natan 67
anarchism 62, 69
Arvatov, Boris 11, 42, 45
Aseev, Nikolai 66
Augustus (Emperor of Rome) 99, 152
avant-garde 42, 67, 157
Avenarius, Richard 38–9
Averbakh, Leopold 23, 25, 72, 74, 141, 144–5

## B
Babel', Isaac 65, 158, 176
Bakhmetev, Mikhail 143
Bakhtin, Mikhail 157

Belomorkanal (see White Sea Canal)
Bely, Andrei 55
Berdiaev, Nikolai 37
Bessal'ko, Pavel 70
Bethea, David 37n
Bezymensky, Alexander 72
biblical allusions 120
Blackburn, Simon 39
Blok, Alexander 62, 64, 65
Bogdanov, Alexander 38–9, 40–2, 44, 47, 51, 52, 69–70, 122, 126, 129
Borenstein, Eliot 118
Briusov, Valery 7
Brodsky, Joseph 162
Brown, Edward J., Jr. 66, 70, 73, 74, 77
Budyonny, Semyon 65, 176
*bugonia* 181
Bukharin, Nikolai 86, 87, 93
Bulgakov, Mikhail 62, 72, 75, 131, 136, 156
Bullock, Philip 118
Bunin, Ivan 62

References to names and topics addressed throughout the text (e.g., *The Foundation Pit*, names of translators, etc.); or to topics obviously addressed in sections of this *Companion* (e.g., Platonov's biography); or to topics of so general a nature as to reveal little of anything specific about Platonov, his writing, or his context (e.g., socialism, communism) are omitted.

## C

Cathedral of Christ the Savior 148–9
Catherine the Great 54, 153
Chaadaev, Peter 153
Chaianov, A.V. 55
Chekhov, Anton 10
Chernyshevsky, Nikolai 49, 145
Chistov, K.V. 54–5
Chizhevsky, Alexander 56
Chudakova, M.O. 158
Chuzhak, Nikolai 11, 42, 43, 54, 68
civil war 6, 62, 83, 105, 116, 155
Clark, Katerina 73, 107, 108
Clausewitz, Carl von 89n
Cohen, Stephen 87
collectivization 90–100, 111, 112, 131, 133, 140, 161
Congress of Soviet Writers 100, 106
Conquest, Robert 91, 93, 94–5
Constructivism 42, 71, 147
Cosmism 70, 71
Cubism 67

## D

Dal', Vladimir 153, 157
Derzhavin, Gavriila 178
Dickens, Charles 135
Dhooge, Ben 163n
Dneprostroi 87
Dobrenko, Evgeny 45, 73
Dostoevsky, Fedor 22, 47, 49, 134–5, 138, 139, 145, 153, 161
dystopia 61, 66, 76

## E

Eikhenbaum, Boris 157
Eisenstein, Sergei 68, 99, 151, 178–9
electrification 86, 90
empiriocriticism 38
empiriomonism 38
Engels, Friedrich 21, 38, 83, 84
Enlightenment 99–100
Erenburg, Il'ya 75
Esenin, Sergei 65

## F

factography 46
Fadeev, Alexander 23, 24, 55–6, 78, 134
Fedin, Konstantin 66
Fedorov, Nikolai 5, 37, 47–53, 117, 118, 122, 123, 124, 126, 129, 135, 144, 145, 150, 177
fellow travellers 21, 23, 63, 65, 72, 73, 75
Field, Daniel 91
Filonov, Pavel 173
Fitzpatrick, Sheila 70, 71, 72, 89, 154
Five-Year Plan 21, 22, 23, 42, 76, 77, 84–100, 105, 111, 122, 125, 127–8, 129, 130, 134, 136, 151, 161, 167, 171, 175, 180
Ford, Henry 44
Formalism 157
Fourier, Charles 48, 145
Frank, Sergei 37
Furmanov, Dmitri 64
Futurism 42, 62, 66, 67, 68, 69, 71, 173

## G

Garros, Véronique 3
Gasparov, Boris 64
Gastev, Alexei 8, 44, 45, 145–7
Genghis Khan 98
Gerasimov, Mikhail 8, 70

Gladkov, Fedor 64, 77, 84, 106, 107–9, 110, 120, 134, 136, 153, 180
Glavlit 63
Gogol, Nikolai 16, 17, 24, 136, 157, 161
Gorham, Michael 155–6, 159
Gorky, Maxim 7, 16, 19, 22, 25, 39, 43–4, 45, 47, 62, 69, 74, 78, 106, 107, 176
Great Terror of 1936–8 175
Grois, Boris 67
Gumilev, Nikolai 63
Günther, Hans 145–7
Gurdjieff, G.I. 56
Gurvich, A. 114

*H*

Harris, Joel Chandler 157
Hellbeck, Jochen 3, 88, 98
Hellie, Richard 91
Herzen, Alexander 92

*I*

Il'f, Ilya 177
Industrial Party (*Prompartiia*) 90
industrialization 53, 77, 81–90, 91, 93, 105, 112, 181
Inozemtseva, E. 5, 6, 7, 10, 15
Ivan the Terrible, Tsar 98, 99, 151
Ivanov, Vsevolod 66, 106

*J*

Jasny, Naum 88

*K*

Kalinin, M.I. 47
Kamenev, Lev 86
Kamensky, Vasily 66
Karazin, N.V. 56

Kataev, Valentin 77, 78, 85, 86, 89, 109–10
Kaverin, Veniamin 66
Kharitonov, A. 132, 133, 135, 136, 137, 139, 141–2
Kharms, Daniil 68
Khlebnikov, Velemir 67, 68, 125
Khodasevich, Vladislav 62
Khrushchev, Nikita 96
Kirillov, Vladimir 8, 70
Klimentov, Platon Firsovich 4–5
Klimentov, Semen Platonovich 131
Kliuev, Nikolai 65
Kol'tsov, Alexei 7
Kornienko, N.V. 10, 12n, 14, 15, 18, 22n, 23, 25, 45, 46, 56, 75, 97, 107, 124n, 140, 151, 178, 179
Kotkin, Stephen 85n, 88, 89n, 99
Kriuchenykh, Alexei 66, 67
Kuznetskstroi 87

*L*

land reclamation 3, 10, 11, 13, 14, 15, 16, 23, 36, 42, 44, 97, 138, 149
Langerak, Thomas 4, 11, 12, 14, 15, 16, 18, 19, 21, 22, 44, 46, 544, 72, 74, 90, 151, 158
Larionov, Mikhail 66, 173
*LEF* 11, 42, 43, 44, 46, 47, 49, 54, 67, 68, 69
left-wing art 42, 44, 45
Lenin, Vladimir 12, 21, 22, 38, 39, 41, 62–3, 70, 83, 86, 87, 123, 136, 138, 144, 148
Leninism 55, 83, 94, 96, 122, 155
Leonov, Leonid 75
Leskov, Nikolai 157
Liashko, Nikolai 8

# Index

Libedinsky, Yuri 72
Litvin-Molotov, G.Z. 9, 19
Lotman, Ju.M. 152n
Lunacharsky, Anatoly 69, 72, 74, 147
Luzhkov, Yuri 149
Lysenko, Trofim 89

## M
McClelland, James C. 38
Mach, Ernst 38–9
Magnitogorsk 11, 85, 87, 109, 110
Maizel', M. 8
Malevich, Konstantin 66
Malygina, N.M. 2, 8, 47, 50, 56, 68, 74n, 131, 132, 138, 139, 140, 142, 149
Mandelstam, Osip 65, 75
MAPP (Moscow Association of Proletarian Writers) 72
Marx, Karl 10, 38, 39, 49, 83, 84
Marxism 23, 38, 39, 40, 45, 55, 62, 69, 70, 73, 83, 84–5, 90, 94, 94n, 97, 100, 110, 122, 129, 155, 168
Masing-Delic, Irene 47, 48, 53, 55, 145
materialism 39, 42, 45, 70, 122, 128–9
Mayakovsky, Vladimir 38, 47, 62, 66, 67, 78, 136
Meerson, Olga 169–71
Meyerhold, Vsevolod 68
Mindlin, Emil' 87
modernism 66, 68
Morson, Gary Saul 110

## N
Nabokov, Vladimir 10, 62, 64, 148
Naiman, Eric 114n, 119, 122, 131, 134, 150n, 178

Nekrasov, Nikolai 7
NEP (New Economic Policy) 83, 87, 91, 180
Nesbet, Anne 114n, 122, 131, 134
Nicholas II, Tsar 92
Nietzsche, Friedrich 13, 36, 89, 138, 142, 163–4
NKVD (Cheka, OGPU, GPU) 3, 5, 83–4, 90, 93

## O
*Oberiu* 68
Old Belief (*staroverie*), Old Believers 108, 153, 177–8
Olesha, Yuri 84, 117–8

## P
Palace of Soviets 148
Paperny, Vladimir 148
parody 46, 110–2, 122, 129, 176
Party, Communist, of the Soviet Union 15, 18, 20, 21, 38, 45, 55, 62, 63, 68, 72, 73, 74, 76, 77, 83, 84, 86, 87, 91, 94, 95, 96, 97, 106, 108, 112, 116, 125, 129, 130, 131, 134, 136, 137, 155, 156, 159, 160, 162, 172, 174, 175, 179, 181
Pasternak, Leonid 47
Pasternak, Boris 47, 65, 66, 78
Pereval ("The Pass") 73, 74, 75, 76
*perestroika* 28
Perkhin, V.V. 25
Peter the Great 17, 21, 22, 78, 85, 92, 98–9, 146, 147, 150, 151, 152, 153
Petrov, Evgeny 177
Pil'niak, Boris 20, 21, 24, 55, 56, 64, 69, 75, 133, 151, 156, 158
Plato 5

Platonov, Alexei 73
Platonov, Andrei Platonovich
journalism—
- "Fabrika literatury" ("The Factory of Literature") 45, 159
- "K nachinaiushchim proletarskim poetam i pisateliam" ("To Beginning Proletarian Poets and Writers") 40, 142
- "O kul'ture zapriazhennogo sveta i poznannogo elektrichestva" ("On the Culture of Harnessed Light and Comprehended Electricity") 41, 118
- "Proletarskaia poeziia" ("Proletarian Poetry") 40, 71, 116, 126–7
- "Protiv khalturnykh sudei" ("Against Crass Judges") 21
- *Razmyshleniia chitatelia* (*A Reader's Reflections*) 27
- "Revoliutsiia 'dukha'" ("The Revolution of 'Spirit'") 41, 45, 129, 143
- "Simfoniia soznaniia" ("A Symphony of Consciousness") 37
- "U nachala tsarstva soznaniia" ("At the Founding of the Kingdom of Consciousness") 41, 118
- "Tvorcheskaia gazeta" ("The Creative Newspaper") 40–1
- "Velikaia glukhaia" ("The Great Deaf One") 75

plays—
- *14 krasnykh izbushek* (*14 Little Red Huts*) 25
- *Dirizhabl'* (*The Dirigible*) 25
- *Duraki na periferii* (*Fools on the Periphery*) 40
- *Sharmanka* (*The Barrel Organ*) 25
- *Vysokoe napriazhenie* (*High Tension*) 25

poetry—
- *Golubaia glubina. Kniga stikhov* (*The Blue Depths. A Book of Verse*) 5, 7, 8, 9, 13, 35, 54, 61, 123

prose—
- "Antiseksus" ("Antisexus") 158
- *Bashkirskie narodnye skazki* (*Bashkir Folktales*) 27
- "Bessmertie" ("Immortality") 26
- "Buchilo" ("The Sink Hole") 149, 158
- "Che-Che-O" 20
- *Chevengur* 18, 19, 20, 26, 37n, 51, 52–3, 54, 55, 64, 114, 118, 119, 129, 135, 138, 140
- "Chul'dik i Epishka" ("Chul'dik and Epishka") 158
- "Dzhan" ("Soul") 26, 28, 51, 53
- "Efirnyi trakt" ("The Ethereal Path") 14, 42, 56, 138
- "Epifanskie shliuzy" ("The Locks of Epiphany") 16, 17–21, 99, 100, 118, 138, 150, 151, 158
- *Epifanskie shliuzy* (*The Locks of Epiphany*) 16, 74, 158
- "Fro" 26, 28
- "Gorod Gradov" ("The City of Gradov") 17, 18, 21, 136
- "Gosudarstvennyi zhitel'" ("A Resident of the State") 23
- "Iamskaia sloboda" ("Coachman's Settlement") 118
- "Iuvenil'noe more" ("The Juvenile Sea") 25

# Index

"Ivan Zhokh" 54
"Kak zazhglas' lampa Il'icha" ("How Il'ich's Lamp Was Lit") 12, 45
"Liubov' k dal'nemu" ("The Love of the Distant") 164
"Lugovye mastera" ("Masters of the Meadows") 13, 150
*Lugovye mastera. Rasskaz* (*Masters of the Meadows. A Story*) 19
"Lunnaia bomba" ("The Lunar Bomb") 13, 42
"Maloletnii" ("The Young One") 140
"Markun" 71, 142
"O potukhshei lampe Il'icha" ("Il'ich's Extinguished Lamp") 12
"Potomki solntsa" ("Descendants of the Sun") 143
"Potomok rybaka" ("The Fisherman's Descendant") 19
"Prikluchenie" ("An Adventure") 19
"Proiskhozhdenie mastera" ("The Origins of a Master") 19
*Proiskhozhdenie mastera. Povest'* (*The Origins of a Master. A Tale*) 8, 20
*Puteshestvie iz Leningrada v Moskvu* (*A Journey from Leningrad to Moscow*) 18
"Rasskaz o mnogikh interesnykh veshchakh" ("A Tale About Many Interesting Things") 51, 56, 143, 149
"Reka Potudan'" ("The River Potudan'") 119
"Rodina elektrichestva" ("Electricity's Native Land") 12, 18, 54, 114, 117, 138, 176
"Satana mysli" ("A Satan of Thought") 13, 42, 51, 138, 143, 149
*Schastlivaia Moskva* (*Happy Moscow*) 18, 26, 77
"Sokrovennyi chelovek" ("The Innermost Man") 18, 22, 52, 128, 140
*Sokrovennyi chelovek. Povesti* (*The Innermost Man. Tales*) 19–20
"Stroiteli strany" ("Builders of the Country") 19
*Tekhnicheskii roman* (*A Technical Novel*) 18
"Tretii syn" ("The Third Son") 51
"Usomnivshiisia Makar" ("Doubting Makar") 22, 23, 106, 141
"V prekrasnom i iarostnom mire" ("In the Fierce and Beautiful World") 5
"V zvezdnoi pustyne" ("In the Starry Wasteland") 142
*Volshebnoe kol'tso* (*The Magic Ring*) 27
"Vprok. Bedniatskaia khronika" ("For Future Use. A Poor-peasant Chronicle") 23, 24, 25, 26, 54, 55, 161
screenplay—
  "Mashinist" ("The Mashinist") 124, 130, 132–3, 138, 142, 150, 175–6, 177, 179, 180
Platonov, Platon Andreevich 14, 15, 27

Platonova, Mariia Aleksandrovna (née Kashintseva) 4, 10, 11, 14, 15, 74n, 90, 118
Platonova, Mariia Andreevna 15
Plekhanov, Georgy 70
Poincaré, Raymond 90
Popkin, Cathy 112
production novel 105–12, 122, 130, 138
production sketches 106
productionism 43, 44, 46, 49
Prokopovich, Feofan 99, 152
Proletkul't (Proletarian culture movement) 8, 16, 53, 69, 70, 71, 72, 122
Pugachev, Emelian 54, 85
puns 167, 172, 177
Pushkin, Alexander 22, 138, 152, 153

R
Radishchev, Alexander 19
railroad 4, 6, 7, 26, 71, 84, 92, 142, 176
RAPP (Russian Association of Proletarian Writers) 20, 21, 22, 23, 24, 45, 74, 75, 76, 77, 133, 144
Revolution of February 1917 69
Revolution of October 1917 (Bolshevik) 4, 6, 8, 9, 10, 12, 40, 61n, 62, 63, 64, 65, 67, 69, 71, 73, 77, 83, 85, 88, 89, 98, 114, 116, 118, 142, 147, 149, 155, 156, 174
Riasanovsky, Nicholas 87, 88, 89, 91, 94, 97
Rimsky-Korsakov, Nikolai 54
Rodchenko, Alexander 68

Rosenthal, Bernice 36
Rozanov, Vasilii 12, 36, 37
Ruder, Cynthia 87
Russian Orthodoxy 8, 49, 149, 179
Rykov, Alexei 86, 93

S
Saltykov-Shchedrin, Mikhail 17, 136
Sartre, Jean Paul 139
secret police (see NKVD)
Seifrid, Thomas 39, 48, 49, 152n, 163n
Selishchev, A.M. 155
Semonova, S.G. 47, 49, 50, 51, 53, 162
Serafimovich, Alexander 157–8
Serapion Brothers 65, 68, 69
sexuality 36, 41, 48, 49, 118–9
Shakhtinsky wrecker organization 175
Shcheglov, Yuri 176–7
Shearer, David 87, 88, 93, 96, 97, 98
Shentalinskii, V. 5, 24
Shklovsky, Viktor 11–2, 36, 66, 169
Sholokhov, Mikhail 27, 78
show trials 90, 175
Shubina, E. 7
*skaz* 66, 157–8, 173
Slonimsky, Mikhail 66
Smithy, The (Kuznitsa) 16, 71, 22
socialist realism 18, 26, 43, 61, 62, 63, 77, 100, 106, 107, 108, 109, 112
Solov'ev, Vladimir 37, 47
Solzhenitsyn, Alexander 18, 128
Spengler, Oswald 37

Stakhanovism 88–9
Stalin, Iosif (Joseph) 3, 19, 21, 22, 24, 26, 28, 54, 75, 83–91, 93, 95–100, 110, 111, 131, 136, 151, 154, 161, 163, 167, 173, 175, 176, 179
Stalinism 20, 27, 35, 36, 45, 61, 63, 67, 72, 77, 83, 88, 89, 92, 98, 99, 100, 110, 111, 123, 127, 147, 148, 152, 159, 163, 167, 169, 171
Stepun, Fedor 37
Strel'nikova, V. 21, 151
Struve, Gleb 72
Suprematism 66
*Svinarka i pastukh* 89
Symbolism 7, 65, 71

## T

Taratuta, E. 171
Tatlin, Vladimir 147–8
Taylor, Fredrick 44
Terras, Victor 68, 76
Teskey, Ayleen 47
Timiriazev, Kliment 56
Timurlane 98
Tolstaia, Elena 36, 55, 56, 139, 163n
Tolstoy, Alexei 75, 78, 151
Tolstoy, Leo 24, 47, 65, 75, 78, 92, 153
Tomsky, Mikhail 86, 93
Tret'iakov, Sergei 42, 66
Trotsky, Lev (Leon) 63, 75, 86, 87, 136
Tsiolkovsky, Konstantin 14, 47, 50
Tsvetkov, A.P. 163n
Turgenev, Ivan 92
Tynianov, Yuri 153–4

## U

Ulam, Adam 87, 92, 93, 95, 96, 97, 98
Uldricks, Teddy 94n
Union of Militant Atheists 180
Union of Soviet Writers 16, 25, 63, 74, 77, 107
Uspenskii, B.A. 152n
utopia, utopianism 6, 10, 14, 17, 37, 40, 47, 48, 50, 52, 53–5, 66, 67, 69, 100, 107, 109, 111, 117, 118, 122, 123, 126, 129, 134–5, 138, 142–9, 150, 162, 167, 169, 171–2, 176

## V

Vaiskopf, Mikhail 88, 97n
Vakhitova, T.M. 107, 136, 140
VAPP (All-Russian Association of Proletarian Writers) 72, 74
Vasil'ev, Vladimir 47
Verin, Vladimir 14
Vernadsky, Vladimir 56
*Veselye rebiata* 89
Virgil 181
*Volga, Volga!* 89
Volkogonov, Dmitri 93, 95, 96, 97, 98
Voloshin, Maximilian 75
von Laue, Theodore 92
Voronsky, Alexander 15, 18, 72, 74, 75

## W

war communism 83, 91, 93
Weiner, Norbert 39
White Sea Canal 11, 25, 87, 106
Witte, Sergei 92–3

## Z
Zabolotsky, Nikolai 47, 124–5
Zamoshkin, Nikolai 19, 173
Zamyatin, Evgeny 20, 66, 76
Zaraiskaia, V.P. 4n
*zaum* (trans-sense poetry) 67, 173

Zholkovsky, Alexander 164
Zinoviev, Grigory 71, 86
Zola, Émile 114n, 161
Zolotonosov, Mikhail 95n, 161
Zoshchenko, Mikhail 66, 132, 158, 162

www.ingramcontent.com/pod-product-compliance
Lightning Source LLC
Chambersburg PA
CBHW050759160426
43192CB00010B/1580